THE GLORY OF
Champagne

THE GLORY OF
Champagne

DON HEWITSON

To Carsar

Here is a chance to
learn a bit about
Bubbly!

Best wishes
Don
Xmas 1990

M
MACMILLAN
LONDON

PICTURE ACKNOWLEDGEMENTS

Illustrations are reproduced by permission of the following: Nic Barlow Photography: pages 3 below, 5 above, 6, 7 above left, 16. Colorsport: 14 below. © 1983 DANJAQ S. A. All rights reserved; still from *Octopussy* with Roger Moore and Kristina Wayborn, Champagne by Bollinger: 14 above. Patrick Eagar: 2. Mary Evans Picture Library: 11. Champagne Krug: 7 above right and below. Montana Wines Ltd: 12–13. Network Photographers/photo Barry Lewis: 5 below. Script, Reims: 1, 3 above. Frank Spooner Pictures/Gamma: 4, 8, 9.

The author and publishers also wish to thank the following for help and advice on the illustrations: Champagne Bollinger, Dent and Reuss Ltd., Michael Druitt Wines Ltd., F. V. M. International Ltd., Champagne Krug, Champagne Lanson, Champagne Laurent-Perrier, Mentzendorff and Co. Ltd., Moët & Chandon (London) Ltd., Montana Wines Ltd., Champagne Mumm, H. Parrot and Co. Ltd., Champagne Pol Roget, Champagne Pommery, Reid, Pye and Campbell Ltd., Richmond Towers, Seagram United Kingdom Ltd., Champagne de Venoge, Champagne Veuve Clicquot.

First published 1989 by
MACMILLAN LONDON LIMITED
4 Little Essex Street London WC2R 3LF
and Basingstoke

Associated companies in Auckland, Delhi, Dublin, Gaborone,
Hamburg, Harare, Hong Kong, Johannesburg, Kuala Lumpur,
Lagos, Manzini, Melbourne, Mexico City, Nairobi, New York,
Singapore and Tokyo

A CIP catalogue record for this book is available from the
British Library.

ISBN 0–333–44893–6

Design by Behram Kapadia
Typeset by Bookworm Typesetting, Manchester
Printed in Hong Kong

To Noelene,
Jessie and Abbey

CONTENTS

INTRODUCTION

New Year's Eve 1965. A night to be remembered. I was working in my university holidays as an academically overqualified and professionally underqualified waiter in one of New Zealand's trendiest restaurants. With only five minutes of the year remaining my boss opened magnums of Moët & Chandon for the staff (thank you, Pierre) and I tasted champagne for the first time. The subtlety of the fizz which gently erupted in the mouth, the delicacy of flavour and of finish produced a taste-sensation totally unlike anything I had previously experienced. I had thoroughly enjoyed my first few months in the restaurant world and these couple of glasses of champagne dashed any thought of a career making use of my formal education. I was hooked.

Over the next few months I tasted as many champagnes as possible; I still remember one night spent comparing Bollinger, Mumm Cordon Rouge, Veuve Clicquot and Perrier-Jouët 1955. Then the Henry Ford II entourage came to town. The Mrs Henry of the moment had sent instructions from Detroit. She would not be crossing our threshold without ready supplies of Dom Pérignon. There was not a bottle in the country because the New Zealand government imposed strict licensing quotas on imported products and understandably the Moët agent preferred to bring in a respectable number of cases of Brut Imperial rather than a few of the Dom. Fortunately some was airfreighted from Sydney; even better, Mrs Ford and associates managed to consume only a few bottles. A friend and I pooled our hard-earned cash and drank a bottle with due reverence. It confirmed the most exciting conclusion from my few but memorable champagne-drinking experiences – there was a wide variety of tastes. A quarter of a century later my enthusiasm has not diminished at all. I am a lowly amateur compared with some of the personalities of the champagne industry. Jean-Charles Heidsieck calculated that he participated in the consumption of more tan 24,000 bottles before retirement at the tender age of seventy – and I shared only one of those. In 1978 I was one of Victor Lanson's guests at his 'favourite London pub' (the Savoy); we were celebrating his eighty-fifth birthday and he was still enjoying every glass. His family estimated that in his lifetime he had shared more than 70,000 bottles!

Champagne is an exciting wine. At times it is as much a concept of style as of taste.

Public-relations people talk about the 'Champagne of Mineral Waters'. The rather dreary financial pages of the London *Times* recently headlined the details of a mutually beneficial takeover as giving the recipient of the bid 'A Champagne Sparkle'. The same paper's news pages reported the demise of Pinewood Studios: 'built with visions of a British film industry to rival Hollywood, on its opening day in 1936 a thousand celebrities gathered for luncheon ... washed down with 1928 Mumm Cordon Rouge.' Why don't other wines have such a charismatic appeal? Despite the presence of such illustrious names as Rothschild, Margaux and Petrus, no one claims to have produced the 'Bordeaux of Fruit Juices'.

But champagne is more than merely style. It is an ideal midday reviver if the morning has been a horror; a relaxing glass and things don't seem so bad after all. It is one of the greatest lunch partners; a few glasses with some lightish food will not affect the afternoon's activities. And the sybaritic delights of a relaxing Sunday brunch with champagne can ease the tensions of the working week. The same 'midday reviver' function applies equally well at the end of the day. It is the perfect aperitif, 'The finest ever conceived by man or provided by nature',* and while not the ideal accompaniment to a main meat course it will transform a modest buffet into a lavish spread.

A sensational wine that complements food and yet shines without it. Is there any wonder that the wine-drinking world has taken such a product to heart?

The Glory of Champagne is not merely a story of wine-production. For centuries, the Champagne region has been in the midst of European battlegrounds, yet the frequent waves of destruction have not managed to subdue the determination of the Champenois. The years of poverty and pestilence have been weathered. Then there is the remarkable fact that the climate of the region is almost unsuitable for the growing of classic grape varieties. The wine could easily have been ignored in favour of more amenable regions. But this did not happen. The central location of the region had a few advantages, one of them being proximity to Paris and royalty. The kings of France came to Reims for their coronations and the guests drank the local wine. Its unique lightness was attractive compared with the heavier wines from the south, and the unusual prickle on the tongue created by an erratic sparkle was considered a virtue.

The character of champagne was developed over the centuries. Dom Pérignon and other monks experimented with the blending of the component grape varieties and with controlling the secondary fermentation within the bottle. This was the beginning of the Champagne we know today. The producers refined the techniques of production, and the travelling salesmen spanned the globe promoting their wines. By the end of the nineteenth century the more adventurous brands were well established

---

*John Arlott, *Krug. House of Champagne* (Davis-Poynter).

in the lucrative markets of Great Britain, Central Europe and Russia, and were sold as far afield as North and South America, and even the Antipodes.

There is a popular misconception which holds that imitation is the sincerest form of flattery, and right from these early days the patience of champagne houses was put to the test. Fake bottles of 'champagne' appeared on the market almost as rapidly as the genuine article. German sekt firms were not beyond reproach, often using corks branded with the best-known names from Champagne. Bismarck's response to the Kaiser's offer of a glass of 'German champagne' is frequently quoted: 'I am sorry, your majesty, my patriotism stops short of my stomach.'

The twentieth century has seen blatant use of the name 'champagne' on wine labels all over the world. Many of the products were sparkling only courtesy of liberal injections of carbon dioxide into bottles of still wine – a flagrant abuse of the name of a specific product from a specific region. This book is not about these wines. Neither is it about the many well-made *méthode champenoise* wines on sale today. I have nothing against these wines; often they offer an attractive alternative to still wine at approximately the same price. They are most acceptable, but they are not champagne.

This book is about the industry, about the best known of the 'grand houses' and the smaller ones, about the growers, the blenders and the wine-makers, about the sales people and about the region's personalities. All these facets are important if we are to understand why there are so many different styles of champagne and how they are created. I am fortunate to be in the wine and restaurant business. As a buyer and seller of the finished products I have monitored the changes and appreciated the best of the wines. I have a tremendous respect for the Champenois: in the past twenty years they have managed to expand their production dramatically while retaining their credibility.

Champagne has never tasted better, nor been more popular. In Great Britain the sales are increasing by nearly 20 per cent every year, and a great deal of the extra consumption is purchased at the supermarkets – hardly the most elitist of outlets. The United States has at times competed successfully for first place on the export market; Italy is similarly keen. The traditional European customers are buying more and more, while the comparatively new markets, such as Canada, Australia and New Zealand, have approached the consumption of champagne with great enthusiasm.

How has all this been achieved? Read on.

THE GLORY OF
Champagne

1

LA CHAMPAGNE –
THE REGION

The champagne vineyards are the most northerly in France. The viticultural region is centred 150 kilometres north-east of Paris, situated on the plains of the Ile-de-France within the territory of a huge province previously known as La Champagne – it is now divided into five governmental *départements*: Marne, Haute Marne, Seine et Marne, Aisne and Aube. There is a defined region of approximately, 35,000 hectares, of which about 25,000 are cultivated – 2 per cent of the total vineyard area of France. The principal growing areas stretch from Château-Thierry, a mere 90 kilometres from Paris (almost suburban!), north-east towards Belgium. Another area is considerably further south – close to the Côte d'Or and spreading to the east of Chablis. For the uninitiated, the choice of vineyard areas may seem strange; when eavesdropping in the bars of local hostelries I often hear the overnight trippers complaining about the vistas of rolling wheatfields: panoramic, photogenic, but never a trace of vine. In fact, despite the seemingly haphazard nature of viticulture, the specific areas are strictly designated with emphasis on soil, on a multitude of microclimates and on the topography.

The three distinct regions of the province are differentiated by soil content.

1. *Champagne Humide* is a large strip of clay stretching from the Ardennes towards the French–Belgian border and then south-east to Burgundy. Wonderful market-garden territory, the traditional regional cuisine abounds with creative use of the superb vegetables. It is also very profitable farmland.

2. *Champagne Pouilleuse*, just to the west of Champagne Humide, is a large area of poor clay soil with no capacity for water retention. For centuries the peasants eked out a meagre existence. There is no great tradition of regional cuisine here as the produce used to be as poor as the soil. All this changed after the Second World War when improvements in farming technology and the realisation of the benefits of correct fertilisation resulted in vast tracts of wheatfields.

3. *Champagne Viticole* is the third region. Until a mere 70 million years ago the whole of the Champagne province was under the sea. After the waters had retreated

Classic Red Grapes

● *Pinot noir*

Classic White Grapes

○ *Chardonnay*

△ *Meunier*

Les Crus de Champagne

 Crus à 100%

 Crus à 95%

 Crus à 89%

 Crus à 85%

■ Towns

 Woods

R. Marne   Mareuil-Le-Port ■

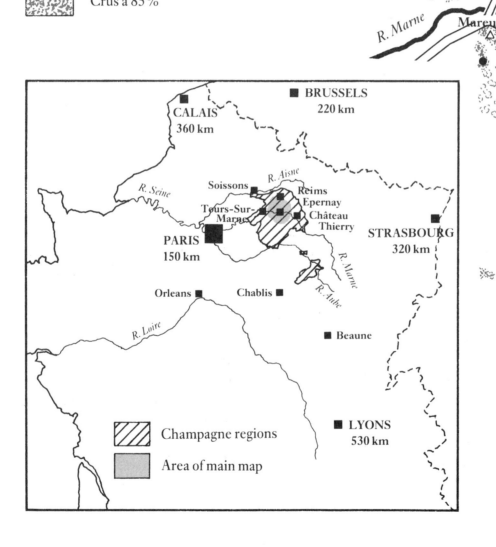

■ CALAIS
360 km

■ BRUSSELS
220 km

R. Seine

Soissons

R. Aisne

Reims
Epernay
Château
Thierry

Tours-Sur-
Marne

■ PARIS
150 km

R. Marne

■ STRASBOURG
320 km

Orleans ■   Chablis ■

R. Aube

R. Loire

■ Beaune

■ LYONS
530 km

▨ Champagne regions

▨ Area of main map

Tinqueux

Reims

Cormontreuil

MONTBRE

*RILLY-LA-
MONTAGNE*

SILLERY
PUISIEULX *BEAUMONT-SUR-*
VESLE

*CHIGNY-
LES-ROSES*

MAILLY *VERZENAY*

*VILLERS-
ALLERAND*

LUDES *VERZY*

*VILLERS-
MARMERY*

MONTAGNE DE REIMS

TRÉPAIL

LOUVOIS

TAUXIÈRES-MUTRY

HAUTVILLERS *CHAMPILLON* *BOUZY*

CUMIÈRES *MUTIGNY* *AMBONNAY*

Damery *AVENAY-
VAL-D'OR*

*DIZY-
MAGENTA* *BISSEUIL*

Mardeuil *AY* *MAREUIL-SUR-AY* Tours-Sur-Marne

Epernay

A MARNE

R. Marne

CHOUILLY

PIERRY

CUIS

CRAMANT

AVIZE

GRAUVES *OGER*

*LE MESNIL-
SUR-OGER*

CÔTE DES BLANCS

VERTUS

| 0 | 1 | 2 | 3 | 4 | 5 | 6km |

| 0 | 1 | 2 | 3 | 4 miles |

there was a series of violent earthquakes which broke up the chalk soil, but one small part on the eastern edge of the Ile-de-France suffered an even more massive upheaval as the bowels of the earth erupted and a huge force pushed through the chalk to create a series of hills. This is the Champagne Viticole region and the cliffs formed are known as the *falaises*. The subsoil is a combination of calcareous marine organisms (Belemnite chalk, named after the belemnite molluscs, is prevalent) and minerals spewed forth from below. Theoretically the soil is poor, yet on the *falaises* the chalk has three great virtues: it stores and reflects the heat of the sun, it ensures the drainage of excess water, and during the rainy periods it can store excess humidity, thereby mitigating the effects of summer droughts. This type of chalk soil encourages the vines to produce grapes with the right amount of delicacy and lightness. The plains surrounding the *falaises* consist of a very different type of chalk, Micraster, which does not offer the same advantages. Cultivation of vines is still possible there but the produce lacks the benefits of the unique Belemnite chalk.

As any keen gardener presumably knows (I am not one), the topsoil is basically man-made and must be renewed regularly if cultivation is to be effective, particularly on the hillsides of Champagne Viticole because the rain washes it down the slopes. The topsoil of the district is extremely thin and must be treated with great care and attention. Nature has helped out considerably – the Montagne de Reims contains crucial deposits of *cendres noires*, a rich iron-filled lignite which is mined and spread throughout the vineyards every few years.

CLIMATE is obviously an essential factor, but the climate of La Champagne has some surprising characteristics. The scientists who lovingly chart and quantify the relative climatic assets in many of the New World vineyard territories would be rather puzzled by Champagne. The region only just has sufficient sunshine and warmth to meet the minimum requirements for ripening of classic varietal grapes. It is wet, with regular rainfall, and unfortunately the wettest months are during the growing season. An average of more than 160 days with rain each year may not seem much to Londoners but it is certainly a lot for a region attempting to produce first-class grapes. As if these problems were not enough, the winters can be vicious, with the vineyards well inland and suffering the vagaries of 'continental cold'. In 1985 mid-January temperatures were as low as −20°C! I was there at the time and it felt more like Scandinavia than one of the major vineyard regions of France. Spring frosts can occur as late as the end of May, violent hailstorms are a regular hazard and the summer weather is erratic. These factors are anything but ideal, yet unbelievably it all works. Why?

The south-facing slopes maximise the sunshine hours on the vines, and the undulating countryside offers hills which provide protection from the frosts. The four rivers (the Marne in particular, plus the Aube, the Ardre and the Vesle) create considerable warmth and provide drainage advantages for nearby vineyards. The neighbouring forests and woods help to maintain the necessary stable humidity level.

All these factors contribute to a fascinating series of microclimates and differences in the quality of the vines.

Not an ideal vineyard region by any means, but this unique combination of factors produces the lightly acidic (in some years this would be considered a euphemism) but fruity style of still wine that is ideal for the making of champagne. Also the unreliability of the harvests – 'The good, the bad and the ugly' – provides the motivation for creating the unique system of blending wines from the current years with stocks of reserve wines from other vintages.

——— THE WINE-GROWING REGIONS ———

There are four quite separate vineyard regions, producing wines with very different characteristics.

THE MONTAGNE DE REIMS is a semi-circle from the southern side of the valley of the River Vesle through to Epernay. The use of the word *montagne* to describe these gentle rolling hills would be a source of amusement and derision in my native New Zealand. But this territory is nonetheless the most dramatic, with vineyards dominating much of the scenery.

THE CÔTE DES BLANCS runs along another semi-circle south of Epernay from Chouilly down to the surrounds of Vertus, offering a glorious panorama of gentle slopes covered with immaculate vines. A few picturesque villages add rustic character. I am convinced that this is the true heaven on earth.

THE VALLÉE DE LA MARNE runs along both sides of the river from Epernay to Château-Thierry. It is mostly flat with much less intensive vineyard plantings. Altogether, there is a more humdrum look to the area. Other agrarian interests vie with the making of champagne and the villages lack the picturesque touch of the Montagne de Reims and Côte des Blancs.

THE AUBE is of considerable interest, more from a historical point of view than a viticultural one. The Kimmeridge clay soils are more akin to their near neighbour Chablis than to the rest of Champagne and the vineyards are on the plains. The Aube is so far from the other three that it is only an occasional map which even acknowledges its existence. Nevertheless the area occupies 15 per cent of the planted area of Champagne. The relationship between the Aubois and the rest of the Champenois has been stormy in the past and it is not particularly warm nowadays.

MINOR REGIONS

As the map shows there are three more small areas of vines: the Aisne, which lies south of Château-Thierry in the Vallée de la Marne; the Côte de Sézanne in the south-west; and Vitry-le-François, east of Sézanne and south of Châlons-sur-Marne. The wines produced here are rather enigmatic, lacking the grace and charm of the produce of the major regions, but possessing obvious varietal characteristics which can be of considerable benefit in boosting flavour in the final blends of the more prosaic non-vintages.

REIMS VERSUS EPERNAY

The region possesses two hubs, each with a strong claim to be the capital of Champagne. The two towns are very different in size and style yet they manage to coexist peacefully.

REIMS is dominated by its magnificent cathedral, which was used for the coronations of the kings of France. It suffered extensive damage during the Second World War but fortunately all has been restored to grace and splendour and it is worth driving from Paris just to see the glorious Chagall stained glass window. The town is a flourishing provincial centre with many industries other than champagne-production; many of the locals have more interest in Les Cornichons (the gherkins) than in *les vignes*. All the same the image of the town is inexorably linked with the wine; there you will find the elegant headquarters of the grand houses, superb restaurants (few of which could survive without the patronage of the houses and their visitors) and a beautiful spread of 60 hectares of sports grounds – the Parc Pommery, donated in 1911 by the family to the citizens of Reims.

EPERNAY is much smaller and less worldly. There is very little activity unconnected to the champagne industry, the town's lifeblood. Unlike Reims it is surrounded by vineyards. Epernay also has the 'Champs Elysées of Champagne' – the aristocratic avenue de Champagne, with many of the greatest names housed in stunning nineteenth-century buildings. This long, wide road is built over a labyrinth of cellars – Moët & Chandon and Mercier alone have more that 40 kilometres of *galeries* winding underneath it.

This is the physical basis of Champagne. Much more than merely one of the great viticultural regions of the world, it is a story of survival. The Champenois are a tenacious breed. They have spent centuries growing vines and making wine in climatic conditions little better than those of England. Despite everything, they have triumphed.

2

THE EARLY YEARS

There are considerable learned disputes about the first appearance of vines in Champagne. Claims that fossil leaves found in the Sézanne district date back to the tertiary era are not disputed but there is general agreement that the 'wild' vines were not capable of producing wine. Anyway, the Ice Age of the quaternary era put paid to all that. The real intellectual quarrel concerns whether the vineyards were in existence before Roman times or were developed by the Romans. There are good arguments for both views but I am inclined to believe in the latter. This harsh climate certainly required a degree of viticultural skill and experience, and the Gauls were lacking on both counts.

The Romans' love of food and wine is legendary, yet at one time they were hampered by a peculiar law. The decree issued by Emperor Donitian makes the thirteen years of Prohibition in twentieth-century America seem quite mild: in AD 90 he forbade both the expansion of vineyards in Italy and the cultivation of the vine in Gaul – and this draconian imposition lasted for 190 years. Of course, his trusty soldiers could not be denied – they could hardly be expected to safeguard the empire without the necessary creature-comforts – and they were allowed to produce sufficient quantities for their own consumption. Fortunately Emperor Probus rescinded the ban in 280, and furthermore he commanded the military to assist in the reconstruction and replanting of the vineyards.

The unique soil structure of the region provided a ready source of building materials for the Roman constructions, and large quantities of chalk blocks were quarried. These superb engineers were able to turn the huge excavations into a most useful asset. The blocks were cut out of the ground in a very unusual fashion – from a smallish aperture at the top the Romans cut downwards, gradually widening the excavated area the more deeply they quarried and so creating enormous underground galleries (*crayères*). The temperature in these *crayères* was cool and varied very little throughout the seasons; they were perfect for storage of foodstuffs and later of the wine. The tremendous advantages of such subterranean chalk cellars were not lost on the Champenois and these *crayères* were the forerunners of the miles of subterranean cellars which were later created throughout the main wine-producing centres of the region.

As the Roman Empire declined, waves of barbarians swept across the plains sacking and looting, then looting and sacking again – Attila the Hun was only one of the many. Fortunately, in the latter part of the fifth century Christianity regained a hold and the clergy and the religious orders established the proper foundations of the wine industry in Champagne – a happy combination of body and soul! The sacramental use of wine had little influence in the establishment of this relationship. The most devout of landowning families were only too happy to endow vast tracts of their best land to the local abbey, and tithes were often paid to the clergy in the form of grapes. Many of the religious houses in Champagne supported themselves by making and marketing wines vastly superior to those of the peasantry. Saint Rémi, Archbishop of Reims, was a great advocate of the wines of the region (and also a notable vineyard-owner). More importantly, he converted Clovis, King of the Franks, to Christianity, finally baptising him in Reims. France now had its first Christian king. It was a significant beginning, and Reims eventually became the city where all French monarchs were crowned.

No doubt the delicacy of the wines was a relief from the heavier, sweeter wines from the south, but one must be honest and admit that their popularity was due to social prestige – the wines from the region of the coronations were tasted and enjoyed by visiting royalty, who usually took some back home. Strangely, the somewhat dubious geographical advantage of being regularly in the middle of a war zone contributed to the growth of reputation: the victors usually grabbed the wine and removed it with the rest of their loot. Thus was the name promoted, albeit in this rather painful manner. The name champagne flourished. In the eleventh century Pope Urban II declared that the wines of Ay were supreme, but then again he would – he was born and·bred in Châtillon-sur-Marne.

Much of the Hundred Years' War was fought in the heart of Champagne – in 1359 Edward III of England journeyed to Reims in an abortive attempt to crown himself King of France. The fact that he didn't succeed was small recompense for the continual fighting which caused havoc among the wine-growing areas. For most of these tempestuous years the vineyards were in effect a perpetual battlefield. While the English soldiers rampaged around the region, the officers concentrated on the cellars and drank vast quantities. Finally in 1429 Joan of Arc dragged Charles VII to Reims for his coronation and the English fled from Champagne, taking a great deal of the local wine with them – once again a very expensive word-of-mouth promotion!

Champagne became increasingly famous, and this process was much helped by two seventeenth-century noblemen. The Marquis de Saint-Evremond offended Louis XIV and was banished from France. He was a great lover of champagne so, naturally, when he travelled to London and joined the fringes of the high-spirited court of Charles II he took his wine with him and his fellow courtiers loved it. At the same time the Marquis de Sillery, a large vineyard-owner and very astute businessman, was successfully promoting his own wines on both sides of the Channel.

The wine of this time had very little in common with champagne as we know it. It was made from a none-too-gentle pressing of the grapes and a small amount of the skin colour from the black grapes entered the blend, giving it a light, often murky, tinge of pink. The aromatic qualities and delicacy of flavour were courtesy of the northerly position of the vineyards. Unfortunately in many years the cool-climate areas were downright cold and the wines were very acidic. At times it was noticeable that the wines had a secondary fermentation, sometimes a great flurry of bubbles and sometimes just a slight *pétillance*. In these times glass was used only for pitchers for serving wine, and these holding vessels were usually stoppered with wooden plugs wrapped in hemp. The wine was stored in casks and eventually the sparkle disappeared.

The growers began to work on the problem of cloudiness and attempted to produce clear white wines from black and white grapes. They also became interested in the unique sparkle. Because of the extremely cold temperatures in early winter the fermentation was arrested and often recurred when the weather became warmer. Considerable carbon-dioxide gas was produced as a result. With most wines this would normally disappear but in champagne it often remained. When this occurred the rather light, sour wine took on another dimension. Definitely a bonus, if it could be controlled.

3

DOM PIERRE PÉRIGNON

Dom Pierre Pérignon is undoubtedly the most famous man in the history of Champagne. Much of his fame is well deserved but unfortunately he has been labelled as ' the man who invented champagne'. Recently, this misnomer has tended to detract from the immensely important discoveries that he did make, refining the developing techniques of making champagne uniquely itself. He was, supremely, the man for the moment.

Born in 1639 on the Champagne–Lorraine border. Pierre studied at the Jesuit college at Châlons-sur-Marne. He joined the order of Benedictines in 1657 and in 1668 he was ordained priest and sent to the Abbey of St Pierre d'Hautvillers in the diocese of Reims. Champagne was by no means the only French wine region where the monasteries were a dominant part of the economy (neighbouring Burgundy possessed a similar relationship) and this particular abbey was rich in viticultural assets.

Soon after his arrival Dom Pierre was appointed *procureur* – a crucial position, basically acting as general manager of a considerable commercial operation. He was responsible for the upkeep of the large spread of buildings and estate, for the organisation and collection of rents from tenants, and for the day-to-day management of the operations of the vineyards, a vital part of the economy of the establishment and a major contributing factor in the material wellbeing of the occupants of the complex organisation. Pierre was highly intelligent and inquisitive, and always did more than merely carry out the duties of his predecessors. First of all he changed the structure of the Abbey's vineyards. Monks and peasants grubbed up vast tracts of land covered with vines suffering from decades of neglect and replanted them with better-quality vines, in particular the local champagne vine which produced a small, soft, black-skinned grape. The vine was anything but prolific, but it was markedly superior in quality to previous plantings. Attention was paid to vineyard management, on concentrating more careful cultivation and rigorous pruning.

DOM PIERRE PÉRIGNON

The role of *procureur* also involved remitting the positive cash flow back to 'Head Office' and this didn't appeal to a man determined to restore some of its past glories to an abbey ravaged by centuries of warfare and trying to create a modern, technically advanced operation. Instead he invested much of the income in the purchase of new vineyards, rebuilt two large wine presses in order to facilitate a style of gentle pressing with little skin contact, and carved large cellars out of the chalk soil. He was meticulous in his approach to wine-making and he created new methods, partly from his own experimentation and partly from using new technical apparatus.

Contrary to the practice of both predecessors and contemporaries, he was meticulous in his attention to the source of the grapes and to their qualities at harvest; he also discovered the secret of blending. Previously, the grapes had been transported to the press-house and merely mixed together. Pierre Pérignon had discovered the enormous advantages of balancing the correct proportion of white grapes with black and taking account of the individual assets of the produce of certain vineyards. He realised that this meant mixing wines from different grapes from different parts of the Champagne region. This was a completely new concept. The other major wine areas considered the product of a single estate to be much more worthy. This degree of meticulous attention was continued in the cellars (*caves*). Racking (the draining off of the clear wine from the cask by gravity, leaving the sediment in the higher barrel) was repeated in order to ensure the clarity of the wine.

There were many other technical advances, some of which have been erroneously attributed solely to Pérignon. A brilliant, innovative man, he was aware of the experiments and inventions of others, and was prepared to use them to maximum advantage. Central Europe was relatively accessible in those days and members of the religious orders were among the most wide-ranging of travellers. By the 1660s the English had manufactured strong bottles capable of withstanding considerable levels of carbon dioxide and were transferring the sparkling wine from cask to glass and using cork stoppers to retain the bubbles. These two factors were of crucial importance to the development work being carried out at Hautvillers – the control and retention of the natural sparkle. Perhaps the cork stoppers were introduced by the wine merchants of Great Britain, who already were dealing with the cork-makers of Spain. Perhaps the crew at the Abbey noticed that monks travelling from the south of France, where the region of Limoux had been producing sparkling wine for years, stoppered their drinking vessels with cork from the nearby Iberian peninsula. Who knows? Historians cannot agree. The important fact is that the Dom was both a mercurial innovator and a fastidious adaptor.

Dom Pierre spent forty-seven years as *procureur* at the Abbey. Whether he invented the process of controlling the second fermentation, hence the key to the production of the ultimate sparkling wine, is of no great importance. Indeed within Champagne there were other monks at work on similar projects, in particular Brother Jean Oudart, who was in charge of the Benedictine Abbey of St Pierre aux Monts at

Châlons-sur-Marne from 1680 to 1742. There can be no doubt that the wine from Hautvillers achieved a special prominence and 'Perignon wines', as they were often called, fetched far greater prices than other wines from Champagne.

Much of the mystique surrounding this key historical personality is related to the fact that there is no painting of Pierre – only the Abbot was accorded such glory. Personal observations of fellow monks at the Abbey attest to his kindness. But, as his own personal records of commercial transactions (on view at Hautvillers) show, he was an extremely diligent and hard-nosed businessman. The detailed files would satisfy the most painstaking of Inland Revenue inspectors. Bottles were nowhere near as strong as they are these days and the wine was much more volatile, yet he was adamant that the customer should pay for all breakages and explosions once the wine had left Hautvillers. Records show that one unlucky purchaser lost over half of his shipment but was invoiced and ended up paying in full!*

There is a popular misconception that Dom Pérignon became blind in his later years – not so, according to Moët. They have a document signed by him in 1715, two months before his death. Whilst the signature is that of a frail old man, it is not that of a blind one.

He was buried in the Abbey's chapel. There is no doubt that this hard-working visionary had established the beginnings of the modern champagne industry.

*Fortunately the first, relatively strong bottles were soon to be imported from England, later they were produced locally.

4

PIONEERING EXPORTERS

The eighteenth century saw a tremendous growth of interest in champagne. This was not achieved easily, although much of the dramatic increase in sales was due to the democratisation of the wine: it was no longer a drink confined to the most privileged of classes. A dubious law which existed until 1728 affected the champagne trade greatly. No wine was allowed to be transported in bottle; theoretically this was meant to prevent tax evasion. Perhaps the resulting, easily accountable large bulk shipments lessened the chances of fiddling the books, but the success of the wines from Hautvillers alone shows the ease with which the elite few simply ignored the laws: those without influence settled for sparkling wine shipped in cask.

In 1739 the city of Paris gave a ball where over 2000 bottles of champagne were consumed. Sales were buoyant. The sparkling stuff from Champagne was achieving great prominence, even though it actually constituted only a small percentage of the overall wine production of the province. The first major houses devoted only to the production of sparkling wines were established, including Ruinart (1729), Fourneaux, the predecessor of Taittinger (1734), Moët (1743), Vander Venken, the predecessor of Henri Abelé (1757), Clicquot (1772), Heidsieck, later to split into three separate houses (1785), and Jacquesson (1798).

Ironically, the French Revolution of 1789 was of great benefit to the most successful of the capitalistic commercial houses. The Church holdings and the large well-known prime-site estates owned by the aristocracy were early casualties of the drastic land reforms. Initially there were considerable problems with sources of supplies of grapes, and obviously the recently established export business disappeared. But the domestic demand for champagne rapidly grew and as the best known of the early 'aristocratic' names of private holdings disappeared, the names of the superior *négociant* houses provided a focal point for the consumers' attention and they quickly flourished under Napoleon's rule. Moët's fortunes at the time illustrate the initial problems and eventual advantages of the period.

In 1792 Jean Rémy Moët, only thirty-four years old, took control of the flourishing house, but soon faced major problems. As Patrick Forbes has recounted:*'In 1798 the Momeron Bank, which held the majority of his capital, failed. Jean Rémy rushed off to Paris, sat on the doorsteps of the bank and asked callers if they had bills signed by him; if they did, he extracted money from a leather satchel and paid the debt. The next day he returned to Epernay without a sou, but with his credit intact.'

A tough way to enhance credibility, but it was very honest and also very effective. As the intense idealism of the times became relaxed, the sales of Moët boomed. In 1802 Jean Rémy became Mayor of Epernay, and provided superior board and lodgings for the Emperor. He built not one but two houses on the avenue de Champagne to accommodate the court on its stopovers from Paris to Germany.** Not surprisingly the appreciative Napoleon became an enthusiastic ambassador of the wines of Moët; he also awarded Jean Rémy his own Chevalier's cross of the Légion d'Honneur 'for the admirable way you have developed your business and all you have done for wines abroad'. Business for Moët and the other prominent names boomed as royalty and prominent citizens of the world clamoured for this renowned wine. The export business had never been better – even after the Battle of Waterloo the Napoleonic connections were of no hindrance to Moët. Jean Rémy's influence continued to reign supreme and he took on a second term as Mayor of Epernay.

Bottles were improving in quality; in 1735 a law was introduced which required that they be made in a number of sizes based on variations of the 'Paris pint', and that the cork be tied down with string. The shape was eventually standardised as a bulbous receptacle, much lighter than its predecessors, but considerably stronger. But, they were still not quite strong enough. This was one of the many technical problems of the moment which needed to be solved if the unique product of consistently sparkling, clear champagne was to continue its success.

Three major technical advances contributed to the quest for better and better wine.

Firstly, in the early years of the nineteenth century the widow Clicquot was worried about the cloudiness of the wines. She persevered with experiments and evolved the system of remuage. At first the bottles were simply shaken and placed upside down in holes cut in tables, remaining in that position until all the sediment had collected around the cork. This was gradually refined and the more gentle manipulation of the bottles at an angle in *pupitres* was developed. The sediment was removed, albeit rather violently, and the recorked bottle now contained reasonably clear wine.

Secondly, the Champenois gradually realised that most of the large numbers of bottle breakages were not only due to problems of the strength of the glass and the manufacturing techniques. The erratic and often violent nature of the secondary fermentation was equally to blame. In the early 1800s Monsieur François, a Châlons-sur-Marne chemist, published a paper which introduced a method of

* *Champagne: The Wine, the Land and the People*, (Gollancz).
** Later these twin glories were to house a galaxy of European superstars from Tsar Alexander I to the Duke of Wellington.

measuring the amount of sugar remaining in the wine after fermentation. This system therefore made possible a strict calculation of added sugar *(liqueur de tirage)*, which controls the degree of sparkle – gentle bubbles rather than a turbulent rush of carbonic gas which aided neither the delicacy of flavour nor the longevity of the bottle. The instrument developed for the purpose was reasonably simple in structure and operation, yet the houses were uncharacteristically cautious and it was years before the system was fully accepted.

Thirdly, dégorgement (removal of the sediment) was still a problem. The widow Clicquot's method was not completely effective; it was also painstakingly slow and required a great deal of highly skilled labour. Members of the firm of Henri Abelé revolutionised the process in the 1880s. The necks of the bottles were immersed in a freezing brine solution, thereby almost solidifying the sediment around the cork. The bottle was then turned upright, the cork was removed, and the pressure within pushed out the unwanted matter, leaving a crystal-clear wine.

These factors were basically the consolidation of production techniques which allowed the Champenois to produce a more attractive wine in much larger quantities. The time was right for the first golden age of champagne.

In the early part of the nineteenth century the more visionary Champenois were actively establishing the all-important export markets. Napoleon's defeat on the Russian front meant that once again their region was under the stewardship of foreign forces, this time the Russians and the Prussians. Fortunately when the former left they took home a great liking for champagne and the Russian market became, until the 1917 Revolution, one of the largest of all. Sales in other countries were promising (even in Great Britain – the years of hostilities never really stopped the consumption of 'bubbly'; it was merely imported from a neutral source). In fact no potential market was ignored. The Champenois were the first of the great travelling salesmen. No market was too small or too inaccessible, if it had potential. Up until now the single most important Champagne personality had been an innovator, Dom Pérignon; now it was time for the appearance of the marketing personalities.

Jean Rémy Moët had blazed a campaign trail in the latter decades of the eighteenth century, and the formidable widow Clicquot was destined to continue the good work.

MADAME NICOLE BARBE CLICQUOT PONSARDIN

In October 1805 François Clicquot contracted a fever and died within two weeks. He was only thirty years old. Four years before he had taken charge of the family business;* he had sold off the textile and banking departments to concentrate on the champagne interests and had immediately launched an attack on the export markets.

*Another of the houses which had actually benefited from the Revolutionary 'reign of terror', it had managed to purchase considerable property in Reims which had previously been owned by the Church.

Despite the instant success of that operation, the family was stunned by his death and lacked the confidence to carry on. Preparations were made for the winding up of the company and notices of liquidation were actually posted.

But no one had considered the resourcefulness of the young man's wife of the past five years. The newly widowed Madame Clicquot came from a family with no commercial wine interests. She was twenty-seven years old, with a two-year-old daughter and no knowledge whatsoever of her late husband's business. And yet she would not consider quitting. A new company was founded and an expatriate Rhinelander, Monsieur Bohn, François' friend and his travelling salesman, was made a partner. A Monsieur Fourneaux was contracted to provide the blend and within a few months the company, La Société Veuve Clicquot-Ponsardin, was ready to commence trading.

The business problems of the time held no fears for the widow. The willing Bohn was immediately despatched to the major markets of Central and Eastern Europe and Russia. Invariably the turmoil of Europe at that time resulted in major problems – defaults on payment, blockades and loss of shipments en route. But by 1806 the company's major export office was established and successfully trading – in St Petersburg Bohn was a supreme salesman, enthusiastic and shrewd. Soon the aristocracy were clamouring for Clicquot and he was determined this should continue. The house of La Veuve Clicquot was to achieve by peaceful means what Napoleon later could not manage by war, the invasion of Russia. In 1806 Bohn wrote to head office, 'I am reliably informed that the Czarina is with child. What a blessing if it is a Prince. Oceans of champagne will be drunk in this immense country. Please do not say a word, otherwise our competitors will arrive here in droves!' Later an important client proposed to visit France. Bohn urged Madame to 'Shower on him all the good things and pleasures that Reims and the neighbourhood can offer. Take possession of him entirely. Do not let him have a second to himself. Either you or your friends invite him for every meal so that our competitors never get near him.'

The records at Maison Clicquot also show that while the widow was raising finance to set up her own production operation (she was dissatisfied with much of the quality of the wine produced by Fourneaux) and looking into the problems of remuage, Bohn was ensuring that the years of hardship and losses were compensated for; the best-known champagne in Russia was able to command the best price. Madame Clicquot, the presiding commercial genius with the flair for taking immense calculated risks, had chosen the right man for the job: between them the company was beginning to enjoy a period of well-merited prosperity. In 1808 Bohn reported,

We have a good, solid trade with the most respected houses of their kind in the North and throughout Europe. We are famous as a concern in the first rank of your profession, the terror of all your competitors by the size of your shipments and all for foreign account. These are the rare advantages which give you a marked ascendancy over your colleagues and only await a general state of peace to flourish.

Alas, Bohn could control markets, but not governments. Napoleon marched on Russia in 1812.

Once again, the Champagne region was in chaos and by 1814 Reims was occupied. Madame Clicquot realised the rather dubious benefits of such a well-known name and constructed a large number of false walls to hide the majority of stocks from thirsty members of the occupying army. But her worst fears were unfounded and after the fall of the Emperor the house was in a position to carry out the most audacious coup in the history of champagne-selling.

Monsieur Bohn may have been forced to flee Russia, but this indefatigable salesman, temporarily bereft of customers, put his mind to other things and hatched a daring plan. Load a vessel as quickly and secretly as possible full of Clicquot and be the first to have champagne for sale after the frontiers are reopened.

> They will suddenly realise you have made a shipment. Everybody will be intrigued. They will write around and maybe even try and follow the ship to discover its destination. In the end they will discover where. In the end, they will come clattering in. If after that we can do nothing, at least we shall have been the first and our wine will have been well and truly sold before the great crowd of sheep have arrived to lower the price.

It all sounds so simple, yet in reality an amount of devious undercover work was required. Complete secrecy was essential, while 10,000 bottles were dégorged within a single month after the abdication of Napoleon, prepared for shipment, transported by carts to the port of Rouen and loaded on to a small ship.

France and Russia had not signed a peace treaty and there was still a Russian embargo on French goods. Bohn, who accompanied the wine on its journey, planned to unload at the East Prussian port of Königsberg and smuggle the wine across the border if necessary. Such measures of stealth were not necessary as the embargo was lifted while the cargo was at sea (and without any hesitation Madame Clicquot had already despatched a further shipment of 20,000 bottles direct to St Petersburg — the captain of the second ship was forbidden to carry any other champagnes).

The heroic Bohn quickly forgot the gruelling circumstances of the journey. He was back selling (or in fact rationing) his beloved Clicquot:

> Your wine is nectar. It has the power of Hungarian wine and the colour of yellow gold. Not the least cloudiness and the *mousse* is such that when the cork is taken out half the bottle hits the ceiling! . . . I need not tell you how my heart jumps for joy to be able to write what you have just read in this letter. The Devil has quit our doors so be of good cheer.

That last sentence applied to the whole of the champagne industry. The next eighty years more than compensated for the trials and tribulations of the past. The houses received ample reward for all the hard work, the brilliant technological innovations and the resilience of the Champenois, as well as for their ability to make the best of bad situations. It seemed that the whole world wanted their wines, and finally they could provide the quantity and the quality. The vineyards were planted to absolute capacity, exports boomed (by now the local market was relatively unimportant) as the major industrial countries of the world became extremely wealthy and both the image and taste of champagne became very fashionable. At the turn of the century the region is estimated to have produced less than a million bottles a year: by 1870 this had increased to 20 million bottles.

The British market was of crucial importance. The country deepened its long-standing love affair with bubbly in the 1860s, after Prime Minister Gladstone reduced the discriminatory tax on French wines. Champagne was much, much more expensive than other wines* and consumption was still restricted to those who could afford it – but its popularity soared. The most celebrated music-hall song of 1869 was George Leybourne's 'Champagne Charlie Is My Name'. The major houses of the time were already engaged in fierce competition for market share of such a lucrative, accessible country. Jacquesson was one of the largest of the time, and Adolfe, son of the founder, possessed the advantage of being married to an English woman. The recently established firm of Krug & Cie had a similar advantage. The founder, Joseph, was first employed in Champagne by Jacquesson and later married the sister of Adolfe's wife; their son Paul spent much of his youth in his mother's homeland. The present generation of the family are extremely proud of the success of Krug in Britain at this time (the house was then virtually unknown in France). It is a mutual love affair which has continued. Madame Louise Pommery established a London office as early as 1861 and was rewarded with the largest sales of any house, a position which the firm zealously defended for decade after decade.**

By the turn of the century the British were drinking the phenomenal quantity of 10 million bottles a year;† 40 per cent of the region's total production. They influenced not only the fortunes of the houses, but also the styles of wine. The existing wines contained a very high dosage of sugar, 12 per cent or more,†† and while the other markets were quite content with this rather sweet style of the wine (in fact the

*Jean-Paul Médard of Moët & Chandon is one of the unsung characters of the industry. A librarian manqué, he has carefully collected among his archives a collection of nineteenth- and twentieth-century catalogues from prestigious merchants which show the exalted status of champagne. In Edwardian Britain Moët non-vintage sold for up to ten times the price of decent still wines; in 1908 Fauchon in Paris listed Château Mouton Rothschild 1896 for FF 3.10 and Moët for FF 15.
**The quality of wine was a major factor at all times, but for the first thirty years of the twentieth century their 'Man in London' was the greatest champagne salesman the English-speaking world has ever seen: the late, great André Simon.
†An amazing total, not repeated until the 1970s.
††More about this in Chapter 9.

Russians preferred the wine very sweet), the British soon preferred their wine much drier. Obviously Pommery & Gréno was vitally interested in the tastes of such a significant percentage of its business; indeed Madame had been concerned about the high dosage for a considerable time as she watched French drinkers begin to treat champagne as an accompaniment to the dessert course. This was *not* the way to increase sales. In 1874 the house launched the first Brut champagne, the forerunner of the modern style; the existence of Brut explains the frequent appearance of slip labels stating 'Reserved for England' (denoting 'extra dry') over the next century.

Do not think that the other markets were ignored. Two of the largest houses were particularly dynamic around the world – Moët & Chandon and G.H. Mumm.

In 1832 ill-health forced Jean Rémy Moët to pass over stewardship of the house to his son Victor and son-in-law Pierre Gabriel Chandon de Brialles, hence the change of name to Moët & Chandon. These two guardians were no playboys (I confess the temptation would have been far too great for me) and vigorous expansion followed rapidly with extensive vineyard purchases and massive construction of cellars to house the increased volume. Production increased fourfold in the next forty years – Jean Rémy would have been very proud of these two. By 1900 sales were in excess of one million bottles, and they were not obtained without considerable effort. In 1914 Alfred Simon, Moët's British agent, privately published his memoirs, *Lest We Forget, 1851–1914*. One chapter is devoted to the 'Moët Crusade in Antipodes', an account of his visit to Australia and New Zealand in 1887/8 on a promotional tour. The cost to Moët must have been astronomical – it paid for the fares of Simon, his wife 'and our faithful manservant Hawkins'. They also allocated 500 cases of the glorious 1884 vintage for samples, together with a credit of £5000 for expenses. The magnificence of his entertaining, chronicled with loving detail, was such that the directors of the present London firm deeply regret that they now have agents Down-under rendering such journeys unnecessary!

G.H. Mumm & Co. only arrived on the scene in 1827. Nevertheless it possessed drive and dynamism and planned its rapid expansion with meticulous attention to detail. Capital was not tied up in vineyard purchases as the German owners, who were growers, winemakers and merchants in their own country, could see that the immediate need in Champagne was for stock not vines. At the time the cost of land was high and the *négociant* houses were comfortably in control of the industry's economy – the poor growers weren't even guaranteed a buyer for their produce at harvest time.

While the domestic market was accorded prime place, the company soon declared its willingness to challenge the firmly entrenched grand names in the export markets. Its wines were of high quality and soon a rapidly expanding export business was operating. In 1876 the company made the finest of its many masterly business decisions; it registered the brand name Cordon Rouge, which eventually became the label for a dry blend. The red sash, achieved by wrapping a Légion d'Honneur-style ribbon around the neck of the bottle, crossing its ends and sealing them with an oval label bearing the words Cordon Rouge, was easily recognised, thereby simplifying promotion. Parisian society loved the new label; this was of great benefit, because visiting *bon viveurs* returned home with memories of the label, even if they were unable to recollect the producer.

Needless to say the enthusiastic champagne-drinkers of Great Britain did not wait for the rest of the world to discover the glories of Mumm. In the first year of operation the company wrote to a hotelier in Brussels: 'We know that your establishment is much frequented by the English and are taking the liberty of drawing to your attention that we know exactly the type of wine these gentlemen prefer. We can say without presumption, that our wine already enjoys a great reputation in England.' Perhaps a slight exaggeration; nevertheless the brand was immediately established, although the dramatic expansion in consumption was still thirty years off.

The royalty of Europe were dedicated customers and the wines were sold all over South America, but it was the initial endeavours and consequent success on the United States market which provides a fascinating example of super champagne salesmanship. Within three years of establishment the house had shipped its first small consignment of 1700 bottles across the Atlantic. The US market was unsophisticated, with little knowledge of champagne; the temperance lobby was vocal, even in these early days; there were considerable periods of economic uncertainty; and of course between 1861 and 1865 there was the Civil War.

Yet sales increased rapidly. By 1877 sales had exceeded 400,000 bottles. François Bonal's history of the house* sums up the reasons for its success:

> North America offered the advantage of a non-saturated market in a continent where wealth grew rapidly and people took delight in displaying it. The owners of Mumm visited the country itself to decide what strategy to follow and, even when the US had been succcessfully won over, its directors continued to visit.

An easily recognised label, an easily pronounced name and a farsighted sales strategy. No wonder Mumm Cordon Rouge was seen throughout the major cities – in the finest restaurants, the most chic nightclubs, even the jazz clubs and brothels of New Orleans. There was a musical piece called the 'Cordon Rouge Gallop'. By 1902 Mumm was firmly established as the largest champagne house of all, greatly helped by the amazing sales figures across the Atlantic: a massive 1.5 million bottles!

The first years of the twentieth century were bliss. Sales were approaching 35 million bottles a year, demand was obviously increasing year by year, both at home and abroad. Even houses who had chosen not to invest in vineyards were now doing so in order to reinvest profits and guarantee sources of supply of the top-quality grapes. The image of champagne was perfect: there was champagne, and then there were all the other wines. The first worldwide wine phenomenon had been created.

Mumm. The Story of a Champagne House (Arthaud).

5

EARLY TWENTIETH-
CENTURY PROBLEMS

B ut most Champenois were ignoring phylloxera, the louse which feeds off the
sap of the vine and at the same time returns the compliment by discharging a
venomous substance into the plant's system. The insect was first discovered
among hybrid vines in the United States, causing no problems whatsoever. It wasn't
until it somehow crossed the Atlantic in the 1860s and found its way into a southern
Rhône vineyard that the nature of the little beast was understood.* The succulent roots
of the classic European vines were a perfect feeding and breeding ground and the
results were disastrous. Vineyards were destroyed, and the hapless owners were
totally bereft of any form of counterattack. In the 1870s and 1880s it spread like
wildfire throughout the southern wine regions of France, then to Italy, the Iberian
peninsula and North Africa.

Yet the pest did not reach as far north as the cool vineyards of Champagne, nor did
it flourish on chalk soils. At least that was the complacent opinion of many growers,
and when only a few affected hectares were discovered there was a certain amount of
justification for cautious optimism. As late as 1898 less than 50 hectares were
reported affected; at the turn of the century that area had expanded, but it was still of
little consequence. Ten years later it was a totally different story. Over a third of the
region's vineyards were wiped out and disaster loomed.

Greed, sheer stupidity and bureaucratic wrangling took their toll before everyone
came to their senses and took positive steps to solve the problem. At least the
Champenois had the benefit of thirty years of research by the earlier-affected regions,
but many growers were loath to spend the considerable sums of money on expensive
carbon disulphide, which had proved effective in killing the louse. Unbelievably they
were even unwilling to exercise these preventative measures when the government
and *négociant* houses offered to provide the necessary finance. Fortunately the

---

*Many wine-lovers who are fully aware that the solution for overcoming phylloxera originated from American
rootstock do not realise that the pest was actually imported from across the Atlantic, and that it equally affected
the classic vines of California.

more pragmatic were learning from the experiments of grafting on to imported American rootstock (Moët had established an experimental laboratory and vineyard as early as 1890 and to this day takes great pains to point out that the results and conclusions were made available to the whole industry). The industry escaped ruin, and it seemed that the effects of the louse could be repulsed.

At the same time there were other troubles in the region. The achievements of the past fifty or so years were of great benefit to the houses and most were honourable in their dealings with suppliers, but others were not. Some growers were paid a pittance and were annoyed that they were missing out on the obvious prosperity of their financial masters. There was also the burgeoning sharp practices of some firms, who were blatantly practising a basic form of oenological skulduggery – bringing in cheap wine from as far away as the Midi, blending it with a percentage of the local produce, bottling it and passing it off as champagne. Continuation of this was guaranteed to destroy much of the remarkable reputation of the name champagne.

There was also the festering problem of the Aube region and its viticultural produce. A brief glance at those maps of the Champagne Viticole which *do* include the Aube is enough to confirm that the Aube district is not close to the region's main vine-growing districts; it's really in a different area. At this time the growers of this southern region, closer to Chablis than Reims and a mere 150 kilometres from Dijon, lacked the ability to produce the correct fruit for the making of high-quality champagne. Georges Vesselle from Bouzy described the problems to me in a very succinct manner,

> In those days there were over 20,000 hectares under vine. They were the wrong grapes – Petit Meslier, Arbanne and a huge amount of Gamay – and they were planted everywhere with little regard for soil and climatic conditions. Forget about the fact that Troyes had been the ancient capital of the province of Champagne. Their wines were traditionally sold to the least knowledgeable of wine-drinkers in nearby Paris. They were quite happy with this arrangement, and not at all worried about the quality, just the convenience of easy sales. In the early years of this century the railway line from Marseilles to Paris opened and this allowed the second-rate, cheap Aube wines to be undersold by even cheaper wines from the south. . . . it ruined their market. It was also time for a political decision – were they going to become part of Burgundy or Champagne? The trouble is that neither province wanted them!

Things were a little more complex than that. In the early years of the century an attempt was made to supervise and control the sale of grapes to the houses. The laudable aim was to prevent the more unscrupulous firms from abusing their power and squeezing the growers. The drastic need for legislation to prevent the fraudulent wines was acknowledged, but if there was to be an empathy between the growers and houses there was an urgent need for a precise definition of the vineyard areas that were allowed to produce grapes for the production of quality champagne. In 1908 the government issued a decree which specified the legal limits of the champagne-producing area – and omitted the Aube. Needless to say the Aubois were furious (even though there was no means of enforcing the decree). In fact the regulations were so vague that no one was happy except the cheats, who were blithely carrying on the ruination of centuries of hard work. In February 1911 another decree was passed, restricting the importation of 'foreign' wines but not admitting the Aube into the delimited area.

This was the final indignity for the Aubois. At great cost they had replanted their phylloxera-ridden vineyards (unfortunately with Gamay grapes, which made such inferior champagne), while enduring a succession of disastrous harvests. Now it had been reconfirmed that they were not allowed to call their wine champagne – yet fraudulent houses were making a mockery of the system by flagrant importation of cheap wine from regions well outside the province of Champagne. So much for decrees guaranteeing authenticity! Enough was enough. Protests became extremely vociferous; demonstrators marched carrying as a symbol of solidarity their unique tools, *fousseux*, hoes with curved tips used for grubbing the rocks and pebbles of the region.*

The situation became extremely volatile, not merely in the Aube. The growers in the Marne were in full agreement with the name champagne being limited to the finest regions but were also desperately short of cash and incensed with the 'stretching' of the produce from their carefully cultivated grapes with vastly inferior wine. They realised that while they were poverty-stricken many dishonest firms were making huge illegal profits. On 11 April of the same year the government, under pressure from the Aubois, cancelled the decree of delimitation and the Aube was back in the region, thereby contributing further to the belittling of their cherished name. When news of the cancellation of the 1908 law reached Epernay, all hell broke loose.

The Marne growers banded together and went on the rampage. During the night roving groups broke into suspected establishments in Damery, Dizy and Cumières, smashed open the casks and poured the adulterated wine on to the streets. The next day the mob had swollen (contemporary newspaper estimates of the numbers vary from 5000 to 15,000) and Ay was sacked. The violence of the pack had by now overtaken events and innocent houses fell victim to the wholesale destruction inflicted by both axe and fire.** One can imagine the anguish of the respectable houses as they pondered the future of their wonderful, unique wine while Ay burned. Within a day

*There are still problems today regarding the relationships between the Aube and 'up north'. A tasting sponsored by the French government in London in 1987 referred to wines from 'Southern Champagne', and many growers of the Côte des Blancs and Montagne de Reims still refer to the Aubois rather contemptuously as 'Les Fousseux', and will tell you in a condescending manner that they have tasted 'some very good *still* wines' from the region.

**There was a certain amount of common sense: Bollinger was not touched and apparently the marchers even lowered the Socialist flag as they passed the doors.

or so more then 40,000 troops were stationed in the area. They remained until harvest-time, but the activities prompted the government into rapid action and on 7 June a bill was passed ratifying two classes of champagne: Champagne from the Marne and a few communes in the Aisne; Champagne Deuxième Zone from the other regions *plus* the Aube. Vin Mousseux was recognised as the term for naturally sparkling wine from other regions, and Vin Gazifié was to describe artificial sparkling wine.

6

THE WORLD WARS

It is ironic that all these seemingly insoluble problems of the time were swept away by a challenge of much greater magnitude – the First World War.

For a short time at the commencement of the war the Germans were back in charge of the Champagne region – but they were soon pushed back. Students of military history need no introduction to the bloody Battle of the Marne. Much of the war was fought among the vineyards of Champagne, and a considerable number of the most highly rated villages of the Montagne de Reims were actually in the midst of the front lines. Trenches were dug throughout the vineyards as the war raged in almost the same spot for four years. The few vines left standing were demolished by a combination of mortar fire and the other instruments of destruction of this horrifying war. The numerous war cemeteries throughout the region bear mute, dignified testimony to the appalling waste of human life. Similarly the village war memorials confirm the sacrifice of a large number of locals innocently caught up in a battle of superpowers.

Yet life carried on. The centre of Reims was literally razed to the ground, with only the cathedral and a few buildings left standing. The remaining populace lived underground in the cellars. Unbelievably some semblance of commercial life carried on with women, old men and children carrying out the dangerous tending of the vines. More than twenty children and countless adults were killed bringing in the grapes of the 1914 harvest. The tenacity of the Champenois was never more sorely tested, fertilisers were very scarce, crops were ravaged, wine-making facilities were wrecked, yet these amazing people produced nearly 50 per cent of the pre-war output. Times were desperate but a failure to continue the business activities would have been an admission of total catastrophe.

Joseph Krug II spent most of the 'activities' as a prisoner of war and his wife Jeanne proved to be another in the line of formidable ladies of Champagne. At the time of the 1915 harvest there was not only constant shelling but also precious little labour of any description and no horses or lorries to transport the grapes from the Côte des Blancs to Reims. It would have been very easy to shrug one's shoulders and let the fruit rot on the vines – but not Madame Krug: she organised the picking and pressing of the Pinot Noir grapes and later blended the wine herself using Chardonnay from the reserve wines. The Krug family treasure the telegram sent on 15 June 1924 from their United Kingdom agents Reid, Pye & Campbell: 'Madame Krug, Congratulations on popular success of your "Private Cuvée" 1915.'

The massive reorganisation of the vineyards after the war damage was a tremendous task but it had its plus factors. Lesser wine-growing areas were not replanted, more attention was paid to the selection of the right grapes for the right soils and microclimates. The vines were replanted in organised rows rather than in a haphazard spread (*en foule*). In fact the number of vines was reduced dramatically but the productivity was much greater. The area under vine was almost halved, the Champenois being convinced that quality was all-important and that the wine-lovers of the world would continue to clamour for their wines. Unfortunately the 1917 Revolution in Russia had already deprived the industry of one of its most profitable markets and in 1920 Prohibition was introduced in North America.

There was not much the houses could do about the problem of the Russian market. The loss of such custom where prodigious quantities of champagne were drunk by the extremely wealthy few (price never being a major consideration) affected the financial well-being of many houses – especially as the bills were left outstanding. No house suffered more than Louis Roederer. In the 1870s it had followed Moët, Clicquot and Ruinart, all well established on the lucrative Russian market – and as the demand soared so did the reputation and sales of Roederer. By the time of the Revolution this market accounted for a massive, irreplaceable 80 per cent of the company's total sales.*

The problems on the other side of the Atlantic were not quite so insurmountable. The era of speakeasies, bathtub gin, bootleg scotch and gangsters has been well documented, but the fact that wine-consumption continued has usually been ignored. Fortunately there was considerable interest in champagne and the more adventurous salesmen were able to continue supplying their clients, albeit by circuitous means.

Prohibition was short-lived in some places outside the United States and in 1923 when Jean-Charles Heidsieck visited Canada he managed to persuade the newly established Liquor Control Board of Quebec to stock his champagne, but this was relatively small business compared with supplying the bootleggers. After a few of the necessary introductions the house was shipping 60,000 bottles to a 'consortium' based on the French islands of St Pierre et Miquelon which are – unsurprisingly! – just off the eastern Canadian coast. Later Jean-Charles was to supply much larger quantities to prominent Canadian businessmen; presumably it was not for either

---

*Louis Roederer was reputedly the forerunner in the commercial development of Prestige Cuvées. In 1876 it created a clear *cristal* bottle for Tsar Alexander II, who refused to buy his favourite bubbly in the bottles readily available to his subjects. (This prompted some of my favourite champagne advertising copy when a Roederer Cristal advertisement of the 1960s bemoaned the fact that after 1917 their orders came to an abrupt standstill!)

personal or local consumption. By the end of the decade the Bronfman brothers, who founded Seagram, were purchasing 60,000 bottles of Charles Heidsieck a year.

This was only one of the major houses. Obviously G.H. Mumm, the Stateside market leader, suffered badly – but once again expediency ensured that lovers of Cordon Rouge were not to be thwarted. Many other brands were also to be found at the top nightclubs and restaurants. While lovers of champagne may not have been able to wander down to the corner shop for a bottle or three, they were not totally inconvenienced. Estimates vary as to the numbers of bottles shipped to the United States via other addresses during Prohibition* – it was most probably all of 70–80 million bottles! Further evidence of the prowess and tenacity of the Champenois; not only were they producers of a unique wine and the greatest travelling salesmen of their time, but when necessary they could adopt a fairly pragmatic approach to their business.

Towards the end of the 1920s the champagne business looked very promising indeed. The French were consuming more and more and Great Britain continued its passionate love affair with champagne. The reorganisation of the vineyards had finally been completed and in 1927 a law was passed defining the limitation of areas in Champagne suitable for viticulture. Density of planting, methods of pruning, harvesting and vinification were specified in order to protect the image of superiority, but there was soon another major crisis – the worldwide economic Depression which began with the Wall Street Crash of 1929.

No matter that the government, growers and houses had agreed on new standards of quality, had finally abolished the deprecatory class of Deuxième Zone and had placed all the regulated wines under a single *appellation*, Champagne,** and that Prohibition was repealed in 1933 – there were very few customers who could afford to celebrate! Sales plummeted as all markets declined dramatically. Both the houses and growers were facing disaster, more particularly the latter as over the next few years their wine stockpiled in the cellars with no buyers.

Once again the resourcefulness of the people triumphed. The houses were desperate for any market at any price, to make room in their cellars and generate some cash flow. Growers were forced to consider another system for the distribution and sale of their grapes and wines. Some of the larger landowners could afford the capital expenditure needed to vinify their own wine, store and then sell direct to the public. Others banded together and formed the first co-operatives: large wine-making facilities with low financial overheads were constructed and the wines were sold direct in bottle to the consumer rather than as grapes or bulk wine (*vin clair*) to the *négociants*. Now the French wine-drinkers had not lost their desire for champagne, merely the means to afford regular bottles. These reductions in prices

*Mexico, the Bahamas and Bermuda were other favourite addresses.
**This acknowledged the wines from the Aube and the Aisne as worthy of the full *appellation*, but the Aubios were legally bound to grub out the inferior plantings and replace them with the three classic varieties.

were sufficient to treble sales over the next decade. In the mid-1930s when the overseas market began to recover, the industry was for the first time enjoying the benefits of a domestic market which readily consumed a major part of production and bought from all the different types of producers, not merely the cheapest nor only the most expensive – a healthy base for expansion of exports.

No sooner had relative prosperity* been re-established within the industry than along came the Second World War. Once again, signs of a rosy future were overtaken by catastrophe.

No doubt it was of some comfort that, although once again the region suffered the humiliation of occupation by foreign forces, at least the battle was being fought across the whole of Europe, rather than just in the Montagne de Reims. The comparatively leisurely build-up of Hitler's invasion of France allowed many houses to construct false walls and hide stocks, an important factor because the Germans were relentless in their demands for shipments of wine back home. At times reasonable levels of accord seemed to have been reached, but at other times there was no such agreement, with the Fatherland demanding impossible quantities of champagne (not altogether surprising given the quality of its own sparkling wines), but presumably conspicuous consumption of such a worldwide wonder was good for morale, particularly as champagne was the spoils of an occupied country. Unfortunately for the Germans the trains carrying stocks were somehow often sent in completely the wrong direction, and often the stock that arrived had a lot in common with the 'champagne' produced by the fraudsters at the turn of the century.

There was very little physical damage to the vines, but times were by no means easy. Ill-health prevented Jacques Bollinger from enlisting, and yet this highly decorated veteran of the French Air Force was still prepared to accept the unenviable post of Mayor of Ay under occupation. He died in 1941 when only forty-seven and another in the remarkable sequence of great ladies of Champagne took the house over. Once again labour, transport, bottles and equipment were hopelessly short. Madame Jacques (or 'Tante Lily' as she was affectionately known by most) suffered the indignity of having her house occupied by the Germans – there are still 'Heil Hitler' carvings on the dining-room table. Yet she managed to be a source of inspiration to all members of the whole of the village community under stress. She was a reassuring figure to all as she bicycled around the region checking the vineyards, a habit she continued after the war when cars were available.

There was one positive aspect of the occupation. In 1941 the Comité Inter-professionel du Vin de Champagne (CIVC) was established under the auspices of the German authorities. The organisation brought both growers and houses together in order to control the industry jointly. Its main purpose was to supervise the 1927

---

*Only relative, because it was only now that total sales achieved a level equivalent to the latter years of the first decade of the twentieth century.

appellation laws and provide a sound platform for mutually acceptable working agreements between the two disparate interests. In its early years the Comité proved invaluable as it presented a unified voice when dealing with the problems of larger and larger shipments of wines to the Fatherland. Comte Robert-Jean de Vogüé of Moët was one of the main instigators of the CIVC:* in 1942 he and his assistant Claude Forman were considered to have been less than helpful – and were sentenced to death by the Gestapo. After a great deal of agitation the sentences were not carried out, but both men spent the rest of the war in concentration camps. The indomitable Champenois character ensured a lively resistance movement in the region and many other personalities suffered the same imprisonment; others were executed.

Inevitably the immediate post-war years were another period of gloom and doom. Obviously the houses and growers suffered serious financial constrictions and there were also the practical problems of neglect of the vineyards and a lack of available technical equipment. The combination of wartime production problems and the swingeing demands from the Germans had severely depleted stocks but that was not a great problem as the total sales in 1945 were down to a mere 22 million bottles, and only 4 million were exports. The economy of Europe was in such a parlous state that the prospects of a significant increase in sales seemed extremely doubtful.

Yet champagne bounced back. Within five years export sales had quadrupled and the worldwide total was a healthy 35 million bottles. After a decade a record 45 million bottles were sold, seemingly the limit of production, yet by 1960 sales reached 50 million.

*See Glossary for more details regarding the structure and functions of the CIVC.

7

POST-WAR AND
THE PRESENT PHENOMENON

The traumas of the first half of the century had taken their toll; many familiar names had disappeared. The champagne industry was more capital-intensive than ever (and was destined to become even more so) and yet as always it was quick to adjust to new developments. Many houses took advantage of post-war reorganisation and modernised their plants, adding much larger fermentation vats and creating more sophisticated means of bottling and dégorgement, ready for the increase in production as newly planted vineyards came on stream,* and new viticultural techniques (especially those minimising the effects of disease and frosts) allowed a more consistently high quality of grapes in larger yields per hectare.

The wars and economic problems were forgotten and the Western world was affluent once again. The home market was drinking vast quantities – in fact, at 35 million bottles in 1960, now over two-thirds of the total sales – but the champagne salesmen were back on their travels preaching the gospel according to St Vincent** with evangelical fervour. In some of the traditional markets such as Great Britain, Belgium and other European countries, it was relatively easy, but other markets were more difficult to regain. Christian de Billy of Pol Roger vividly remembers his first few years with the family firm,

> When I joined I soon became used to travelling. After one year's experience in Epernay I was sent to the United States for five months. I visited twenty-two cities in all – from New York down to Miami, across to Texas then California, Denver, Chicago, St Louis and many others.
>
> In those days I was a little naive and thought that because the States had been a huge market for champagne in the early part of the century all I would have to do was turn up and my order book would be filled. The trouble was that in those days the public had lost the habit of drinking champagne. After three whole

*Despite these new plantings only 40 per cent of the delimited area of 1927 was planted. The seemingly ever present financial problems had not allowed for the expansion, and also much of the unused vineyard area was in the poorer-quality regions.
**The patron saint of the French wine-growers, in particular those of Champagne.

weeks of promotion in New York my agent persuaded me to throw a 'Champagne Pol Roger Party' and I was horrified to find the caterers had stocked a large spirits bar. I was even more horrified to discover just how necessary this was. At least half of the delightful, friendly people who attended didn't even bother to taste a glass of Pol Roger!

The next year Guy Pol Roger sent him off again, this time on another five-month jaunt – through the South Americas, returning to California and then on to Ontario and Quebec.

At the time South America had some very important markets, especially Venezuela, where there were many parties where they did actually drink the Pol Roger. Panama was a very enthusiastic customer – it was a duty-free zone and a large number of countries sent military planes to collect huge shipments of untaxed goods. I am pleased to say that Pol Roger was well represented.

Victor Lanson was the driving force behind the rapid growth of his family house at this time. Stories about him could easily fill a book of this size. Many are genuine. Having had the good fortune to enjoy the company of this greatest character of the twentieth-century champagne world I have no hesitation in believing any that involve his legendary drinking ability or his wicked sense of humour.*

Apparently he was a dinner guest in one of the larger cities of the United States and was annoyed that only hard liquor was offered before dinner. With difficulty he managed to extract a glass of Lanson Black Label, but there were further horrors – only iced water was served as accompaniment to the meal. A few years later Victor had the opportunity to return the hospitality in Reims. No spirits were offered as an aperitif and the Lanson flowed. When the guests were seated for dinner they noticed an elegant glass in front of them, filled with water ... and a goldfish. Finally one plucked up the courage to ask Victor about this strange fact. He smiled and said, 'In Champagne we understand the correct use for water.'

The missionary work certainly paid off. As production increased in the 1960s so did exports, sometimes in unusual places. I well remember Victor's eldest son, Pierre, visiting New Zealand in 1968; a small, geographically remote country (this was before the days of Jumbo jets) was gradually becoming aware of the delights of champagne as compared with the locally produced sparkling muck which flaunted the same name. The promotional work done by Pierre benefited Lanson enormously (it was well established by then and has continued to be one of the dominant brands) and was also a tremendous boost to the image of all champagne. Laurent Perrier, newcomer to the international scene and merely ninety-eighth largest house in 1959, realised that the older houses had spent a great number of years and millions of

*No doubt many are apocryphal, but whenever I query the authenticity of a particularly funny tale with Mario Snozzi, General Manager of G.H. Mumm for thirty-five years and a *bon ami* of Victor, they are usually verified.

francs establishing their brands on most markets, so Laurent Perrier's own initial export drive was to the almost untapped markets of the expatriate nationals in colonial West Africa. It seemed a gamble but the company had done its homework and while the British colonies in Africa were great whisky- and beer-drinkers the French territories were extremely enthusiastic wine-drinkers ... and they loved champagne.

Replanting was continued, with another 6000 hectares planted this decade. The average harvest for the period 1959–69 was 88 million bottles with no year exceeding 102 million bottles. Suddenly in 1970 the region was blessed with a yield of 220 million. The Champenois had never had it so good and their good fortune was richly deserved.

The houses were overwhelmed with wine, and storage became an acute problem. G.H. Mumm even resorted to hiring tank barges at the port of Rouen. The co-operatives, which had been gradually increasing in number, simply did not have the storage capacities and they suffered the consequent oenological problems after using less than perfect facilities.* The growers selling their own wines direct to the consumers were in a marvellous business position; plenty of stocks of high-quality wines and a booming home market (yes, as the economy prospered the French drank even more champagne).

In 1972 I attended the Champagne Academy course, the greatest fortnight in my life. As a guest of the major houses we attended lectures by the most knowledgeable members of the champagne trade, we were tutored in tastings by some of the most superb palates – members of the families responsible for the blends and the *chefs de caves*, and we discussed the achievements of the champagne houses and their futures. At the time sales were buoyant (124 million bottles compared with 42 million only ten years before, and the export market had grown at the same pace as the domestic). Despite this expansion quality was not suffering – the superb 1964 and 1966 vintages being sold at the time, and the 1970 still lying in the cellars, were positive testimony. The progress was expected to continue, but gradually. Few could envisage that this was only the beginning of the most incredible growth of all. There were a few hiccups provoked by the financial insecurity of the Western world after the oil crisis of the mid-1970s but these problems were soon pushed aside. A new, classless generation of worldwide champagne drinkers was spawned as the increased production allowed the Champenois to sell a previously élitist wine at a reasonable price.** Exports increased market share to nearly 40 per cent with Great Britain foremost. The United States momentarily assumed the position of largest export market in 1984; Italy,

*Many foresaw future problems and created larger tank storage establishments. The mammoth Centre Vinicole de la Champagne at Chouilly, actually a union of co-operatives, began life in 1972 as a storage centre which took in the must – the unfermented grape juice – from the member co-operatives; later it was returned for vinification. (See Chapter 14.)

**When I first arrived in London in 1972 petrol stations offered free beer glasses; later it was wine glasses – now it is champagne flutes!

Belgium, Switzerland, West Germany and Canada have continued growing; and in certain years, currency permitting, Australia and New Zealand have performed prodigiously. Nowadays total sales average nearly twice the 1972 figure.

This recent dynamism in the champagne world has taken its toll as many firms have not managed to survive. The French inheritance laws, with the associated problems of whingeing death duties and inter-family disputes which make television's *Dynasty* seem rather relaxed, and the sheer sums of capital needed for stock financing have resulted in dramatic change since those heady days of the early 1970s when the great Champenois families were in control of virtually all major houses.

Christian Bizot, nephew of Madame Bollinger, was one of my tutors in 1972. The Bollinger firm is not exactly the most flamboyant of houses, but because of the carefully controlled tradition of excellence it is, along with Krug and Roederer, in a unique position of exercising great influence within the business despite relative modesty of size. Bizot is one of the most astute of all present *directeurs-généraux*, and his innate modesty belies the fact that his firm has resisted many temptations and very skilfully balanced the quality ideals with the tremendous expansion of production.

> We have a responsibility to maintain the quality. Not only for ourselves, but also for the growers. We have always had an excellent relationship with our suppliers – they are proud to sell their grapes to Maison Bollinger – and I tell them we have no future worries whatsoever, as long as we continue to produce top-quality wines.
>
> The mergers and buying and selling of companies can continue without affecting ourselves. We are small enough to be able to stay financially independent. There will always be room for individualistic houses.

Some others have not been quite so astute, others have not had the chance. More about these aspects later.

8

THE 'SOUL' OF CHAMPAGNE

Many words have been written on the *méthode champenoise*, and many other producers both at home and abroad would have us believe that merely by adhering to certain aspects of the creation of champagne they offer products of similar quality and stature. I recently spied a bottle of Loire sparkling on a Florida supermarket shelf which featured a back label boasting: 'The unique, centuries-old technique perfected by the French in the Champagne region has been used to produce this finely balanced wine with a magical sparkle.' Arrant nonsense. Any wine-maker with the right equipment and a measure of skill can make a wine sparkle using the technical aspects of the *méthode*, but this is only a part of the complex and unique soul of champagne.

—— THE GRAPES ——

Over the centuries a number of varieties have been cultivated, but nowadays production of champagne is confined to three varieties.

CHARDONNAY. The Côte des Blancs is the heartland of Chardonnay territory. In many respects it is surprising to find this grape in such a northerly clime as it produces open buds very early and is therefore very susceptible to the late spring frosts which beset the region. It is a shy bearing (yielding smaller quantities of grapes than most other varieties), subtle grape which produces wine with great elegance and a good deal of fresh, zippy character. It is not disparaging to point out that the Chardonnay here doesn't produce the extroverted, 'up front' style of wine found in New World wine regions as this is often due more to oak than to fruit. Many a reasonably knowledgeable wine-lover confuses the flavour of this rather introverted variety and actually associates its style with the results of barrel fermentation and ageing in new oak. The subtlety of flavour needs time to develop, and the early years of Chardonnay-dominated champagne blends are often characterised by an excess of acidity. The character of the wine varies immensely, from the appley delicacy of the Côte des Blancs to the slightly more full wines dotted around the Montagne de Reims and the fragrant, yet quite earthy, wines from the Vallée de la Marne.

PINOT NOIR. The majority of the vineyards of the Montagne de Reims and the south-facing slopes of the Vallée de la Marne are planted with this noble but delicate grape variety. A great deal of the still red wine of the region (Coteaux champenois) proves that the grape which produces such velvety, voluptuous still wines on the better slopes of the Côte d'Or and Côte de Beaune doesn't manage quite the same in Champagne (I won't be discussing the still wines of the region in much detail) — and yet the grape produces a considerable depth of flavour and a prominent bouquet when made into champagne.

PINOT MEUNIER. A poor relation of the Pinot Noir, and often unfairly disparaged. The Meunier doesn't produce buds as early as the other two; it therefore doesn't have the same battle with the climate and is quite happy on the colder north-facing slopes of the Marne; it also produces a significantly higher yield. Meunier is the workhorse grape of Champagne — it is the most widely planted of all varieties and the least talked about.* The wine produced lacks the elegance of the other two varieties but it is soft and flavoursome — easy drinking, if a little one-dimensional. Many houses will place great emphasis on informing the world at large that they use no Meunier whatsoever, others will talk loosely about their 'Pinot' content and hope they won't be asked 'which?' or 'how much of each?'. Yet major houses such as Moët & Chandon and Veuve Clicquot have never disclaimed the considerable percentage in some of their blends. The Meunier has the other great advantage of maturing early. Unfortunately it has a reputation for lacking staying power, which is probably unfounded. Just ask one of the Krug family, who revel in their use of considerable quantities of Meunier. No one could accuse their champagnes of being shortlived!

These three grape varieties of Champagne are unique. The two 'noble' ones are not ideally suited to a region with such a short summer but do possess an important attribute for such a northerly climate: they are early-ripening. And they thrive on the clay soil. The other has never succeeded anywhere other than Champagne. While certain areas can make excellent (or in the case of Meunier 'good') wines from the one grape the vast majority of the fine champagnes are made from the unique blending of the characteristics of the different varieties.

—— THE VINEYARDS ——

As I have said, the area currently under production is about 28,000 hectares, approximately 2 per cent of the total vineyard area of France. Seventy-five per cent are in the Département de Marne, 17 per cent in the Département d'Aube and 8 per cent in the Départements d'Aisne and Seine et Marne. The total area demarcated

---

*Latest CIVC figures show that it accounts for 39 per cent of all vineyard plantings. Pinot Noir 33 per cent. Chardonnay 28 per cent.

under the champagne *appellation* is approximately 34–35,000 hectares. Only another 3,000 to 5,000 of the remaining hectares could be planted as the remainder is occupied by nature reserves, land unsuitable for vines, roads and, of course, buildings.

Merely being the proud owner of vineyard land within the delimited area doesn't allow barter on the open market for the best-possible price for the grapes. Champagne has a unique system of classification, the *'Echelle des Crus'*. The CIVC rates the vineyards by percentage – from 80 per cent to 100 per cent, according to the quality of the grapes cultivated. Prices paid to the growers relate to these assessments. Each year, just before the harvest, the CIVC sets a binding price for 100 per cent grapes according to a number of circumstances, most importantly the size of the harvest and the average wholesale price of a bottle of champagne in the previous year (this seems rather complicated; the theory is that taking the price of the finished product into account ensures the producer of the grapes approximately a third of the bottle price). In 1987 there was a giant harvest equivalent to 270 million bottles, and 100 per cent grapes fetched FF22 a kilo; 1988 produced a relatively modest 225 million bottles and the price was raised to FF24. Growers in all the different villages are paid according to their rating figure. A certain amount of leeway is allowed for negotiations, and a supplementary price for premium grapes may be allowed, but this is sometimes exceeded, especially in years of stock shortages. Many people have told me of considerable underhand deals which have pushed up the cost of the crop, 'not done by me, you understand, but by a friend'.

There are seventeen villages with 100 per cent status. This allows them to be termed GRAND CRU: Ambonnay, Avize, Ay, Beaumont-sur-Vesle, Bouzy, Cramant, Louvois, Mailly-Champagne, Puisieulx, Sillery, Tours-sur-Marne (Pinot grapes only) and Verzenay have enjoyed this status since the introduction of the system with the establishment of the CIVC. Chouilly (Chardonnay only), Le Mesnil-sur-Oger, Oger, Oiry and Verzy were added in 1985. These Grand Cru villages contain just 17 per cent of the cultivated area. Interestingly Chardonnay is in the majority (52 per cent) with 46 per cent Pinot Noir and 2 per cent Pinot Meunier.

The villages with status between 90 and 99 per cent are entitled to the term PREMIER CRU:

90%   Bergères-les-Vertus (Pinot), Bezannes, Chamery, Coligny (Chardonnay), Cuis (Pinot), Ecueil, Etréchy (Chardonnay), Grauves (Pinot), Jouy-les-Reims, Les Mesneux, Pargny-les-Reims, Pierry, Sacy, Tours-sur-Marne (Chardonnay), Villedommange, Villers Allerand, Villers-aux-Noeuds.

93%   Avenay, Champillon, Cumières, Hautvillers, Mutigny.

94%	Chigny-les-Roses, Ludes, Montbre, Rilly-la-Montagne, Taissy, Trois Puits.		(Chardonnay), Dizy, Grauves (Chardonnay), Trépail, Vaudemanges, Vertus, Villeneuve-Renneville, Villers-Marmery, Voipreux.
95%	Bergères-les-Vertus (Chardonnay only), Billy-le-Grand, Bissueil, Chouilly (Pinot), Cuis	99%	Mareuil-sur-Ay, Tauxières.

These Premier Cru vineyards (once again with a predominance of Chardonnay) account for only another 18 per cent of the total area, leaving the vast majority of vineyards within the 80–90 per cent ratings.

—— THE CHAMPAGNE *APPELLATION* ——

In 1927 the Champagne region was defined and a number of other restrictions were instituted. These were refined and expanded by decree in 1935 and put into practice with the establishment of the CIVC in 1941. The most important of these laws are:
– Definition of types of vines (nowadays only Chardonnay, Pinot Noir, Pinot Meunier) permitted in the production of champagne. Furthermore, no other grapes may be planted in the delimited region for other purposes.
– Strict regulations regarding the planting, management and pruning of vines.
– Limitation of the yield per hectare.
– Ratifying the minimum alcoholic strength of musts harvested.
– Enforcing the maximum yield from pressing.
– Ensuring that only wines with a certificate of origin of *appellation* Champagne may be taken into the cellars of the region.
– Insisting that all wines produced must be bottled in the region.
– Prohibiting the making of any 'sparkling wines' other than *appellation* Champagne within the region.
– Stating that the wine cannot be bottled before the first day of January after harvest, and it then cannot be despatched until it has been stored for at least a year.

This is all regulated by the CIVC with the assistance of the industry, which is aware of their common interest in protecting the quality image of champagne. More about the committee later.

—— THE VINEYARD YEAR ——

After the harvest the vine branches are cut back severely to enable the plant to have as few worries as possible during the freezing winter months when all energy must be concentrated on revitalisation of the roots. The home gardener's favourite fertiliser (well, it was certainly my father's), super phosphate, is added to the soil. In mid-winter general tidying-up is carried out, the vineyards are a little forlorn but there is a certain haunting beauty in the austerity, especially during the really bitter winters. The topsoil is augmented with the *cendres-noires* lignite (see p.6), the dried refuse from the last vintage's pressings and, less evocatively, the refuse from towns (*boues de ville*). The latter may be organically desirable but its effect leaves a lot to be desired aesthetically because the distributed rubbish is always full of bits of the bright-blue rubbish sacks used by the French. The Champenois claim they are using less of this form of manure, but I haven't noticed any lessening of the 'blue bags' effect, scattered along the rows.

Spring is the time for planting any new vines. In pre-phylloxera days the vines were planted in a haphazard manner, *en foule* — not in any particular line and certainly not in rows along wires. Left to themselves the vines would rapidly propagate themselves, thereby overrunning the vineyard; in fact even with the attention of the growers there were up to four times as many vines per hectare as now. When reorganisation and replanting were carried out, two important factors influenced the planting of vines in rows: firstly, the ease of cultivation, because the space between rows allowed horse-drawn (later mechanical) cultivation equipment; and, secondly, the extra space allowed the sunshine easier access to the fruit. The *appellation* law demands that the rows must be 1.5 metres, or less, apart and along the rows the vine plants must be at a distance between 0.9 and 1.5 metres — providing a total spacing and distance in between vines of at least 2.5 metres — in order to limit the strength and size of each plant. This enables the total harvest to be spread over the maximum number of vines, rather than having only the strongest survive. The cuttings have been grafted on the American rootstock (now propagated in France). New plantation of vines can only be carried out with the governmental authorisation related to the planned development of the small amount of suitable remaining land. Replantation can only be carried out when a vine covering the same surface in the same holding has been rooted out.

Spring is also the time when the sap rises from the roots and the buds begin to form. This is indeed a crucial time for the *vigneron* because the region is known to suffer from late frosts. Every time there is a mild winter, with the consequent early rising of the sap, the growers shake their heads as they mutter about their fears of 'another 1957', when frosts devastated the vines, which had budded early after a very mild winter. It is also time for pruning, and once again there is cause for anxiety because the earlier the *vigneron* prunes the more chance he gives the vine to concentrate its energy — yet it is also being exposed more to the perils of a frost. Mid-March or a little later is the accepted balance of desirability versus the risk factor. (The *vignerons* don't just sit around resigned to fate, they have two reasonably effective means of deterrent: paraffin-fired braziers which are placed strategically throughout the vineyards; and spraying with water (the frost freezes the water, not the bud, and a layer of thermal protection is formed). The systems of pruning are strictly regulated in order to keep the grapes close to the soil so that they can benefit from the reflection of heat and the restoration of the humidity hoarded by the chalk soil. The Chablis and Cordon de Royat systems which allow the bud to be no more than 0.6 metres from the ground must be used for Chardonnay and Pinot Noir. The Vallée de la Marne and Guyot methods, while different in style, must result in the buds being 0.5 metres from the ground. The former is only allowed for Pinot Meunier, the latter for the other two varieties, but not in Grand or Premier Cru vineyards.

In about late May or early June the vines begin to flower followed by the setting of the grapes – another time for anxiety. If the flowering is early the danger of frost lurks, and ironically if the weather is suddenly very sunny after the prolonged cold spell there is a danger of *couluré*, a viticultural form of sunstroke when the vine reacts illogically and wastes most of the vitality gained from the sun and warmth, and channels into propagation of the vine itself, ignoring the leaves and fruit. The vines are carefully trimmed so that the warmth reaches the fruit, but a covering foliagè must be left perfectly in place in order to protect the grapes from the direct rays of the sun. The vines are sprayed at regular intervals to counteract the problems of fungal diseases and insect pests. (Birds are another matter but not to the destructive extent in Britain, where netting almost covers whole vineyards.) Chemical solutions may not appeal to believers in organic cultivation but the problems of mildew in wet summers and other diseases are even less appealing.* The ground is broken up by hoeing and by August the vineyards present a beautiful picture, combining the joys of nature and the meticulous husbandry of the *vignerons*. The rolling hillsides look as if they have been trimmed by a manicurist. I have travelled around most vineyard regions of the world and have never seen such splendour.

—— THE VINTAGE ——

The comparatively cool spring means that the amount of heat received in August is crucial to the ripening of grapes; fortunately September often provides much-needed dry warmth. In exceptional years such as 1976 the harvest (*vendange*) can be carried out as early as the first weeks of September, while it may be as late as mid-October. In many years the few weeks before harvest is a very tense time as the vineyard owners anxiously wait for the grapes to ripen and hope the rain stays away.

The decision on the beginning of the harvest is set by the CIVC, approximately 100 days after the spring flowering of the vines. Previously there were two rigid dates, one for Pinot and a later date for Chardonnay, nowadays the CIVC have adopted a more relaxed approach with a variation of localised starting dates. *Vignerons* in the other

*Also the improvement in both fertilisers and spraying solutions has contributed significantly to the higher yields and more consistent quality.

major viticultural regions of France rightly consider that the setting of the harvest dates by their respective committees is a crucial matter – but here it requires the very finest of tuning. As Bernard de La Giraudière of Laurent Perrier points out:

> In other regions the amount of sunshine is very important but not exact. In some of the New World countries even a few weeks is not of crucial importance either way – but in Champagne just a few extra hours of sunshine can mean the difference between a thin, undistinguished wine or a good harvest.

Ideally the dates set for the harvest will provide grapes with a satisfactory sugar content (sufficient to produce wine of 11° alcohol), but also with a degree of acidity which would be unwelcome elsewhere in the wine-making world.

Picking the grapes is a serious, hectic, back-breaking affair, though one accompanied by a degree of gaity. Many of the pickers are industrial workers from the big cities of the north and their families. This work offers fresh air, communal festivities (especially at the end of the harvest) and some extra money. These are the regulars who return year after year. Students are also an important source of labour; many of my friends say they wouldn't have missed the experience, but 'never again, thank you.' Gypsies trek up from the south. All in all it is a polyglot affair with a great deal of hard physical effort and great spirit in the evenings in the large dormitories where the pickers are housed.*

The harvesting is slow, and takes weeks. In some years this length of time works in the growers' favour, in other years the latter part of the picking may produce over-ripe grapes lacking the necessary acidity, or be carried out in the autumnal rains with consequent rot problems. However, despite these disadvantages the much more rapid mechanical harvesting is forbidden. Anyone who has seen these machines in action will be fully aware of the fearful shaking received by the vines, and the thin skins of the champagne grapes must be kept in pristine condition for the gentle pressing. No doubt a suitable machine will eventually be developed and, as the terrain is certainly amenable, hand-picking will be replaced.

The 1987 harvest was an excellent example of the trials, tribulations and occasional success stories of such a prolonged harvest. After a patchy summer and damp early September there was nothing but gloom and doom. One grower in Verzenay muttered to me that he didn't enjoy being reminded about the disastrous, damp 1972 harvest. Picking started as early as 28 September in some areas and as late as 10 October in others. In the beginning there was considerable rain, although the temperatures were so low that the problem of rot was avoided; however, suddenly the sun came out and the rest of the crop was harvested in near-perfect conditions. The late-picked Pinot Noir was of reasonable quality, the Pinot Meunier flourished –

---

*I once asked Christian de Billy of Pol Roger whether they strictly enforced the segregation of the sexes in the dormitories. His eyes twinkled as he replied, 'Not if their children are persuaded to carry on the tradition of harvesters.'

but the late burst of sunshine could not compensate the Chardonnay vines for the lack of the vital 'real' heat of August. I have been around during years of despair (1972, 1977), years of benevolence (1976, 1982) but never a year of such fascinating irregularity.

—— THE PRESSING ——

Most of the major firms have press-houses dotted throughout the region, so the grapes never travel too far. Once again the pristine condition of the grapes is of paramount importance if the pigments within the skins are to be kept from blending with the juice. The co-operatives have their own press-houses and a considerable amount of the harvest passes through these establishments. Many of the medium-size producers will press for other growers who do not have the facilities. It is a busy, bustling operation with vast quantities of grapes being turned into must with great care and attention. Once again the regulations are very strict. The presses may be the traditional vertical *coquard* or the more modern horizontal ones. The *coquards* are either round or square and are made of wood. They are very shallow as the requirement is not only fast, gentle pressing but also as little contact between juice and skins as possible. The grapes are placed in the container which is basically a series of pieces of wood joined together and then a large wooden lid is pushed down squeezing out the juice. All very simple and effective, and basically the same operation as that performed more than a century ago. When I first began visiting Champagne the CIVC had just permitted different forms, in particular a horizontal operation with a large inflatable cylinder – the grapes are placed inside and pressed as the cylinder expands. In the early years of these presses there was much talk of the benefits. Theoretically the speed of the process was particularly advantageous for the extraction of maximum flavour and fruit. Nowadays the enthusiasm seems to have waned – giants such as Moët have retained the *coquards* and when Bollinger had to buy new presses recently it chose to replace with the same. In fact Deutz even shipped a *coquard* out to California when it built Maison Deutz in Santa Barbara.

The presses are quite small for such a giant operation. They have a capacity of 4000 kilos and the yield must by law be limited to 100 litres per 150 kilos of grapes. So one pressing must not yield more than 2666 litres of must entitled to bear the Champagne *appellation*. The law also dictates four different qualities of pressing:

The CUVÉE: the first 2050 litres of juice extracted. This is the most gently pressed juice with more freshness and delicacy of flavour.

Some houses such as Krug use only this category. Others make certain wines (in particular Prestige Cuvée) from only this. After this pressing the sides of the press are opened and the solid mass of skins and pips is chopped and replaced in the middle for much heavier pressing which yields:

The PREMIER TAILLE: the next 410 litres.

The DEUXIÈME TAILLE: the next 205 litres.

The REBÊCHE: whatever is left – if desired. The most profitable use for this is distillation. Very occasionally it is used to produce very ordinary table wine.

The heavier pressing of the almost dry skins results in small quantities of free-flowing juice with a much higher tannin content. Many houses do not use the deuxième taille at all (in fact I am sure it will soon be outlawed) and some like Bollinger use the premier taille sparingly and only in certain years. Often it is sold off to lesser houses which produce cheaper styles of wines; often it is swapped for much lesser quantities of cuvée.

For a large percentage of the Champagne growing industry, the whole year's cycle has now come to an end. For others the work is really just beginning. The different grapes from the different vineyards are pressed separately, the juice is allowed to settle briefly for about ten hours (either on the site or rushed through the narrow, winding roads and villages by tanker drivers who are all desperately seeking to prove that they are faster than Alain Prost) and is then fermented.

The vines in winter.

ABOVE *and* **RIGHT** *Despite technological innovations, champagne viniculture remains a very labour intensive industry – from the back-breaking work of winter to harvesting.*

OPPOSITE *This view of Cumières shows the essential characteristics which make up the micro-climates of the region. South-facing slopes maximising sunshine hours on the vines, the warmth-providing river Marne, and the woods helping to maintain the humidity level.*

ABOVE *and* RIGHT *Different approaches to the first fermentation.*

OPPOSITE *The traditional 'coquard' press. To avoid unnecessary contact between juice and skin, this batch of 4000 kilos will soon be wheeled over for fast, gentle pressing.*

At this stage, the individual wines taste little better than they look! Prince Alain de Polignac of Pommery makes his initial assessment.

Sur lattes

Remuage

Sediment

Sur pointes

9

THE *MÉTHODE*
CHAMPENOISE

I consider that it is rather misleading to refer to the method of vinification as such because basically the *méthode* begins with the choice of vines, and continues with the painstaking and carefully regulated cultivation in a unique region; it is not confined to the wine-making. Basically champagne is the product of two fermentations, the first outside the bottle, the second inside. When the must enters the vats the yeast enzymes which have been lurking on the skins cause a reaction which converts the sugar into alcohol and carbon dioxide. (I know this sounds terribly boring, but pay attention for a short time – it is important!) This fermentation is quite a vigorous affair with the juice bubbling with considerable ferocity. The temperature is all-important: in the past the natural conditions used to suffice, the cellar doors were opened and the chilly draughts would bring the casks down to a suitable temperature level (between 15° and 20°C). It would take around three weeks before the yeasts worked themselves into an early death after reducing the sugar level to almost nothing (less than 2 grams per litre), then dropped to the bottom to form the lees. Nowadays sophisticated technology does the job more simply and more precisely. Most oenologists (wine-makers) prefer the first fermentation to be carried out rapidly as this preserves aroma and delicacy of flavour.

—— MALOLACTIC FERMENTATION ——

The considerable amount of natural grape acidity contains a high percentage of harsh malic acid. In the past when the cellars warmed up in spring a non-alcoholic fermentation, the 'malolactic', often took place whereby this tart, hard acid was changed into softer lactic acid. According to eminent personalities such as Christian Bizot, Henri Krug and Jean-Baptiste Lanson, previous generations of wine-makers quite frankly did not fully understand this process. In the days of oak fermentation, it simply happened – a fully integrated but unrecognised part of the process of softening the harsh base wine.

Nowadays *malo* is the buzz word. Oenologists realise that either they can prevent it, by treating the musts with sulphite and then, after fermentation, keeping the temperature of the still wine at 15°C or below, or they can ensure that it occurs by raising the temperature above 15°C and adding yeast cultures. It must be admitted that the majority of the houses are in favour and many consider that the process is vital for the making of sound, soft wines, while some others (in particular Krug, Lanson and Piper Heidsieck) consider that the effort of prevention is a necessary step in making full, fruity wines and they point out that the wines will soften naturally with age, and that their wines will age better than those which have undergone the process. (Bollinger sums up the mixed opinions by making wines under both conditions.) There doesn't really seem to be a straightforward answer – no one can accuse Moët & Chandon's vintage wines of ageing anything but gracefully, yet they have undergone an induced *malo*. Similarly I have drunk many, many bottles of reasonably youthful, fresh and fruity Lanson without any traces of excess acidity.*

When the alcoholic (and most probably malolactic) fermentation has been finished the wines are 'racked' – the clear wine is drawn off from the vat leaving the sediment. New stainless-steel technology means that this can be a relatively simple and speedy affair, pumping the wine from one vat to another a couple of times, whereas the traditional cask-fermentation techniques requires the use of gravity and much more time and manual effort to ensure the clarity; this can take most of the winter.

At this stage, even with the largest of houses, the wines are still kept individually – village by village, grape variety by grape variety. It is an immense task of organisation on a grand scale, which has been helped considerably by new technology. It does take away some of the mystique, but the fermentation cellars with their lines of giant stainless-steel tanks and a computerised control board looking like a set from a James Bond movie allow a much more efficient and foolproof method of keeping track of numerous individual cuvées (700 tanks containing wines from more than 100 crus at Moët).

—— THE BLENDING (*ASSEMBLAGE*) ——

Just when most white-wine producers are ready to sit back and relax – and prepare for the receipt of their monies – the real work begins in Champagne. Rémi Krug repeatedly states:

> Anyone can grow grapes, anyone can make sparkling wine by the *méthode* if they are prepared to invest the time and money, but only we can capture the secret of champagne – the importance of the blend. The creation of a wine from numerous different communes within the region and from reserve wines from a number of older vintages.

*Jean-Baptiste Lanson is always keen to point out that the average bottle of Lanson Black Label has about four years of bottle age, and shrugs his shoulders and changes the subject when queried about the possible fruit/acid balance of a non-*malo* wine which is not at least twice the legal age.

THE *MÉTHODE CHAMPENOISE*

In spring the still wines (*vin clairs*) are very much an acquired taste – all but the most forward are extremely sour with little of the attractiveness of varietal character showing. At first the blenders, usually the *chef de caves* and other directors (who in the old days were invariably members of the family) taste all the new wines. They will have to make an initial decision on the quality of the harvest. The serious houses are searching for the continuation of the all-important 'house style' and many decisions are based on the year's ability in allowing them to do so. Which will marry most successfully with which? How are they going to age? Which are not up to the standard required of a constituent part of the style? How much of the company's reserve stocks will be needed to achieve the balance? Are the best wines of a quality suitable for vintage champagne? And if so, has the house sufficient liquid assests to allow this (sometimes it is more necessary to bolster the reserve wines with top-quality stocks). The questions are almost unending.

The reserve wines are of crucial importance. When nature has blessed Champagne with a succession of good-quality, plentiful vintages most producers can turn out a decent product, but after poor years the skill of the blender will be negated if there are not sufficient stocks of wines from other vintages. The major houses keep vast stocks – up to five years' sales, or in the case of Krug in excess of six, an expensive proposition in these days. (Many of their neighbours in Chablis have forgotten the meaning of the word 'stockholding'.) Judicious blending of these high-quality wines will add depth and maturity to unattractive base wines from the present year. Perhaps the current vintage is poor on Chardonnay, yet the house takes particular pride in highlighting the delicacy and appley flavour of this grape in its non-vintage blend, then the blenders will add some white grape reserve and the style and flavour are continued.*

There is nothing simple about this crucial process. There is no substitute for experience and memory (and money!). In some houses it is passed down from father to son, but as ownership of many houses has changed it is now passed down through the technical employees – from the *chef de caves* to his assistant oenologists. These superb tasters learn the house style and get to know its vineyards, its sources of grape purchases, and its extraordinary individual qualities. It is interesting that despite a lack of family ties these people so often remain with the same house throughout their careers, unlike in California and Australia, where wine-makers seem to change allegiances as often as football managers change clubs. Loyalty is one reason, but another is that their knowledge has been built up over the years around the style of 'their' house in particular, not the style of Champagne in general.

---

*The subtleties of blending never cease to fascinate. For example Perrier-Jouët and Pol Roger, two close neighbours on the avenue de Champagne, both have overt Chardonnay characteristics which are very different: the former light, flowery with a delicate hint of apples and the latter more pungent, aristocratic with a delightful firm finish. The superb intense quality of their white grapes from only the finest of cru allows them to obtain these dominant flavours with only a minority of Chardonnay in their respective blends.

THE GLORY OF CHAMPAGNE

There will always be small growers who make exciting, well-balanced wines from a limited part of the Champagne region. There are some perfectly agreeable wines from large co-operatives and delicious wines from smaller ones, but more about these in later chapters. The reputation of champagne lies with the large houses, and the centuries of tradition and carefully honed skills passed on from generation to generation. These are the names that evoke the image of champagne all around the world, and whilst the rest of the *méthode champenoise* is very important their reputation and subsequent commercial success or failure are very closely allied to the skills practised in the blending room.

Obviously many smaller producers tend to play down the importance of blending and of the reserve wines. My assertion can be proved with a simple tasting experiment. Two years after a poor vintage (considered sufficiently newsworthy to receive a great deal of newspaper space at the time, and it will always be reported in wine magazines early in the new year) buy a couple of bottles of different *marques d'acheteur** non-vintage wines and also a couple of bottles of well-known brands. Taste them blind. The cheaper wines will inevitably have a much larger proportion of the recent poor vintage and will be unbalanced and lacking in depth whereas the others will have a much more round taste as the house style will have been maintained – the art of the blender and the benefits of the finances of an international operation.

The time has now arrived for the theories of the tasting room to be put into practice. The individual wines are now mixed in vats with the aid of a propeller type of apparatus which works as if a giant of a chef was stirring a massive cauldron of sauce. The wines are thoroughly mixed and ready for one more cleansing to achieve perfect clarity. A 'fining' agent, normally bentonite, gelatine or occasionally isinglass, is added to the blend to attract any unnecessary objects still within the wine.** This all stays together and is simply removed. Afterwards there is a final precaution, one last racking – and the wine is ready for bottling.

The wine has been 'fermented out', that is virtually all the sugar transformed into alcohol. Perfect for making bone-dry wine – but a still one; so just before bottling sugar is added (mainly beet, sometimes cane) in a solution with *vin clair*, the *liqueur de tirage*, to reactivate the yeasts within the wine and produce the secondary fermentation sparkle. The amount of sugar added has been carefully calculated since the days of Monsieur François to control precisely the degree of sparkle in the wine. Occasionally selected yeasts are also added to the *liqueur*, if needed, to prompt a recalcitrant blend. Nothing is left to chance – it can't be as the bottle will eventually contain carbonic gas with a pressure up to six atmospheres, which is approximately the same as in the tyre of a long-haul truck. A temporary enclosure is now attached to the bottle, formerly a cork with a metal band across the top hooked around the neck

*See Chapter 11.
**A form of clay, Bentonit is being used increasingly instead of the more traditional isinglass; the latter may be less 'efficient' but some houses continue to use it because they claim more character remains.

--- 48 ---

(*liège et agrafe*), but nowadays normally a 'crown cap' – a metal or preferably a more expensive stainless-steel bottle top with a plastic seal inside.*

____ THE SECONDARY FERMENTATION ____
THE *PRISE DE MOUSSE*

The wine is now ready for the second-most important stage of creation, the ageing in the cellar and development of the secondary fermentation, the *prise de mousse*. The bottles are taken to the deepest parts of the cellar where they are laid on their sides separated only by thin wooden slats (hence the term *sur lattes*, which crops up later in the commercial life of some champagne) or more often nowadays in huge pallets. Two important factors determine much of the character of the wine in the bottle: the time allowed for fermentation and the amount of ageing afterwards. A very cool, constant temperature at around 10°C as found in the deepest sections of the traditional chalk-walled cellars allows the wine to undergo a leisurely fermentation which creates fine bubbles and a wine with more depth of flavour. Once again the yeasts die and fall to the side. It is important to age the wine for a considerable time on these lees as the wine gains added character. Only the most commercially minded and least quality-conscious houses will leave the wines in this state for the bare minimum legal time of one year for non-vintage and three years for vintage; most will leave it for at least two to three years for non-vintage and five more years for vintage.

Now comes the most publicised feature in the *méthode champenoise*, although many think that it is only a contributory factor.

The second fermentation in the bottle produces more unwanted material than just the dead yeasts – there are also other substances both chemical and organic. Fortunately they all merge together in a sticky solution, considerably easing the problem of a further fining within the bottle. The bottles are shaken and then stacked in *pupitres*, two large boards hinged at the top and stood upright in an 'A' position. The holes for the necks of the bottles are carved in the wood and allow the storage to begin almost horizontally. REMUAGE is now carried out as the means of gently easing the sediment down to the end of the neck of the bottle. At first it is deliberately spread throughout the entire contents of the bottle in order that all the constituents of the sediment will collect together. Highly skilled workmen, the *remueurs*, move the bottles every day, a combination of vigorous shaking and delicate turning to prevent the sediment firmly attaching itself to the side of the bottle. Also the bottle is gently moved on its way towards an almost vertical position. No batch of wine is the same as

---

*Corks are obviously much more expensive, and also more time-consuming as they require manual dégorgement. Some houses still consider they are necessary for wines that are to receive long ageing in the cellars. It is significant that even though most houses use 'crown caps' for non-vintage and vintage wines, they still use corks for their Prestige Cuvées.

It is easy to tell which has been used. The crown cap is merely clipped around the bottle so the lip is quite normal. The metal band around the cork has to be fastened to a pronounced edge which rings the bottle top.

any other and the *remueurs'* skills are more than merely manual. They have to judge the best means of achieving the end result of all the sediment in a compact agglomeration on the tip of the capsule with none left straggling around the sides.

Some wines are easy and the task is completed in about six weeks; with others it is difficult and much more time and effort are required. No wonder that the proud wizards who handle up to 50,000 bottles every day refer to them as 'my wines'. Years ago at Krug the workers could not work out why one batch was even slower than the most difficult wines. They were even more mystified when it happened again and to bottles in exactly the same place. A *remueur* searched the establishment and found a window slightly ajar on the ground level. The faintest of breezes were wafting down through the different floor levels and creating a small, but consistent, draught around these bottles – imperceptible but enough to change the character of the wine.

The subject of remuage is still one of the great debating points of the industry. Traditionalists such as Krug and Bollinger are firmly of the belief that the wines are too individualistic for anonymous treatment. Jean-Claude Rouzaud of Louis Roederer points out that even his *remueurs* do not make their own decisions on the necessary degrees of turning and shaking; the *chef des remueurs* checks the *pupitres* regularly, analyses the sediment and instructs his workers. Some batches have a much lighter deposit and require less vigorous handling.

Many other houses disagree. Jean-Baptiste Lanson takes an opposite approach: 'Now that we use the more efficient bentonite for fining the sediment is nowhere near as concentrated, therefore the remuage is now one of the more simple parts of the process.' A large number of the producers now use various means of automatic remuage. A little-known fact is that machines have been used in Champagne since the 1930s.* Some of the early 'present generation' of equipment looks more like one of Baron Frankenstein's inventions but most have the very expensive but labour-saving *gyropalettes*. It is interesting that very few firms have completely changed and that some of the largest (Moët & Chandon, Laurent Perrier, Mercier) have no automation at all.

Moët has devised *les billes*, the encapsulated yeast balls which trap the yeast deposits within their porous skins and which may revolutionize the whole means of collecting the sediment. The CIVC has given permission for Moët to begin commercial production using this method in 1990.** I for one would mourn the passing of the *remueurs*, the most highly skilled artisans of the wine world, and the wonderful sound they make when at work in the cellars – as the bottles knock against the wood the sound is similar to a horde of pigeons chattering away to each other. No doubt there will always be a position for a number of *remueurs* as I would doubt that the more

*Many happy hours were spent researching this book in the archives of Moët's Jean-Paul Médard and he triumphantly produced the photograph of this grower's cellars.
**More about this in Chapter 12.

special, individualistic cuvées will ever be produced by anything other than the traditional method.

After the remuage is completed the bottles obviously remain vertical! They are stored in huge banks *sur pointes*, and look extremely vulnerable. In fact the neck of the bottle fits neatly into the punt of the bottle below. The wine receives more bottle age. Many firms consider that a further lengthy ageing period at this stage is needed to encourage the yeast sediment to continue influencing the character and increase the complexity of the wines.

The final part of the *méthode*, DÉGORGEMENT, is carried out at the last moment, just before shipping. The immersion of the neck in a brine solution with a temperature as low as −28°C turns the sediment within the confines of the plastic 'inner capsule' into a semi-frozen quantity of murky sludge, almost in the form of an ice bullet which is ejected upon opening. The rest of the wine is considerably warmer and forces out the frozen part. When corks have been used the task is done by hand as the *agrafe* is removed − another advantage of the crown cap is that it can be done mechanically as if opening a bottle of beer on an assembly line. In fact the whole dégorgement, corking and packaging line initially seems boring. In all but the smallest of concerns it has the outward appearance of any light industrial operation ('You've seen one, you've seen them all'), but not so. After the sediment has been released there is a vacuum which must be replaced and this is done immediately with the addition of the dosage (*liqueur d'expédition*), a mixture of similar champagne and cane sugar. The addition of sugar is a very particular operation as it can transform the character of the wine so carefully created in the vat and bottle. In the old days, especially in the glory days of the sweet-toothed Russian market, the amount of sugar was up to twenty times as much as that added today. The relative levels of dosage now receive legal definition, in terms of grams of added dosage sugar in grams per litre:

EXTRA BRUT: Between 0 and 6 grams. The most severe of these are called Brut Zéro. Brut Sauvage or other names reminiscent of aftershave lotions, and are among my few dislikes in the world of champagne. Houses such as Krug and Bollinger, which are renowned for 'dry' wines with great depth of flavour and, dare I say, a certain amount of austerity, still add a small amount of sugar. They rightly claim it accentuates the flavour of the fruit.

BRUT: Under 15 grams. This is by far the most common category. Previously wines which were exported to Great Britain as 'Brut' were often named similarly but shipped to other markets, in particular North America, with a higher sugar content. But nowadays, all the major markets are uniform.

EXTRA DRY: Between 12 and 20 grams.

SEC: Between 17 and 35 grams.

DEMI-SEC: Between 33 and 50 grams.

There is very little present-day interest in these last three categories. When the sweeter-toothed South Americans were still a flourishing market, sales of demi-sec were considerable. But those days are over and their substantial purchases have been replaced by extra sales on the Brut markets.

DOUX: More than 50 grams. Genuinely sweet, often rather poor-quality fruit masked by the added sugar. There are a few notable exceptions, in particular Louis Roederer Rich – a wonderful dessert wine.

—— THE FINAL FLOURISH ——

The bottle is now ready for corking. An expensive and carefully selected wedge of the finest that Portugal can offer is forced into an aperture about 40 per cent of its size. It is then wired, for the important reason that all and sundry would like to see it stay in the neck of the bottle. Next the bottles are 'dressed' and packed.

Finally, after all this time, the wine is ready for despatch. Years after the harvest and after all this careful control and handling the champagne producer is ready to receive a return on investment.

10

STYLES OF CHAMPAGNE

—— NON-VINTAGE ——

This category accounts for nearly 90 per cent of total champagne sales. The main theme is consistency of the house style – the blend, the amount of dosage and the amount of bottle age are crucial factors in maintaining the image and sales. Many firms are quite candid about their concentration of efforts on their non-vintage. After all, the health of their balance sheets depends on this wine.

Non-vintage wine must have a minimum of one year's bottle age. The CIVC laws do not allow the wine of the previous harvest to be bottled before the following January, so even the cheapest is approximately eighteen months old before release. The wines from the serious houses receive much, much more – most keep their wines for three to four years, Bollinger at least five and Krug six or more. I make no apologies for being a devotee of the non-vintage wines from the larger houses. Their reliability is most important and I would rather pay a little more to enjoy this. Some small houses and growers make delicious wines in certain years but they do not own sufficient reserve stocks to achieve the consistency. Similarly the BOB (Buyer's Own Brand) wines which are supplied by the huge companies and co-operatives to wholesalers, supermarkets and large retail chains can be marvellous, when the recent vintages have been favourable. Recently we have experienced the ups and downs. The cheap champagnes were most attractive when the glorious 1982 and 1983 wines were predominant in the blend, yet the next shipments with a large proportion of 1984 wine were very average.

Ask any of the senior personnel of the houses and with very few exceptions they will admit that style and quality of the non-vintage are the most important factors in their operation. The major names have spent a fortune building their brands and are not about to ruin all the hard work by presenting unbalanced, unripe wine. As early as 1809 when the widow Clicquot was encountering quality problems, the ubiquitous travelling salesman Monsieur Bohn was quick to pen a letter of warning from

St Petersburg: 'I like big eyes everywhere except in champagne!* Never forget that only the best will do.'

They have not forgotten. Even in these days of clamouring demand, when there has been a shortage the houses have always restricted supply to ensure adequate mature stocks. Louis Roederer's Jean-Claude Rouzaud considers his firm's reserve stocks of 650,000 litres to be the 'jewel in our crown'. He has a strict rule: every single litre removed and used in the year's blend must be replaced with the next vintage, no matter what the consequence. This was managed even in the lean years of 1980 and 1981. If 1982 had been as poor the system would still have continued and sales reduced accordingly.

—— VINTAGE ——

At the turn of the century most of the champagne shipped to the major export markets was vintage, but things gradually changed and the houses began to be recognised by the style of their non-vintage. Nevertheless, vintage still retained great importance and even as late as the 1960s the major houses celebrated their new releases with a combination of reverence, pomp and circumstance.

The laws state that vintage champagne must be made only from the wines of the year stated on the label, and that in no year can more than 80 per cent of the total crop be used – the rest must be put into the reserve wine stocks. The wine must be aged in bottle for a minimum of three years, although once again the serious firms keep the wine much longer: Krug launched its 1981 in 1988. While the declaration of the vintage is not as relevant as in the port-wine business, there is a common factor: the decision is not universal; the individual houses make up their own minds. As I have mentioned, the quality of the harvest is only one consideration, because the reserves are all-important. The climatic conditions usually dictate the style, but the superior wine offers the *chef de caves* and his team of blenders the opportunity to flaunt their techniques. The ideal wine is that which allows the house style to complement the wine, not dictate, producing a distinctive degree of rich intensity of flavour. The 1983 Moët is an excellent example. Even in the past few decades when interest has waned this house has placed great emphasis on its vintage wines, in particular a glorious 1966, elegant 1971 and a stunning, fruity 1982. This splendid vintage produced excellent Chardonnay, so Moët used much more in the blend (50 per cent compared to its normal 25–30 per cent) and the result is a rich, creamy wine with a luscious ripe finish.

Over the years it is these top vintage wines that I remember most vividly – the state-of-the-art champagnes. I will never forget the fulsome, classic 1966 Bollinger, one of the great taste-sensations of my life, both when first tasted in 1972 and when

*An allusion to large bubbles.

recently tasted in 1985. There have been many other beautiful wines – G.H. Mumm has the knack of creating excellent wines in erratic years: the creaming soda style of the 1973 Georges Goulet; the aristocratic 1975 Heidsieck Dry Monopole only just reaching its peak now; the rich and powerful 1976s from Veuve Clicquot and Lanson made in a year that produced many fat, blowsy wines; the flowery, subtle 1979 Pol Roger; and recently its superb racy, extrovert 1982.

The recent decline in the importance of vintage is a disturbing trend. Krug excepted, there is little of the previous excitement now that the marketing effort is concentrated on non-vintage and prestige wines. Some houses now produce a vintage wine virtually every year, thereby undermining the special-quality aspect of the wine. No region as northerly as Champagne can make absolutely top-quality wine every year. Bollinger has registered its disapproval by renaming its wines Vintage Grande Année, hopefully reminding some others of the concept of single-year champagne. Finally, there are the claims of the public-relations departments of some houses that all vintage wines are perfect for drinking the moment they are released. This is usually wishful thinking. I tend to work on the principle of drinking the vintage previous to the one on release. (Occasionally this can go wrong. The classic example is 1975 and 1976: the latter was ready for drinking almost immediately on release, while the former needed years more bottle age. Also most of the 1982 and 1983 wines were ready on release.)

However, the lack of attention to these wines has produced some beneficial aspects. Many of the wines cost only about 20 per cent more than the non-vintage. Careful selection of the right wines from the right houses allows very classy drinking at only a slightly greater cost!

—— RECENT CHAMPAGE VINTAGES ——

1988 A mild, wet winter followed by a dry, hot April ... perfect for budding. A sunny June allowed satisfactory flowering but an extremely wet July upset development of the grapes. Fortunately August was dry and hot, and good fortune continued through to a harvest of very good quality, and reasonable quantity.

1987 A poor summer followed by a warm, sunny September. It rained during part of the harvest but temperatures were low, so the grapes did not pick up any rot or disease. The Pinot Meunier had a fine year, Pinot Noir was adequate in certain areas, but the Chardonnay really suffered. A year to test the skill of the blenders.

1986 Favourable summer temperatures followed by excellent conditions at harvest allowed the production of a large quantity of high-quality wine. Most will declare.

1985 Lowest January temperatures for 150 years were followed by a freezing

February. Serious damage to the vines was aggravated by severe frosts in April. A patchy summer followed by unseasonally high temperatures in September enabled a high degree of ripeness and reasonable quality. A vintage will be declared.

1984 Poor quality.

1983 A dream. The largest ever yield and excellent wine. Yves Bénard of Moët, a man not given to hyperbole told me, 'Neither myself nor any other of my fellow Champenois have ever experienced such a vintage in the Côte des Blancs – superb both in quality *and* quantity. According to the text books this is impossible.'

1982 A wonderful summer produced a record yield, promptly eclipsed the following year. The last time there were two successive years of such outstanding quality was 1927 and 1928!

1981 A late frost in April, followed by almost every unfavourable climatic condition possible in May and June, ensured a small harvest. However the weather improved and the quality of the small crop was very good. Most will be used for blending.

1980 Another poor spring and summer were rescued by a warm lead-up to the harvest. Small quantity but good quality. Once again will mostly be used for blending.

1979 A welcome type of year much needed after the disastrously small harvest of the latter was 1978 and 1977 (also very poor in quality). A large yield of light, easy-drinking stylish and forward wines.

—— ROSÉ CHAMPAGNE ——

There have been dramatic developments in the making of pink champagne. In the 1950s this was the stuff to be drunk out of actresses' slippers. The image was elitist and frivolous. I am only just old enough to remember the newspaper headlines about the flamboyant British socialite Lady Docker – a glass of pink bubbly always seemed to be close at hand. Fortunately the days (or should I say nights) of the débutante balls and the ancillary occasions where it would seem that the privileged few desired to prove how they could afford to waste their money spraying champagne around the place are over (replaced to a certain extent by motor-racing drivers). Champagne's image became more serious and pink was suddenly out of fashion.

In the 1970s some houses carried on making this style in small quantities. I have fond memories of the light, subtle Roederer Rosé and the more full-bodied Veuve Clicquot, and I loved all the vintages of the extroverted, raspberry-flavoured G.H. Mumm Cordon Rosé. Towards the end of the decade the style suddenly became fashionable again, but this time as a 'serious' wine.

Not all Rosé is made in the same manner. There are two totally different methods. One is the standard Rosé formula of 'maceration', when the black Pinot grapes are allowed to ferment for a short time before pressing, allowing 'free run' juice of the highest quality and a degree of redness. This needs great care and attention in order to achieve the required amount of colour and fruit flavour, and houses using this method, such as Laurent Perrier, stress that there will be a certain amount of variation of style from year to year. The second, and more common, method is simply adding a portion of the still red wine from the region before the secondary fermentation has begun. This is obviously simpler and less chancy, and there is the further advantage of allowing the house a consistency of style. Interestingly, Champagne is the only region in France allowed to make Rosé by this method. The pros and cons of these two methods are widely debated.

These variations in method do not explain the amazing differences in style. A line-up of thirty or forty different wines will show a range of colours from the palest of pink with almost no Rosé character to rich, deep-reddish wine which looks more like sparkling burgundy. I am not keen on either extreme. I look for an attractive, genuinely pink colour with an uncomplicated Pinot fruit nose and whoosh of raspberry or strawberry flavour.

In the early days of the Rosé renaissance the houses seemed to concentrate on making only vintage wines and for some reason charged a price closer to the Prestige Cuvées – this rankled. After all, surely in these modern times, and when most of the wine was made by the *addition* method, there is no longer the risk of spoiling the whole cuvée – so Rosé did not cost a lot more to produce. Fortunately there has been a pronounced move in the direction of good sense, and pink champagne is now available at all ends of the market, from the exotic Taittinger Comte de Champagne Rosé, Dom Pérignon Rosé and Perrier-Jouët Belle Epoque Rosé to the excellent-value, easy-drinking non-vintage wines from Lanson, Mercier, Pommery and many others. A good positive sign which augurs well for the future for we lovers of Rosé champagne.

—— BLANC DE BLANCS ——

This style has suffered a serious image problem, and much can be blamed on Ian Fleming, creator of James Bond. In the early books the hero regularly ordered bottles of Blanc de Blancs (Taittinger Comte de Champagne actually)* and the term caught on. Unfortunately wine-makers throughout France regard this popular but essentially meaningless description of wine made from white grapes as a manna from heaven; even the coarsest table wines were eligible for this trendy name.

*Claude Taittinger proudly points out that his firm's prestige champagne was most frequently mentioned in the actual books, and the only one to appear in the early movies. Later when the marketing of recognisable products via the screen ('product placement') became an important source of income to producers the bottles changed.

However, in Champagne the term is relevant. It guarantees that the wine is made from 100 per cent Chardonnay. A decade ago very little Blanc de Blancs was made other than the Prestige Cuvées, but now it is a totally different matter. At a recent tasting in London I sampled wines from nearly seventy houses and growers who were actively selling Blanc de Blancs on the United Kingdom market. Like Rosé champagne, the range of styles is quite amazing, varying from the flowery, light and zippy wines from Grand Cru Côte de Blancs villages such as Chouilly. Cramant and Le Mesnil-sur-Oger to the less expensive wines from the Vallée de la Marne, which were more full in flavour and yet perfectly acceptable. One of the most interesting wines was from Landragin, made from grapes from Verzenay, right in the heart of Pinot Noir country in the Montagne de Reims.

The delicacy of top-quality Blanc de Blancs cannot be underestimated. Even champagne lovers who previously dismissed the wines as a marketing gimmick are having to admit that the fresh, fragrant, appley flavour offers a unique, attractive style of champagne.

—— CRÉMANT ——

Literally this means 'creaming' – a more gentle champagne with less sparkling (under four atmospheres of pressure compared with six atmospheres) created by adding a smaller amount of *liquer de tirage*. It is less common nowadays: although the method is perfectly legal, EEC regulations are soon to outlaw use of this term on champagne labels. Other French sparkling wine-makers will be forced to forgo the term 'Méthode Champenoise'; in return they will enjoy the exclusive use of the term 'Crémant'.

—— BRUT ZÉRO ——

I have already discussed this. It is sometimes of interest in the tasting room but it is not for drinking.

—— BLANC DE NOIRS ——

More common in the Champenois' United States operations than at home. White wine made from Pinot. Most of the wines I have tested have been made by growers without Chardonnay grapes (i.e. more out of necessity than desire) and the wines have been rather ungracious and unsubtle, but there are some full, flavoursome wines with an overt yet balanced depth of Pinot character.

—— CUVÉES DE PRESTIGE ——

The Russian Revolution halted sales of Louis Roederer Cristal and the concept of an elite 'superior' cuvée stagnated. Until 1936 that is, when Robert-Jean de Vogüé, at the outset of a dynamic career with his family firm Moët, created a new 'super blend' of the finest wine from the first pressing. The combination of the excellence of the wine and instant snob appeal proved successful and Dom Pérignon was well on its way to worldwide fame and fortune. The unique yet simple shape of the bottle (a reproduction of one of the original champagne bottle shapes) and an evocative yet simplistic label unlike any other created a wine that wealthy wine-drinkers loved. Not only was the taste superb, but anyone with a little knowledge could instantly recognise that this was something special.

Nowadays there are many Cuvées de Prestige, some equally stunning (in particular Taittinger's Comte de Champagne and Louis Roederer's Cristal – this time for all the world). The success of these wines, particularly in the United States, has even resulted in Perrier-Jouët, previously a small house, expanding rapidly from sales of 1.2 million bottles in 1974 to 3.5 million. More Perrier-Jouët is now drunk in New York than in Paris, the house has climbed from nowhere to third-largest sales across the Atlantic – and this is mostly due to their Belle Epoque cuvée, which not only provides the instantly identifiable image of the house but constitutes nearly 40 per cent of their total sales!

The best of these wines are described in loving detail in later chapters. Are they worth all the money? It must be pointed out that even the success of the finest of these wines has bred some rather poor imitations; even co-operatives are making Prestige Cuvées – surely one term negates the other? It is important that these wines should only be made under circumstances where the quality of the product is of paramount importance and the quantity is restricted if necessary. Then they give value for money, because if the consumers can afford them they are also experiencing some of the finest champagnes.

11

THE BUYERS AND SELLERS AND HOW TO READ A LABEL

NÉGOCIANTS MANIPULANTS (THE HOUSES OR 'SHIPPERS')

The carefully nurtured image of champagne centres on the Grandes Maisons growing and cultivating their vines then making their wines. But that image is only partly correct. As their name suggests, they are similar to the large names in Burgundy, and are 'merchants in the trade of wine'. Fifty 'serious' _négociant_ houses account for nearly every bottle of the merchants' production.* They own a mere 13 per cent of the vineyard land yet control 70 per cent of the total production and 94 per cent of exports.

Students of the social history of Great Britain in the 1960s fully realise that the 'big is beautiful' claim did not work – the motor industry in general and the British Leyland fiasco in particular offer conclusive proof. Similarly the quality sector of most of the wine world has shunned the large producers – whether they are called _cru classé_, _clos_ or _boutique_ matters not – as long as the common denominator is scarcity. This is not so with champagne. The combination of viticultural and vinification superiority with the aggressive yet charming promotion and sales techniques have favoured the larger, more flamboyant houses. In fact the twenty-four largest account for 85 per cent of the merchants' share of production. They are the creators of the _de luxe_ image of Champagne and the product amply supports their claims. As early as 1841 champagne salesmen were described as:

> having nothing in common with Burgundy brokers and their cavalier behaviour. They dine at Lé Vefour, have a horror of drunkenness and speak of their wares in moderate tones only. They generally conduct their business in private salons, on public promenades or in the foyer of the Opera. After extolling the virtues of sparkling champagne in an elegant manner, they always end the encounter by

---

*There are actually 110 houses registered. A few make insignificant quantities, many are dormant and a large number are used merely as _sous marques_ – see later in the chapter.

saying with an innocent air: 'I will send you a case, but don't consider yourself under any obligation to keep it.' With that, they button up their white gloves, or play with their lorgnon. The subject of their wine is dropped, and the topic of conversation is changed to Lord Seymour's horses, or the mineral water of Bagnères.*

Business life is not quite as relaxed now. But the major houses do still employ a coterie of some of the world's finest roving commercial ambassadors promoting both their company champagnes and those of their competitors.

Many have floundered: a meal at the Restaurant Le Vigneron in Reims is a salutary experience for any budding champagne mogul. The walls are covered with a wonderful collection of originals of advertising posters, some from early this century and many from the last – the houses still surviving are very much in the minority. These present-day giants are theoretically categorised by membership of the Syndicat de Grandes Marques de Champagne, and the term Grande Marque (a colloquial translation would be either 'Big House' or 'Big Blend') is widely used, although virtually meaningless. Granted, most of the well-known members are present, but so are many moribund names and some shoddy producers, while a number of important houses are omitted.

A few of the largest houses own large spreads of vineyards, which provide a substantial, though not predominant, percentage of their grape needs. A few of the medium-sized houses also own large holdings, and buy in only a minority share of their grapes. Others, of varying sizes, own small amounts of land . . . and some none at all. All this means that the relationship between the *négociants* and growers is crucial, and the monitoring task of the CIVC is by no means easy.** In the past many houses grew rich on their successes and, while many of the growers had genuine grievances, others harboured grudges without considering the financial risks and costly promotion sustained by the houses throughout both good and bad times. The politics of envy have often overlooked the fact that without the houses' marketing flair the grapes would fetch considerably less.

—— *RÉCOLTANTS* (GROWERS) ——

Eighty-seven per cent of the vineyard area is owned by the extraordinary number of 15,000 growers. Over half cultivate less than a hectare; even with the high prices obtained for grapes in Champagne these holdings are not economically viable – many of the owners are only part-time growers, often leaving the bulk of the vineyard work to their wives; others lease the land to other growers. These 8000 or more part-timers account for a mere 12 per cent of the vineyard territory, whereas fewer than 2000 proprietors with holdings in excess of a modest 3 hectares control 40 per cent.

*Adolphe Ricard, *How the French See Themselves.* 1841.
**See Glossary.

I have mentioned the tough times experienced by growers. For a long time they were undoubtedly at the mercy of the houses as the well-known brand names were the only purchasers of their grapes. Nowadays things are very different and they have three choices: they can sell their grapes to the houses, or to a co-operative, or they can make and market their own champagne and become *récoltants manipulants*.

RÉCOLTANTS MANIPULANTS (GROWER-PRODUCERS)

Approximately 4500 of the growers are in this category. The image of the man of the soil tending his cherished vines and creating the finest possible champagne may be attractive to the writers of romantic novels, but reality is rather different. There are without doubt some superb growers' champagnes which are a product of excellent-quality grapes and top-notch wine-making, but the market-place is even more of a minefield than Burgundy – for four major reasons.

1. *Lack of 'vineyard spread'.* A vast majority of growers own land only within a limited area. They are not allowed to buy in more than 5 per cent of their stock* and therefore are restricted in their scope for blending.

2. *Lack of finance.* The stockholding required for top-quality champagne-making is much greater than for any other wine region. For every bottle sold the large houses have to lay down at least another three, and these sums do not always make much sense to bank managers. Few growers can afford the finance for sufficient reserve wines. This is of no great importance in bountiful times, but is a major problem when there have been a few poor vintages.

3. *The cost-consciousness of the home market,* where almost all these wines are sold. A great deal of growers' wines are made with price the most important factor, and the wines are released almost the moment the minimum legal age has been satisfied. The style is undoubtedly fresh, perhaps with a touch of fragrance, but also with a great deal of excess acidity.

4. *The bewildering labelling anomaly.* Previously nearly 20 per cent of the growers' labels were on bottles not actually made by themselves. Grapes were sent to the co-operative for pressing and vinification along with those from all the other members. Some remained with the co-operative for marketing while the rest (or all) of this anonymous wine returned to the grower who sold it implying that it was made on the premises according to family tradition'. In other words a grower from a Grand Cru village could have his wine made at a co-operative and yet no reference to this would be on the label – instead it would most probably feature his name and village and flaunt the term '100% Grand Cru'. Needless to say the genuine *récoltants manipulants* were just as aggrieved as the *négociants*. It was an unbelievable loophole

*Otherwise they become liable for the stiff 'commercial tax' of a *négociant* house instead of enjoying the many benefits of the much less avaricious 'agrarian producers'.

in the laws of the region. Fortunately it was rectified by a new CIVC law of 1 January 1989 which decreed two new, more exact, descriptions within the general *récoltant manipulant* category:

Récoltant-Cooperateur when the grower's wine is made by a co-operative.

Société de Récoltants when the wine is also not individually made but is part of a group of producers.

This has to be stated on the label. Admittedly only the knowledgeable consumer will be able to tell the difference but don't worry you are soon to be informed!

―――― CO-OPERATIVES AND *COOPÉRATIVE* ―――― *DE MANIPULATION*

They are the newcomers on the scene. The economic woes of the 1930s spawned the co-operative organisations, more out of commercial pragmatism than ideology. Their initial success was noted and since the Second World War they have expanded rapidly, with the assistance of the CIVC. In recent years the co-operatives have become an important, if rather prosaic, feature of the commercial world of Champagne; as a source of BOB wines for large retailers and as a source of extra stock for some of the houses. They vary from small operations that merely offer pressing facilities to those that also make the initial still wine and others that create the *prise de mousse*.

Then there are the *Coopérative manipulants* which assume the role of a quasi-*négociant* house and complete the grape-to-sales process. *Coopérative manipulants* vary in character almost as much as the houses: many are merely functional with products totally lacking in character. The high-tech, high-quality Union Champagne at Avize is anything but. It incorporates 1000 growers and produces 5 million bottles a year, including the Marks & Spencer champagnes, yet is dwarfed by the nearby Centre Vinicole de la Champagne (CVC). In comparison La Goutte d'Or, also in the vicinity at Vertus, bears more resemblance to Pol Roger than to either of them.

Two organisations epitomise the dynamism of the present-day *coopérative manipulants*: the CVC and the CRVC (Coopérative Régionale des Vins de Champagne).

The CVC building sprawls across the top of the hill at Chouilly, the first village of the Côte des Blancs. The centre has storage capacity for 35 million bottles (second only to Moët) and annual sales in excess of 12 million bottles. There are 4000 *vigneron* members controlling 1500 hectares, and all grapes are pressed at the facilities of the eighty-five member co-operatives. In the early days nearly all of the wine was returned to the growers for sale, but nowadays the centre markets more than 6 million bottles a year, through large sales under BOB labels and a combination of its own labels – Nicolas Feuillatte is the best known – and significant *sur lattes* sales to the *négociants*. Their relationship with their largest customer, Mercier, is revolutionary. In 1987 Yves Bénard, President of Moët–Mercier–Ruinart, announced a contract whereby the CVC will make in excess of a million bottles of Mercier each year under the direct supervision of Moët's *chef de caves*, Dominique Foulon. Control will be exercised from start to finish and the co-operative will receive a percentage of the added value of the product (the difference between cost of the grapes and wholesale price) thereby linking the members and management to the quality of Mercier. As Bénard explains, 'The members and technical staff of the CVC and our company have to work together to ensure quality of good-value champagne. It is not buying *sur lattes*, more a partnership where we lease buying contracts, technical expertise and cellar space.

Who knows where this could lead? Sales of the CVC's own brands have not yet matched their efforts; the money spent on marketing the Nicolas Feuillatte brand will not be recouped for many years unless there is a sudden surge in worldwide sales. Perhaps another example of the often quoted (by the *négociants*, naturally) stories about co-operatives making sound wines but lacking the necessary commercial expertise? If so, more contracts similar to the Mercier one seem to offer the best prospects.

The recent successes of the Jacquart brand seem to dispel the idea that this is the only choice for the large *coopérative manipulants*. The CRVC, only twenty years old, produces an attractive range of wines from the produce of 650 growers and 1000 hectares in the main regions. They also have Christian Doisy, a youthful and dynamic general manager with the marketing flair of a president of one of the largest of houses, and an advertising budget to match. The brand has been in existence only since 1981 and yet on a recent visit to Reims I checked the windows of the food and wine stores – every single one displayed bottles of Jacquart. It is also the 'house champagne' in a majority of the medium-priced restaurants I dine at in France. The wines are not expensive, they are well made, perhaps lacking excitement – but they are very easy drinking and very good value.

Either of these choices offers considerable challenges with promises of healthy financial returns to the more adventurous organisations.

NÉGOCIANTS NON-MANIPULANTS: MARQUES AUXILIAIRES AND 'BUYER'S OWN BRANDS'

In theory these are merchants without production facilities who deal in large quantities of poorer-quality wines. In reality both have certain areas of respectability. *Marques auxiliaires* are basically what the rest of the French wine trade calls *sous marques* or, to put it quite bluntly, a host of other labels of long-departed firms, which allows the producers/wholesalers a stock of options. Numerous clients benefit from the series of 'exclusivities'. Genuine *sous marques* do exist offering cheaper wines from serious houses (Masse from Lanson and Théophile Roederer from Louis Roederer) but they are few and far between. 'Buyer's Own Brands' (BOBs) have long been a traditional part of the British wine trade with every merchant having his own cheap and cheerful 'house brand'. The label looks authentic and possesses a fancy French name — most purchasers assume the wine is from a reputable, long-established firm. Anything but. In my early days in the United Kingdom the merchants used to refer to this wine rather contemptuously as 'wedding fizz'. Sometimes the wine was perfectly sound, other times not. The improvement in viticultural and vinification techniques, the increase in production of sound, safe co-operative wines, and the sterling work done by houses specialising in this market have lessened the chances of 'horror' wines and nowadays they are a good deal more serious in content and style. But the fact remains that the label is no guarantee of consistency of quality or supply. In September 1988 *The Times* wine correspondent, Jane MacQuitty, complained that 'Sainsbury's previous cavalier approach to labelling their own-label Rosé champagne (one label for five different pink champagnes) has sadly repeated itself with their 1982 Blanc de Blancs vintage champagne ... the bottle you buy today could come from three different suppliers.'

The complaint about the Sainsbury's Rosé had been raised before. In fact Sainsbury was required to withdraw an advertisement claiming that all its Rosé champagne was made by the maceration method and from a family house. Robin Young, a *Decanter* magazine columnist, had noticed that two different purchases provided him with two different styles of pink champagne, and he complained. At least the 1982 Blanc de Blancs variation was only of houses, not of actual method.

The salient feature of this complaint is that a few years ago no one would have expected better from a supermarket champagne. It was the lowest of the low. Today this part of the market has become much more important with the dynamic growth of supermarket wine sales. In a matter of years, new labels have appeared on the British shelves; suddenly Sainsbury's own label is one of the ten largest champagne brands in Great Britain. Tesco, Marks & Spencer and Waitrose are also prominent.*

The wines sold by these four regularly do well in consumer-press blind tastings and hopefully all the supermarket buyers will continue their policies of strict quality control. In 1988 the *Observer* published a survey of the spending trends of the British public and began the section on wine: 'A major trend is the staggering increase in Britain's consumption of champagne. In the first six months of this year France exported 8,729,622 bottles of champagne to the UK, 11.62 per cent more than in the equivalent period last year.' The confidential CIVC export figures for the houses show that a large percentage of this increase was generated by the supermarket 'own labels'. This democratisation of champagne has been an added bonus to the industry,

---

*It is noticeable that Sainsbury now print the name and address of the product on their labels.

and the high quality of most of the big-selling BOBs nowadays is also producing a beneficial side-effect: the purveyors of the lowest quality are being rapidly forced out of the largest export market and it is being left to the French to drink the stuff!

—— THE LABEL ——

The requirements are strict, but the label is simple. Champagne is the only *appellation controlée* French wine that doesn't need to state the fact on the label. The word Champagne alone, in large letters, is sufficient.

Note: any label that mentions *méthode champenoise* is not champagne! This terminology is soon to be outlawed in the countries of the EEC.

The details required by the CIVC: (1) Name of the house or brand; (2) Village or town where produced; (3) Alcohol content; (4) Produce of France; (5) Contents of bottle; (6) Degree of dryness (or sweetness); plus at the bottom, the CIVC registration number for the producer or brand.

There may also be specific details – of style (vintage, Rosé, Blanc de Blancs, etc.), or of rating (either Premier Cru or Grand Cru may be used when applicable).

Two letters preceeding the CIVC numbers are all important: **NM:** *Négociant-Manipulant*; **CM:** *Coopérative-Manipulant*; **RM:** *Récoltant-Manipulant*; **RC:** *Récoltant-Coopérateur*; **SR:** *Société de Récoltants*; **MA:** *Marques Auxiliaires*.

When the owner of the brand has not made the wine then a further line must be added–**Elabore par** followed by the status and CIVC code. This states that it is made by an outside source, and which type of producer. The houses can no longer buy in wines *sur lattes* and not acknowledge the fact. Nor can the growers using co-operatives pretend that their wine is made by themselves, neither can bogus brand names pretend to be established houses.

A major series of correct decisions. I am only sorry that the actual producers are still unknown to those of us disinclined to visit the offices of the CIVC and look up the register of names. I applaud Sainsbury's new policy – an object lesson for all.

12

MY FAVOURITE HOUSES

The selection of a few houses is not an easy task for a dedicated imbiber of champagne. When I am drinking a glass of top quality wine with a distinct Chardonnay flavour I instantly become a convert to the lighter champagnes – but replace that glass with a Pinot-Noir-flavoured wine of equal quality and I will happily renounce my previous conviction and swear undying allegiance to the products of black grapes. I just love good champagne!

Yet there is something very special about the houses in this chapter. They all produce distinctive wines in all categories, and their excellent quality has been remarkably reliable over the past twenty-five years of tasting – in both the Champagne region and on their major export markets. Their house styles have been the most consistent. Obviously there are many others I was tempted to add to the list, and obviously it is a very subjective selection. It has turned out to be a cross-section of the industry – from the small to the largest, from companies dedicated to self-promotion to one whose owner does his best to avoid it. Read on and be prepared to make some different New Year resolutions and try a few more house styles!

—— BOLLINGER ——

ESTABLISHED: 1829.
LOCATION: Ay.
YEARLY PRODUCTION: 1.5 million bottles.
VINEYARDS: 120 hectares, mainly in Avenay, Ay, Bisseuil, Champvoisy, Cuis, Louvois, Tauzières and Verzenay.

Lovers of fine champagne can be thankful that the French nobility of the early nineteenth century considered that the commercial production and selling of wine was a task for tradesmen. The de Villermont family, who owned 11 hectares in Ay and Cuis, decided to 'commercialise' their grapes but did not want their name associated. In 1829 they selected two ambitious salesmen – a Frenchman, Paul Renaudin, and a German, Joseph-Jacob-Placide (Jacques) Bollinger – and the firm of Renaudin, Bollinger & Co. was founded. The former stayed only for a couple of years but the twenty-five-year-old man from Württemberg was much more determined. Over the years Jacques expanded the vineyards in both villages, created a new one in Verzenay, and most important of all, in 1837 he married the boss's daughter.

The next generation continued the vineyard expansion, and in 1918 the twenty-four-year-old grandson Jacques took over. His reign was characterised by consolidation of the 'Bollinger heritage' with much upgrading of the existing vineyards and the replanting of the highly rated Ay gem La Côte-aux-Enfants. Jacques' tragically early death and the wartime valour of his widow Lily have been discussed, but this remarkable lady's influence continued in peacetime. Jacques had taught his wife the complexities of the business and her judicious administration of the company's fortunes strengthened its supreme vineyard holdings, expansion being confined to only the very finest of sites. Bollinger's reputation for quality was never compromised, yet she managed to increase production (and sales) from 400,000 to 1 million bottles.

At the start of the Second World War Great Britain accounted for 85 per cent of the house's total production. Despite the serious stock problems and the consequent need for strict allocations for even the best of customers, Madame Jacques decided that the company could not rely on one market alone and she was the first member of the family to cross the Atlantic and develop the North American markets. Visits to other countries followed – despite her lack of pretence when around Ay she was more than happy to assume the role of ambassadress to the important export markets. Apparently she had few qualms about giving orders to agents and expected them to be obeyed.

I must now admit to a certain amount of bias. To attend the Champagne Academy study course in October 1972 I paid my first-ever visit to France. On my first day in this wonderful country I lunched at Madame Bollinger's house and sat on her left. I was captivated by the wonderful 1966 vintage served, and enchanted by the manner in which this remarkable seventy-three-year-old lady entertained six young members of the British wine trade with a series of anecdotal tales from her experiences at home and abroad – combined with a great deal of equally fascinating technical detail. In the midst of this her eagle eye espied one guest playing with his *oeuf en gelée*. When quietly asked if there was a problem, the young man murmured that he didn't care for the taste of egg. I wouldn't describe Madame's answer as a schoolmistress's rebuke, but she managed to register her disapproval by recounting her problems during visits to the United States where a large proportion of her hosts went to considerable trouble to obtain escargots and served them in her honour:

'I couldn't tell the people that I hated them. I always managed, with the help of much bread, to swallow them.' Game, set and match to Lily. A wonderful lady. When she died in 1977 the world was a much poorer place.

There were no children and the Bollinger lineage was now at an end. Nephew Claude d'Hautefeuille, a member of the firm since 1949, had taken control in 1970 and his eight-year stint in charge was crucial in combining Madame's family tradition with the rapidly expanding market. In 1978 another nephew, Christian Bizot, took over the stewardship with his nephews, Arnould d'Hautefeuille and Michel Villedey. In the recent decades the house's motto has been 'independence at all costs' and its policy has been to expand sales steadily, to purchase its own means of distribution wherever possible, and to form partnerships in other aspects of the wine business.

In 1960 it purchased Mentzendorff & Co., its United Kingdom agents since 1858. In 1967 it purchased its French distributors. In 1973 it acquired Langlois-Château, a medium-sized Loire sparkling-wine producer. Recently it has taken 40 per cent in the enterprising Petaluma winery in South Australia and has joined forces with Whitbread (owners of the United States agents) and Antinori in a still-wine making operation in the Napa Valley. All this expansion away from champagne is to allow the company to continue its cautious, traditional policy at home – independence and the production of highest quality wines is much easier to achieve when finances are healthy and worldwide distribution is strong.

Only 30 per cent of the grapes are bought in. At pressing only the cuvée is used (in exceptional vintages a little of the premier taille may be kept). The wines considered to be of vintage material in need of lengthy ageing are fermented and blended in oak, the rest in stainless-steel vats. The non-vintage wines are stoppered with crown corks but Christian Bizot is yet to be convinced that these are suitable for the lengthy ageing received by Bollinger's vintage wines.

The house commits itself to enormous trouble and expense keeping its vast reserves (five years' stock – about 7 million bottles) in magnums. Can you imagine a cost accountant's reaction to that? And yet, if you listen to Christian Bizot, it is quite logical: 'Experiments haven't convinced us that there is any other solution.' No one can accuse Bizot and the others of slavishly worshipping the past. They merely pick and choose which aspects of modern wine-making they wish to utilise. At the moment they are experimenting with a new strain of yeast, L'Aglomerante, which sticks together and could provide easier remuage. Bizot emphasises:

We are not devout traditionalists. The team keeps abreast of the latest technical developments ... but the family is all-important and I am bound to ensure the continuity of the 'Bollinger tradition'. If some people's tastes change that's fine – just as long as they don't expect Bollinger to change its style.

THE WINES
Non-Vintage Special Cuvée Brut

An uncompromising wine which usually has the bottle age of most vintage champagnes – and invariably benefits from a little more. Aristocratic and firmly structured with a considerable length of finish. Not a 'champagne for all occasions', it demands attention and rewards the drinker with a superb example of a Pinot-Noir-dominated blend. Interestingly, although it is the house's flagship, it accounts for only about 40 per cent of production.

Vintage Grande Année Brut

Also at least two-thirds Pinot Noir. The same classic ingredients and yet the character of the year is not totally dominated. As always Bollinger sticks firmly to its beliefs, rebutting the claims of some houses who consider that with modern viticultural and oenological techniques vintage wines can be made in nearly every year. Bollinger produces its not inconsiderable quantities in only the finest of years – hence the term Grande Année.

Rosé Vintage Grande Année

One of the very finest. A sensuous, enticing nose complemented by a beautifully balanced character. Plenty of the raspberry fragrance of delicious Pinot Noir fruit. I once shocked a magazine editor by describing this as 'the perfect dirty-weekend wine'. I still consider the phrase apt.

Vintage Année Rare

Produced from only the most exceptional of vintages. The wine has remained on the lees for at least ten years, giving a very full, yeasty flavour.

RD Vintage

Bollinger's answer to the Prestige Cuvées, but without any fancy-shaped bottle or exotic label. Vintage wine is aged on the lees for seven or more years, and this storing *sur pointes* allows the wine to develop complexity without losing freshness. When the wine is sufficiently full-flavoured the bottles are disgorged and shipped, hence the name *récemment dégorgé*. The expression is used in the industry but somehow Bollinger managed to register it as a trademark. On one social visit to Australia I was fortunate to be served 'RD' on each of my first four nights – that says a lot either for Australian taste or for my reputation as a discerning champagne-drinker.

Vieilles Vignes Françaises Vintage Blanc De Noirs

There are many champenois who claim to make small quantities of 'exclusive' champagnes, but none can match this. For some unknown reason the phylloxera louse failed to penetrate two tiny vineyards in Ay and Bouzy owned by Bollinger. The original vines still stand ungrafted and Cyril Ray, author of the excellent history of the house, suggested that wine should be made separately in 1969 to celebrate Madame Bollinger's seventieth birthday. The tradition has continued in vintage years (sometimes the production is less than 2000 bottles) and needless to say the price is incredible! I am fortunate to have tasted three vintages. Without a doubt it is the most individualistic of all champagnes – rich, fruity, with an incredible intensity of Pinot flavour that demands years of keeping even after dégorgement. A fascinating wine with great interest value. Not really for 'drinking', more for 'tasting'. If you ever see a bottle on sale (no mean feat in itself), buy it, and share the taste (and cost) with a few friends. Unless you manage to buy another bottle you will never taste anything like it again.

A Remarkable Tasting

In August 1985 I was invited by Mentzendorff & Co. to taste an astonishing range of Bollinger vintages. It was a treat to discover just how well many of the older wines had stood up to the tests of time. It was also a marvellous affirmation of the quality of the wines. We first tasted the complete range of all vintages released from 1959 to 1975, plus an amazing rarity from an earlier vintage.

1975: Glorious yeasty nose with a depth of intensity and almost overpowering fruit flavour balanced with an elegant finish. A wine that will last for years.

1973: One of the few very good wines from this year. A delicate nose with a fragrant flavour.

1970: Not much bouquet but a pleasant, elegant character with rather light finish compared with most Bollinger vintage wines.

1969: Yeasty nose. Showing its age, but gracefully, and still retaining intensity of Pinot flavour.

1966: Fond memories: drunk regularly during my first exciting years in one of the world's most exciting cities. Would it stand up to such memories . . . or would it let me down? I am delighted to report that the wine was still sensational – an alluring flavoursome Pinot nose and still a beautifully consistent *mousse*. The flavour was a revelation with hints of the finest of Meursault. An aristocrat of champagnes.

1964: No disappointment, even following the 1966. A lighter nose with a little less flavour but a delightfully subtle biscuity finish.

1961: All the worst aspects of old champagne. Little *mousse*, fat and flabby with a touch of maderisation.

1959: Not ageing gracefully. Some fizz remaining but no charm.

1952: A deep, golden colour with plenty of vitality. A honeyed Château d'Yquem nose and a ripe, intense flavour with a lengthy, gutsy finish – a magic wine.

After these wines we had to suffer two vintages of the *Vieilles Vignes Françaises*:

1973: The Pinot Noir shrieks. More flavour than you would ever reasonably expect in champagne. An idiosyncratic wine. Nowhere near ready for drinking.

1969: Once again a unique style. Deep colour with a very rich nose — at times the taste is more red burgundy than champagne. A superb finish with a beautiful balance of fruit and oak. It was drinking well at the time but I have no doubt that another ten years' bottle age will help.

I realise that very few people in this world have the good fortune to spend a few hours tasting (and retasting!) such a stunning array of wines, but as well as the sybaritic delight of such an occasion it was also welcoming to see the house achieving its goals. In Christian Bizot's words: 'Bollinger has remained faithful to its past in today's world, where all too often the notion of quality is dying out.'

—— VEUVE CLICQUOT-PONSARDIN ——

ESTABLISHED: 1805.
LOCATION: Reims.
YEARLY PRODUCTION: 8 million bottles.
VINEYARDS: 275 hectares, mainly at Ambonnay, Avize, Ay, Bouzy, Le Mesnil-sur-Oger, Oger, Verzenay and Verzy.

An intriguing house. Veuve Clicquot has an image of impeccability, the highest of quality – they call it more 'artisanal' than 'industrial', basically enjoying the image of a boutique winery while benefiting from the considerable advantages of being the third-largest brand of all.*

At the risk of oversimplification, one can say that none of these achievements would have been realised without Madame Nicole Barbe Ponsardin, who took over a small family business and transformed it into a considerable international operation.** Not only did the widow have a great aptitude for commerce, she was also adept at choosing the right person for the job. Her original partner, Monsieur Bohn, was the ever faithful, peripatetic supreme salesman, responsible for the remarkable achievements on the Russian and Central and Eastern European markets while she stayed at home supervising the business at base and handling the finances. On Bohn's death she appointed another young German, Edouard Werlé. He proved just as devoted to his stringent duties as his predecessor and contributed enormously to the continuing success of the house.

Sadly for such a dynamic lady (or perhaps as a result of her ruthless determination) her daughter Clementine was extremely shy and reserved and inherited none of her mother's business acumen. She married a likeable but irresponsible aristocrat, the Count de Chevigne, who enjoyed the good life and

---

*After Moët & Chandon and G. H. Mumm.
**See Chapter 4.

considered money to be little more than a means for gambling. Not the man to entrust with the hard-earned family fortune.

Extravagant perhaps, but the Count certainly possessed cunning. He was usually pressed for cash but he found an easy solution. He wrote some rather salacious literature which became a best-seller – simply because it was reprinted about a dozen times as the highly embarrassed mother-in-law bought up every copy of every edition in order to prevent distribution. Despite her disapproval of the Count's lifestyle, Madame Clicquot seemed to be fond of him; apparently, despite his many failings, he was still an attentive and loving husband. He managed to persuade the widow to invest vast sums of money in his project to restore the Château de Bousault, where she was able to live in luxury until her death in 1886 at the grand old age of eighty-eight. Her attachment to her son-in-law was not totally unrealistic and her will was quite pragmatic: the business and a portion of the vineyards had been endowed to the faithful Monsieur Werlé and the remaining vineyards were left to her granddaughter, Anne de Mortemart, the Duchesse d'Uzes – later to be sold back to descendants of Werlé.

At the time of her death Veuve Clicquot-Ponsardin was selling the astonishing number of 3 million bottles per annum. Her motto was 'Only one quality: the finest', and she had built up a portfolio of vineyards that enabled her to achieve this. Business continued to boom; first Edouard Werlé then his heirs ran the business with the principles established by Madame and Bohn. Their reward has been this *boutique* image of a carefully crafted product of outstanding quality, but produced in vast quantities.

Nowadays the firm owns the third-largest vineyard holding in Champagne, with an average rating of 97 per cent. The sheer size of the operation is such that these estates account for only 30 per cent of the company's grape requirements; the rest is bought in from 1000 hectares of similarly rated estates.

The company has not been reticent in adopting the most modern methods of vinification, when suitable. It was one of the first to use *gyropalettes*, but they are hand-turned cages, not the vast mechanical monsters currently in vogue. Visitors to their cellars cannot help but be impressed by the obsessive attention to quality control. At no stage in the production does the company accept that its size is a problem – it prefers to consider it an asset. Six oenologists are employed to create the wines and one is responsible for nothing other than continual quality assessment.

In 1955 Veuve Clicquot-Ponsardin became a company quoted on the Paris Bourse, and since then there have been a certain number of diversifications and commercial changes. In 1978 the house of Canard-Duchêne was purchased, followed a few years later by a majority shareholding in Parfums Givenchy. In 1986 there was a short-lived takeover/merger (everyone called it something different) of the Henriot–Charles Heidsieck–Louis Vuitton luggage group. The Heidsieck company was then sold to the cognac house Rémy Martin and in 1987 the Clicquot group was 'merged' with the Moët–Hennessy group – forming the giant LVMH conglomerate.* After a few battles, which threatened to rival *Dallas*, Joseph Henriot succeeded Alain de Vogüé (great-grandson of Eduard Werlé) and the new breed of merchant banking–business administration whizzkids joined the more traditional Champenois-trained executives. Henriot felt the firm had become complacent and needed revitalisation if it was to hold on to its eminent position in the market. No one suggested the product wasn't right, but he thought there was a lack of attention to the details of the commercial world of the 1980s. In 1988 I questioned Henriot about the well-publicised rift between himself and Alain de Vogüé. At the time the LVMH grouping had been finalised for less than a year, and Henriot was already quite emphatic about the 'sleepiness of Veuve Clicquot in the recent past' and realistic about the competitiveness of others very close to his corporate home.

> Whenever a major champagne house relaxes, as we did in Australia for example, our partners Moët prove their experience in expanding their efforts and grabbing the extra market share ... We are now small in the USA and yet eighty years ago we had 35 per cent of the market. We should be able to acquire at least 10 per cent.**

Another champagne story of present-day board-room skirmishes which fortunately have not affected the wonderful product.

As a restaurateur I (with my accountant, bank manager and doctor) am aware of the stresses of a far from easy profession – but it does have its glories. One of these is to enjoy frequent glasses of Veuve Clicquot at around midday, to celebrate getting through the dull business of the morning and looking forward to the excitement of the 'real' working day.

THE WINES
Non-Vintage Brut Yellow Label

If asked to sum up the character of the wines of Veuve Clicquot I would use just one word, 'richness'. This full, flavoursome wine reeks of gutsy, yeasty Pinot Noir flavour and has a glorious lingering, soft, yet robust finish. One of the easiest of all non-vintage wines to pick in a 'blind' tasting.

The instantly recognisable label certainly doesn't harm business. Interestingly the house recently purchased a painting at a New York auction entitled 'Wife, Wine and Song'. The bottle chosen to represent wine? You've guessed right.

Vintage Brut Gold Label

Only grapes from vineyards rating 97 per cent or more are used for this wine. Ageing

---

*See page 160.
**A week after this Clicquot announced that Bernard Ganter, one of the greatest modern day champagne salesmen, had been persuaded to join Clicquot and would control the United States subsidiary company. I have no doubt Henriot will now achieve his desired market share!

on the lees varies according to the style of the vintage but is approximately five years. A 70 per cent Pinot Noir content produces a revelational rich, luscious wine with a little less vintage variation than many other houses who tend to 'let the year speak for itself'. No house, apart from Krug and Bollinger, has been so consistent recently – the 1973, 1976 and 1979 were gems, and the 1982 is even better, with an alluring floral bouquet counterbalanced by an almost overpowering intensity of rich, ripe, biscuity flavour. This will keep for years.

Rosé Brut Vintage

A full-coloured, deep-flavoured wine, as is to be expected from a house which owns nearly a third of the total vineyard area of Bouzy. Made by the addition of approximately 10 per cent of wines from this cru to the normal blend. Clicquot proudly claims to be the first house to have produced a pink champagne – in 1780. Despite its depth of flavour I prefer to drink the youngest possible vintage on the market.

Demi-Sec White Label

Very popular in the halcyon days of the South American market and still enjoying significant popularity in Spain.

La Grande Dame Vintage

One of the more attractive of the secondary echelon of Prestige Cuvées. I enjoy the full style (over 60 per cent Pinot Noir), which is quite different from most of the lighter wines of this class. The wine was first launched in 1972, the house's bicentenary year, and has remained a product of only the vineyards owned by *la grande dame* herself. It has only one real problem: when the vintage champagne of the same house is superlative it is very difficult to find the rationale for spending double the money on something that does not taste twice as good.

—— HENRIOT ——

Established: 1875.
Location: Reims.
Yearly production: 1 million bottles.
Vineyards: 125 hectares, mainly in Avenay, Ay, Beaumont-sur-Vesle, Chouilly, Cramant, Epernay, Mareuil-sur-Ay, Le Mesnil-sur-Oger, Mutigny, Oger, Trépail, Vertus, Villeneuve-Renneville and Verzy.

I first tasted Henriot on a balmy spring evening, sitting in the Monaco football stadium on the night that John Conteh threw away his chances of fame and fortune. He decided not to turn up to defend his recently acquired world boxing title. Unfortunately for the atmosphere on the 'big night', the majority of the fans didn't seem to fancy watching a last-minute replacement battling it out with the challenger and they followed Conteh's example and stayed away. The problem was that no one seemed to have informed the caterers, and I will always remember the forlorn sight of dozens and dozens of large tubs at the end of the rows of seating stacked with iced bottles of Henriot, and hardly a soul to empty them. My friends and I did our best but it was a mere drop in the ocean. Despite these rather bizarre surroundings I was still amazed by the quality (of the bubbly, that is, not of the licensed brutality as the jet-lagged American substitute was pummelled on to the floor) and surprised that such a deliciously soft, fruity and mature non-vintage had never come my way before.

Over the years I looked out for the name and it was obvious that it may have lacked penetration on the export markets but was certainly well established in France. The name Henriot regularly appeared in the best Michelin starred restaurants. None of the wines appeared in the supermarkets but they graced the shelves of most of the upmarket stores. My neighbour in the south of France bought it by mail order and poured it before Sunday lunch. In fact it seemed that the French were determined to keep this wonderful wine for themselves.

Gradually Henriot started to appear overseas. I have drunk the wine at Stars Restaurant in San Francisco and bought it in shops in Australia, and it is now a regular feature at the better eating and drinking establishments in Great Britain. But even now it is hardly one of the better-known champagne houses despite being one of the largest vineyard owners in the Côte des Blancs, and one of the most self-sufficient of the major houses, with 90 per cent of production coming from these company-owned vineyards.

The Henriot family have owned vineyards around Reims since 1640, before the appointment of Dom Pérignon as cellarmaster of the Abbey of Hautvillers. In 1809 Apolline Henriot, née Godinot, was widowed and, instead of genteel retirement, she took over the business affairs of her in-laws and formed the champagne house Veuve Henriot Aine, which combined the Henriot holdings with her father's considerable vineyards. In 1851 her grandson Ernest helped his brother-in-law Charles-Camille Heidsieck establish Champagne Charles Heidsieck, and Veuve Henriot became major suppliers to the firm – a relationship to be repeated, in rather different form, 125 years later. In 1875 Ernest left and took over the family firm which was renamed Henriot & Cie. Expansion was considerable and while some successful family companies of this time were using their profits to maintain luxurious mansions with a lifestyle to match, Monsieur Henriot was investing his proceeds. Over the years he purchased vast areas of the very finest of Côtes des Blancs vineyards. In those days many of the houses were not particularly interested in vineyard ownership and the rather down-market agrarian activities that accompanied this; they preferred to leave the business of growing grapes to the farming classes. But not Ernest. He was an incredibly smart businessman who could see the relative bargains in the low cost of the land and the great advantages of controlling one's own production at source. A visionary.

The family have continued to run the company through a succession of sons. Now the house is firmly under the control of one of the most dynamic men in Champagne, Joseph Henriot. The 1970s and 1980s have seen many changes in the champagne industry: the increasing power of the growers, who began to sell their own wines rather than sell all their grapes to the *négociants*; the slump in sales during the mid-1970s; the spiralling costs of refinancing new stocks when the sales resumed their upward trend – all these factors helped to change the balances of power within the industry and caused problems for many houses. There was much wheeling and dealing, and Joseph was right in the thick of it. In 1976 he expanded dramatically by taking over Charles Heidsieck, a house with much greater sales and a worldwide sales organisation – but no vineyards. For a brief time he also owned the De Venoge–Trouillard group. In December 1985 Charles Heidsieck was sold to the Rémy Martin group and a month later Henroit merged with the much larger Veuve Clicquot–Canard-Duchêne–Givenchy group. Despite being owner of the smallest component Joseph ended up as the largest shareholder. A year later the group was sold to the Louis Vuitton luggage company and Joseph retained a seat on the board. Later there was the merger with Moët–Hennessy, followed by bitter infighting and the Guinness involvement.

All seemingly complicated, but the fact remains that Joseph Henriot is President of the Clicquot group of companies and very happy. All three houses are totally different and complement each other rather than compete. The future of his family firm is totally secure and he is free to run it precisely as he desires.

> There will always be the majority of champagne drinkers who enjoy drinking the famous names. Henriot is another story, a relatively unknown smaller house.* I don't want to please everyone, I want to make the finest of champagnes with a Chardonnay dominance in most blends. I am not in a hurry, I don't need the money, therefore I can build a long-term *boutique* champagne with no need for any compromise whatsoever. I want to sell it as the finest product of our own vineyards. Well done, properly done, for very demanding people.

Who are we to argue?

The Wines

Recently I was discussing champagnes with the excellent *sommelier* at the Auberge Le Grand Cerf, just outside Reims. He described the Henriot wines as being 'the champagnes that the growers order when they dine here. They love wines made from such a wonderful selection of the finest cru of the Côte des Blancs.'

*Not totally unknown – Henriot is the house champagne at the Upland Goose Hotel on the Falkland Islands!

Non-Vintage Brut Souverain

A beautifully balanced wine combining depth of rich, creamy flavour balanced with the delicacy and fruit of the significant Chardonnay percentage (30–35 per cent). 'No Pinot Meunier whatsoever, because I don't like it,' says Joseph rather bluntly. It was almost as if I had suggested a bottle of cheap Spanish sparkling!

Blanc de Blancs Brut Non-Vintage

Who better to make a Blanc de Blancs? Luscious, fragrant fruit with a light, flowery finish. It has many of the refined qualities of the premium wines made solely from Chardonnay, but at a fraction of the cost.

Vintage Brut

Forty to forty-five per cent Chardonnay. A wonderfully full, toasty and luscious no-compromise flavour. The 1976, 1979 and 1981 were three stars of these vintages, and the 1983 is simply superb – search for it and buy as many bottles as you can afford. You won't be disappointed.

Rosé Brut Vintage

Pinot Noir with a goodly percentage of Chardonnay (the exact quantity is not divulged) and the addition of red wine. A delicacy of colour and style but with a clearly defined Pinot character. The full flavour makes it an excellent champagne for a buffet on the patio – even in an English summer!

Cuvée Baccarat Vintage

One of the best-value Prestige Cuvées. A fifty–fifty blend of Pinot Noir and Chardonnay, it needs time in bottle but patience is rewarded – I consider the 1975 vintage one of the finest commercially available champagnes I have ever drunk. A *Cuvée Baccarat Rosé* is soon to be introduced; it will be made in very small quantities and only in very special vintages.

Réserve Baron Philippe de Rothschild Vintage

Very rare – and very expensive. Another fifty-fifty blend which also needs considerable bottle age. A wonderful wine but I cannot come to terms with the price when the superb Baccarat is easily available, and much more cheaply. Perhaps this wine may even be discontinued with the death of the Baron. A word of caution – if you see 'Rothschild' champagne, and the price is reasonable, it has nothing to do with Henriot. 'A. Rothschild' is one of the hundreds (thousands?) of names used by the giant BOB specialists, Marne & Champagne.

—— KRUG ——

ESTABLISHED: 1842.
LOCATION: Reims.
YEARLY PRODUCTION: 500,000 bottles.
VINEYARDS: 15 hectares: 9 at Ay, 6 at Le Mesnil-sur-Oger.

One of the least ostentatious champagne marques, also the most idiosyncratic; Hell will freeze over before a large bottle is seen being sprayed over the crowd at a motor race. Self-promotion is not one of the great desires of this house – the family prefer to let the wine speak for itself. Ask any senior member of the champagne establishment which champagne they rate the most highly (after their own, naturally). The answer will inevitably be Krug. Why?

The reason is quite straightforward: Krug is a dynasty dedicated to the creation of the greatest individualistic champagnes, made in a manner totally unsuited to the larger operations. In 1972 I sat across the table from Paul Krug, sipping the wonderful 1964, while he explained the family philosophy. It was quite simple really: 'There is champagne . . . and then there is Krug champagne.'

Johann-Joseph Krug was one of the many Germans to make his way to Champagne. In 1834 he began work as a clerk with the well-established house Jacquesson in Châlons-sur-Marne. The champagne world appealed to the young man and within a short time he was handling much of the important administrative work of the company and had been appointed a partner. Adolphe Jacquesson and Joseph (he had long dropped the Germanic Johann) succeeded in creating a major force within the industry, selling huge quantities of champagne across Europe. In 1841 Joseph married an English girl, Emma Ann Jaunay, Adolphe's sister-in-law, and life seemed to be successful and settled. Suddenly in 1842, for no apparent reason, Joseph parted company with Jacquesson and moved to Reims.

Prospects were hardly rosy. Joseph was forty-two, with a wife and baby son Paul, and little else. Fortunately, in a relatively short time he had established a formidable reputation as a businessman and blender, and this talent was not lost on a wine merchant, Hippolyte de Vives, who was happy to become a financial partner with Joseph, as long as he could retire and leave to Krug the running of the company. French law did not allow the use of names of partners not actively involved, so in 1843 the house of Krug & Cie was founded, in rented cellars in the rue Saint-Hilaire. Joseph immediately established the name on the major export markets, and by 1844 the wines were well known as far afield as St Petersburg, London, Amsterdam, New York – even Rio de Janiero, albeit with other houses' wines. The first actual Krug blends were not made until 1845.

Times were not easy for a new house with limited capital and only small quantities of wines. But Joseph's blending skills were in great demand and in some years he was making as much wine for other houses as for Krug – the ultimate in BOBs! By the time of his death in 1866 Krug & Cie was well established with a great reputation to match the hard-earned financial stability. Paul had joined the business three years previously and proved to be a marvellous asset. He was given 50 per cent of the company, his mother 25 per cent and de Vives also 25 per cent (on his death these were purchased by Paul). The name Krug was promoted, although financial restraints forced Paul to continue the considerable amount of blending for others. This was the great boom time for exports to wealthy Britain, and Paul was able to profit from his firsthand knowledge of the market — he had spent much of his childhood in the homeland of his mother.

Paul ran the house for forty-four years, during a time of great prosperity for the Champenois, and Krug's customers across the Channel were by no means the only lovers of good champagne. In 1873 he purchased the cellars, buildings and land on the rue Coquebert (the house is still there). He also found time to father ten children; unfortunately none was interested in carrying on the family tradition. Somehow the eldest son, Joseph II, was persuaded to relinquish his career in the army and he 'enlisted' with the family establishment. He helped his father run the firm for seventeen years until Paul's death in 1910.

Joseph Krug II was not the larger-than-life character which his father had been, didn't particularly want to work in the world of champagne and was considered to be easy-going ... yet when the going was tough the steeliness of the family character became evident. He married Jeanne Hollier Larousse, who proved her worth to the business during Joseph's absence during the First World War.

Joseph returned in 1918 but the rigours of prison-camp life had taken their toll and his health was failing. In 1924 his only son, Paul II, was still only twelve, so a nephew, Jean Seydoux, was appointed General Manager. No family could have wished for a better guardian of their affairs. Seydoux proved to be a consummate businessman with both organisational abilities and flair for the champagne world. Not only did he help Joseph steer the company through the vicissitudes of the years between the wars but he was a prominent member of the CIVC, dedicated during the German occupation to foiling the Nazis' desire to seize as much fine champagne as possible. Ironically Joseph II lived to the ripe old age of ninety-eight, dying five years after Seydoux in 1967. Despite having joined the firm in 1922, Paul II had to wait until the passing of both these grand old men before officially assuming total control. In actual fact after the war he had been supervising the regeneration of the firm and the inevitable replenishing of stocks.

At this stage the house owned no vineyards. In the 1880s Paul I had purchased 20 hectares around Mailly, but he later sold them. The Krug attitude had always been to leave cultivation of the grapes to others; they would concentrate on what they knew best — the selection of grapes and the blending. This might work in a *négociant*'s ideal world, but the realities of the modern champagne world demanded that Paul II protect the firm against external economic forces. In the early 1970s it purchased some extremely expensive vineyards, including the Clos de Mesnil. This involved a great deal of money and outside investment. Long-standing business colleagues Rémy Martin provided the capital. Initially they were minority partners, now they are majority, although the family are still very much in control. Paul has officially retired but still assists at blending time, and the house is now run by his two sons: Henri, who makes the wine, and Rémi, who sells it.

Many of the Mesnil-sur-Oger vines were too old, and large-scale replanting was carried out over a number of years, though some of the older vines were kept to achieve a balance. Now that all vineyards are fully productive the Krug holdings account for about 30 per cent of the company's requirements; the rest of the grapes are bought under contract. The house is justifiably proud of its relationships with growers: in Ambonnay it has contracts with families that span five generations and in Avize it has a contract whereby it receives half of the produce from a 30-hectare property. The grapes are bought from an intriguing mixture of Grand and Premier Cru villages plus a host of lesser-rated villages in the north, giving the house a not particularly impressive 91 per cent rating on the quality scale. Also, contrary to many other major houses, it has always been a firm believer in the lowly Pinot Meunier.

At harvest it is not unusual to find the most senior personnel out in the vineyards checking the quality before pressing – after all, the grapes are the property of the house from the moment they are put in the basket. At the pressing only the cuvée is kept for Krug; the remainder is made into wine and then sold. Forget about stainless-steel fermentation vats: Paul II and Henri haven't chosen to ignore the new technology of recent decades – they simply don't approve. The wine is fermented in 205-litre oak barrels with the date of picking noted on the side along with the vineyard – very important in years of uneven harvest conditions. The fermentation cellar at the rue Coquebert is a reminder of the old days, with nearly 4000 casks stacked neatly. There is no mechanical equipment as the wine is never filtered, only racked by gravity twice using the same equipment that was in operation when the house was established. Obviously this is an expensive, labour-intensive process, but the Krugs maintain that their wines lost complexity and aroma when they experimented with stainless steel. Also the small amounts in each cask allow close supervision of the wine. If a problem occurs then the cask can easily be rejected. And such a large number of different wines allows much more scope for individuality at blending time.

The family conducts their first tasting as early as the end of November, before even the first racking. This is to pronounce judgement on the vintage. All wines are tasted individually and a decision is taken whether to continue with the barrel or reject (in poor years up to 20 per cent of the total harvest may be rejected at this stage). The second crucial tastings occur late February–early March, and once again it is strictly a family affair. Rémi even stops travelling for two months. Henri describes the blending as 'the creation of a symphony . . . in an orchestra each musical instrument is essential, from the violins and cellos to the flutes, oboes, bassoons, etc. . . . each one of them playing its part and contributing to the harmony of the "whole" work.'

Henri, Rémi and Paul have up to 300 base wines from the present vintage plus the resources of the vast quantities of carefully preserved reserve wines kept in 4000-litre stainless-steel tanks ('they prevent oxidisation'). After the decisions the wines are blended in ceramic-tile-lined concrete tanks and then put back in cask. It is fascinating that, although the bottling takes three to four months, the last bottle tastes the same as the first. This is because the casks are so old that they don't interfere with the wine (rather different from Burgundy, Bordeaux, California and Australia). When I first visited Krug, crown capsules were scorned, but now that the quality has improved they are used. Needless to say remuage is all by hand, performed about two or three years after bottling. The wine is then kept for at least three more years, possibly more – on average the cellars hold six years' stock.

THE WINES
Grande Cuvée Non-Vintage

The house proudly claims that it is 'the only house to specialise 100 per cent in the production of Prestige Cuvées'. The logic involved in the creation of this wine is quite complicated, but it seems quite rational and simple when one of the family explains the reason for the wine being the cheapest (well, relatively the cheapest) and accounting for over 80 per cent of the total production.

Despite the house's great reputation for production of long-lasting, powerful, majestic vintage wines – many wine-lovers become quite misty-eyed when the 1928 is mentioned, and I confess to the same emotions regarding the 1953, 1964 and 1966 – the Krug name was established by its Private Cuvée. While this wine was essentially a non-vintage, the house always considered it much more prestigious. The Krugs believed in the principle of non-vintage – Rémi prefers the term 'multi-vintage' – but felt that as their wine didn't merely consist of a blend of recent years (the Grande Cuvée on the market at the time of writing is composed of forty-seven wines from eight vintages) it merited more consideration. No true champagne-lover could dare argue!

In 1978 this remarkable wine was replaced by Grande Cuvée, with totally new packaging including a replica of one of the early champagne bottle shapes. The style was considerably lighter, using the fruit of the newly purchased vineyards in the Côte des Blancs. The wine is quite remarkable, with an average content of 50 per cent Pinot Noir, 35 per cent Chardonnay and 15 per cent Pinot Meunier. The elegant biscuity nose hints of a lightish, floral style and yet it actually possesses considerable depth of glorious, mature fruit flavour. The finish is firm but soft . . . the taste sensation lingers for hours.

Vintage

The family have an equivocal attitude towards their wonderful vintage wines. Rémi and Henri are quick to insist that the Krug style prevails over the style of the vintage, but I should quote Joseph II: 'Krug Cuvée is my baby. For vintage champagne I have to share the credit with God.'

The wines are so good – don't even bother thinking of an average-quality vintage from this house. The leisurely ageing process means the wines are not released until the competition are on to at least their next vintage, and in my opinion they always benefit with even more bottle age. The blend varies considerably from year to year. The 1979 has 28 per cent of Pinot Meunier, which by common consent has a short life, but Rémi says, 'The remarkable 1928 had the same percentage and is still going strong!' Beg, steal or buy a bottle or three of the current year on sale, keep for another four or five years . . . and share with one of your best friends.

The Krug Collection

It is all very well discussing the longevity of the vintage wines, but poor storage will destroy this great asset. This problem is alleviated, admittedly at some cost, by the house's periodical releases of older vintages, in bottles and magnums, that have been resting untouched in their cellars. They are individually numbered in descending order as the stock is released – a two-magnum collection, one each of the 1963 and 1973, was auctioned in Bordeaux in 1987 and Australian wine merchant Brett Crittenden paid the princely sum of 10,500 francs!

Rosé

In 1983 the family introduced their first Rosé. Made by the *addition* method it still has a considerable amount of Chardonnay (approximately 25 per cent). A very, very pale colour and an almost too delicate flavour. I will save the not insubstantial sum of money required and continue enjoying the Grand Cuvée and vintage wines.

Clos du Mesnil Vintage

This exceptional walled vineyard is right in the heart of the village Mesnil-sur-Oger, and has been there since 1698. The 1.9 hectare property belonged to the Benedictine monastery of Le Mesnil until 1750. It was purchased in 1971 in a very parlous state; extensive replanting meant that the wine was not ready for release under the estate label until 1979. Krug proved with the first release that the 'masters of the Pinot' were equally mercurial with Chardonnay and the wine is fragrant and vivacious, yet with a magnificent rich intensity quite unlike any other Blanc de Blancs. It slips down the throat leaving the most glorious, honeyed aftertaste. I shared a bottle with Henri in March 1988 – and was still quietly smiling to myself in May.

Production varies from a mere 9000 to 17,000 bottles according to the vintage, so don't expect to find it easily. Like the Bollinger Vieilles Vignes, it is an inordinately expensive curiosity, but must be tasted at least once in a lifetime. It is another reminder of the pre-eminent position the house retains in a volatile industry. At no stage does the family ever compromise quality. Krug isn't cheap but neither is the taste. As Rémi says, 'Our customers must always find the Krug taste, which is so special that they expect and recognise it.'

—— LAURENT PERRIER ——

ESTABLISHED: 1812.
LOCATION: Tours-sur-Marne.
YEARLY PRODUCTION: 7.5 million bottles.
VINEYARDS: 80 hectares.

The phenomenon of the post-war champagne industry. This family-owned company based on the outskirts of the region was almost extinct at the start of the 1950s. Now it is the fourth-largest brand. This spectacular rise has not been the result of selling cheap products with a label to match the buyer's purse. Anything but. An attractive, individualistic house style with consistency of quality has been one of the dominant characteristics of Laurent Perrier.* How has this been achieved?

The house actually dates back to 1812 when Eugène Laurent, a cooper from Chigny-les-Roses, settled in Tours-sur-Marne. Records are hazy due to the devastation of the company's files during the First World War, but it would seem that he set up business as a champagne merchant. His son, also named Eugène, married a Mathilde Perrier who, in the great tradition of champagne widows, grasped the reins of the company after the demise of her husband and launched into extremely vigorous expansion. However, several of her next-of-kin were killed in the war and when she died without children in 1925 things had started to run down. Another widow, Marie-Louise de Nonancourt (a sister of Victor and Henri Lanson), bought the company in 1939, planning to pass it on to her son Maurice. Tragically he was captured by the Germans when attempting to escape conscription and he died in the deportation camp of Oranienburg. His younger brother Bernard avoided the clutches of the occupying army, joined the resistance and in 1944 moved on to the 501st Tank Regiment, with which he fought until the end of the war.

After hostilities had ceased Bernard de Nonancourt returned home and proceeded to embark on a crash course in the making and selling of champagne, courtesy of experience gained working at a number of houses. He soon realised that breaking into the international champagne market was not going to be easy.

---

*Granted the champagne houses do work together very well, as the worldwide reputation of the *appellation* testifies – but there are obviously many rivalries and jealousies. I have never heard a derogatory word about Laurent Perrier. As one prominent President put it, 'Don, I am envious of the ease of their success, but I am also full of admiration for their standards. We didn't think there was room for another brand of this size. They have proved us wrong!'

Laurent Perrier's initial export drive was to the almost untapped markets of the expatriate nationals in colonial West Africa: quite a gamble. It was a long way from France with a climate that rapidly ruined wines (and reputations if stored incorrectly and for too long). The company had done its homework and realised there was a promising future for champagne with a youthful, fresh, early drinking style and they duly created the ideal blend. They also realised that the stocks would have to be carefully monitored and that lengthy storage periods had to be avoided at all costs. It would be preferable for the agents occasionally to be out of stock while awaiting fresh supplies than always to be in stock of tired, out-of-condition wine.

On the home market the company initially concentrated on promoting its still wines. This was before the *appellation* Coteaux champenois was created, and the wines were usually excess production and termed 'Vin nature de Champagne'. They discovered that despite the negative opinions of their competitors there was a market, especially with restaurateurs. The still wines were an invaluable key to the door, introducing the name Laurent Perrier to many influential hotel and restaurant customers. Also, as the wines had to be sold young, there was a much faster return on the invested capital, and the profits were then reinvested in the booming champagne part of the business.

Laurent Perrier's rise as one of the largest houses is astonishing and legendary. Much of the incredible expansion is a tale of Bernard's business acumen, which involves his selection of associates as much as that of cuvées. Bernard de La Giraudière, a whole four inches shorter than de Nonancourt and yet still the height of an international rugby forward, is one of the great natural champagne salesmen of his time. He joined the firm over twenty years ago after university and spells in the French section of the BBC and the administrative side of the industry at the CIVC. François Philippoteaux was appointed on the administrative side, and for the past twelve years a dynamic Bordelais Alain Terrier, a protégé of Professor Ribereau-Gayon, has been *chef de caves*. Delegation seems to work extremely well; the vital constituent members of the administration regard the company as part of their heritage and the dedication certainly produces the right results.

The company vineyards provide only a tiny percentage of Laurent Perrier's vast grape requirements, yet it doesn't seem to have any problems with supply even in the years when other houses are complaining. Both Bernards firmly believe in the philosophy that 'A good contract with the right grower is better than owning a poor vineyard producing bad wine.' They are proud of their creation of a network of conscientious growers. Bernard de La Giraudière also points out that many have been dealing with them since the early days of the house's rejuvenation and 'remember the fact that the house paid reasonable prices for the grapes for their still wines in days when others were haggling over centimes'.

The two Bernards and Terrier believe that the finest champagne is achieved when the final taste is dominated by the flavour of top-quality grapes, hence their fresh, youthful, racy style. Prolonged ageing on the lees is avoided as they concentrate on obtaining this overt fruit flavour. The house is run by perfectionists, the cellars are the most up to date of all the major houses* and the massive operation exudes an aura of calm efficiency.

THE WINES
Non-Vintage Brut

One of the most reliable of all non-vintage wines. Bernard de Nonancourt has always adopted a strict policy of limiting vintage sales in order to provide sufficient wines of top years for the non-vintage blend. I love the fragrance and the attractive Chardonnay flavour which is counterbalanced by the refined Pinot body.

Vintage

More depth of flavour with usually about 70 per cent Pinot Noir. An agreeable wine, but I have to admit a preference for the non-vintage. Then again, the vintages are not readily available and the house practises what it preaches – in three recent visits to the establishment I have been offered many a bottle, of everything but the vintage.

Rosé Brut Non-Vintage

One of their success stories. A luscious, fragrant wine made by the maceration method with only Pinot Noir. The skin contact at pressing is for only a very short period in order to produce a pink wine with considerable delicacy in colour, aroma and flavour. An ideal introduction to the glories of Rosé champagne (and relatively inexpensive).

Cuvée Grand Siècle

Simply one of the finest of all champagnes. It is an assemblage of 100 per cent wines from three outstanding vintages. Sometimes the Chardonnay content is 50 per cent, sometimes considerably more. It is always a beautifully balanced, complex classic wine which flaunts both the art of the blender and the advantages of large stockholdings of the finest reserves. It is a shame that the American market is so vintage-conscious that the house must compromise and release a Grand Siècle of a single year. The Americans are the losers.

Vintage Millésimé Rare

An occasional release of small quantities of the reserve wines of the most exceptional years that have been used in the Grand Siècle (over the years 1959, 1961, 1966, 1969 and a sumptuous rich, toasty 1975).

*A little easier for a house which is by far the youngest member of the establishment. Also most of the central houses are united in a need for more space whereas in outlying Tours-sur-Marne expansion has not been a problem and construction work has been able to reflect the technical needs rather than available space.

Ultra Brut

They assure me that many people love this wine. I reserve judgement.

Coteaux Champenois

I have deliberately avoided evaluating the few still wines of Champagne, but as Laurent Perrier has been such a pioneer of this *appellation* I must acknowledge the Blanc de Blancs de Chardonnay, which is an attractive, lemony wine from the Côte des Blancs. Alain Terrier is experimenting with different forms of maturation for still Pinot Noir, including new American oak casks. The results should be interesting but nowadays these wines no longer form such an important part of the company's cash flow.

—— MOËT & CHANDON ——

ESTABLISHED: 1743.
LOCATION: Epernay.
YEARLY PRODUCTION: 26 million bottles.
VINEYARDS: 500 hectares, with particularly significant holdings in Chouilly, Cramant, Le Mesnil-sur-Oger, Hautvillers, Ay, Mareuil-sur-Ay, Verzenay and Jaulgonne.

Throughout the history of champagne the performances of the large houses have been impressive, but none has achieved the phenomenal growth of the Moët & Chandon group (Moët, Mercier and Ruinart). In 1986 they accounted for 30 per cent of all champagne exports, a revenue figure equal to 40 per cent of all Bordeaux exports, 69 per cent of Burgundy, 124 per cent of Beaujolais and 180 per cent of Côtes du Rhône! Moët is now the leading brand on the domestic market, having recently overtaken stablemate Mercier, and is also in first place in the top eight export markets – Great Britain, the United States, Germany, Switzerland, Italy, Belgium, Australia and the Netherlands. Total sales have increased by a staggering 92 per cent since 1971.

Even the greatest of houses produces the occasional disappointing bottle, but one of the most important aspects of Moët in the course of my champagne-drinking life has been the remarkable consistency of the wine. This has not been achieved by chance and good fortune. One has to go back to the beginning to understand the present-day position of this amazing house.

In 1792 Jean Rémy Moët, at only thirty-four years old, took over control of the house of Moët, founded by his grandfather in 1743. The business was the third-oldest champagne house and was flourishing, despite the fact that the Revolution was doing the same. There were problems with sources of supplies of grapes, and obviously the recently established export business disappeared, but Jean Rémy proved to be an adept survivor. The Napoleonic years heralded a period of tremendous growth in both the size of the house and the profile of Jean Rémy, who lavished hospitality on Napoleon, Josephine and the rest of the entourage, and in return enjoyed the patronage of the Emperor and benefited commercially from the connection without any effect on export sales afterwards. European royalty and prominent citizens of the world clamoured for this renowned wine. The hospitality and promotion were not in vain. I consider that it was at this stage that the traditional Champenois blend of flamboyant and warm-hearted hospitality combined with hard-nosed realisation of the long-term benefits of such promotion was created, and Moët was the pioneer.

Jean Rémy's successors were equally determined businessmen and reinvested the company's proceeds. By the beginning of this century Moët was one of the major (but by no means the largest) houses, with a formidable portfolio of vineyards. While other less secure houses struggled in the first decades of the century Moët continued to flourish, although by the time of the Depression even it was feeling the pinch. Robert-Jean de Vogüé joined the company in 1932 and immediately proved the right man for the job. While most of Moët's competitors were worrying about the cost of champagne in tough financial times, he created Dom Pérignon, which was an immediate success. When the economic gloom finally retreated and other houses were beginning to re-establish their businesses, Moët was already in the midst of a great expansion drive spearheaded by Robert-Jean's promotional and sales abilities. After the Second World War sales increased at a bewildering rate. Moët assiduously promoted its own name around the world and also contributed considerably to the necessary bolstering of champagne's image. In the 1960s, when total annual production of champagne was about 70 million bottles, Moët was producing 10 million. In 1962 the company's shares were quoted on the Paris Bourse and consequent regular expansion programmes saw the purchase of Ruinart, Mercier, Christian Dior perfumes and many ancillary activities at home and abroad – plus a merger with Hennessy Cognac.* Recently there have been the traumas of the merger with the Louis Vuitton–Veuve Clicquot–Henriot–Canard-Duchêne–Givenchy group to form the giant LVMH 'super company' and the subsequent realignment with Guinness. But at no time has the financial wrangling interfered with the main aim. As champagne sales have increased dramatically in the last two decades the group has ensured that its sales have also expanded at the same rate and it still controls this remarkable share of the industry!

Its huge vineyard holdings, by far the largest in the business, meet about 20 per cent of Moët's needs. Traditional *coquard* presses are used, although they are experimenting, with the CIVC's permission, with a horizontal press capable of handling 12,000 kilograms (three times the traditional amount). In the past, when harvesting the grapes was even more leisurely, *épluchage* (the hand-sorting of

*They now own their agents in many countries. The largest acquisition of this nature was the 1980 purchase of their United States agent Schieffelin & Co., which in turn brought ownership of the superb Simi Winery in the Napa Valley and 50 per cent of Sichel & Söhne of Mainz, producers of Blue Nun Liebfraumilch.

grapes) was carried out. This is not practical on the huge estates, now that speed is also important along with care and attention. Moët has developed an alternative system. The first 200 litres of the cuvée are used basically as a cleanser of the skins and are separated after pressing and join the deuxième taille, not used by Moët.

On entering the fermentation cellars one suddenly realises the awesome 'might of Moët'. Row after row of giant stainless-steel fermentation tanks look more like a scene from a science-fiction movie than a winery. And they are dwarfed by the 6000-hectolitre blending tanks (that's just 780,000 bottles per tank). Total capacity is 300,000 hectolitres, which adds up to 15 per cent of all champagne production! In 1982 the crop was so large that these blending tanks were used for first fermentation and, in the opinion of oenologist Richard Geoffroy, 'made the best cuvées'. Fermentation is rapid – first fermentation lasts only one week. The wine is left on yeast for three weeks while undergoing malolactic fermentation. All rather different from a few decades ago when the wines were left in the cellars more or less alone for six months or so.

Over 150,000 people visit the vast 28 kilometres of cellars underneath the avenue de Champagne each year, passing by a few thousand of the millions and millions of bottles, an impressive sight. At the moment everything is still very traditional – all remuage is still done manually – but things are changing. Throughout its history Moët has been one of the great innovators of the world's wine industry. At the start of the phylloxera crisis, Comte Chandon de Briailles pioneered the reconstitution of Moët's (and the rest of Champagne's) vineyards by building an experimental grafting centre. The first mechanical cultivator of narrowly spaced vines was built by Moët in 1945, and it was one of the first champagne houses to use stainless-steel vats (as recently as 1964). Prime emphasis has always been placed on viticultural and oenological research. But there has been no change for change's sake. Philippe Coulon, Director of Oenology, proudly states, 'There have been no revolutions in the champagne industry, only evolution, as we have gradually adapted modern techniques to our needs.'

Moët's laboratory is the prime source for the development of *les billes*, which are expected to be in operation by 1990. These are encapsulated yeast balls made from a neutral alginate derived from seaweed. There will be no free-floating yeasts in the wines after their first bottling; instead minute yeasts will be trapped within the balls. As they are porous the wine in the bottle can penetrate and normal reactions occur – but without clouding the wine. 'Remuage made easy.' All that is required is the addition of these balls, and the normal horizontal storage, and when it is time for the remuage the bottles are simply placed vertically and *les billes* dutifully fall downwards into the capsule. I have tasted wines made both by traditional methods and by use of *les billes* and have not been able to ascertain the difference. A certain amount of wine made by this method will be released in 1993.

I personally consider that the house handles its premier position extremely skilfully. The opulence of image is balanced with careful financial calculation. I recently congratulated a senior member of the family on the success of the 'softly softly' approach to Domaine Chandon California (wine was made in rented facilities for the first few years until the company was convinced of the viability of the operation) and the reply was 'Ah, yes, but we still had to sell one of our French châteaux to pay for it.' Similarly there has been an estimable willingness to restrict sales of Dom Pérignon rather than sacrifice the quality and the bankable excellence of Moët's vintage wines. The greatest compliment I can pay this house is to report that they command immense respect from the rest of the industry. A friend, head of one of the finest and most highly respected houses, summed up their position succinctly: 'Moët are not my competitors. They are in a world of their own. They do a marvellous job for all of Champagne . . . and I am proud to consider them my friends.'

The Wines
Non-Vintage Brut Impérial

The champagne which is known the world over – light, fresh flavour with plenty of fruit. Always seems to taste much lighter than one would expect of a wine with an average of 50 per cent Pinot Noir and 20 per cent Pinot Meunier.

Vintage Brut Impérial

One of the delights of the champagne world. Usually a Pinot-dominated blend which can achieve true greatness in some years; the virtues of these wines have already been extolled. I recently tasted a magnum of 1959, disgorged in 1985. A wonderful voluptuous, biscuity nose and flavour which lingered on and on.

Rosé Vintage Brut Impérial

No compromise. All Pinot Noir made by the *addition* method. A full flavour with just a hint of what good sparkling red burgundy would taste like . . . if there were such a thing! A considerable softness on the finish, perfect for aperitif, first-course or main-course drinking.

Dom Pérignon

What is there left to say about this remarkable wine? Louis Roederer may have made a special wine for Tsar Alexander II in 1876, but 'the Dom' was the first of the 'real' Prestige Cuvées by a good many years (the Tsar's personal bubbly was sweet for a start) – and is still the one associated with first-class travel, caviar dinners and all the facets of the good life that are escapist ideals to most of us. Moët have succeeded so spectacularly with 'DP' because, although the wine is very soft and delicate, it still possesses a wonderful toasty nose and spicy, biscuity character.

Alice King, of London's *Daily Mail*, organised a blind tasting of twenty non-vintage wines. Unknown to us tasters her editor had insisted she add a bottle of the Dom, on the assumption that this wine was an example of outrageous, unjustified extravagance (i.e. an affectation, little different from other champagnes). The editor was a little miffed when I immediately spotted it. Quite frankly, it was very easy!

Dom Pérignon Rosé

Sixty per cent Pinot Noir, made by the *addition* method. Even more exclusive. A wonderfully refined wine combining the delicacy of flavour of the finest grapes with a subtle Pinot flavour. One of the most deliciously subtle aftertastes of all. I have only tasted it once, and that was in the United States with a group of people who paid little attention to the wine in the glass. My heart bled.

—— POL ROGER ——

ESTABLISHED: 1849.
LOCATION: Epernay.
YEARLY PRODUCTION: 1.3 million bottles.
VINEYARDS: 80 hectares, mainly in Chouilly, Cramant, Cuis, Epernay, Moussy and Pierry.

Winston Churchill christened the Pol Roger house at 44 avenue de Champagne in Epernay 'the world's most drinkable address'. Sometimes when I am in a reflective mood (or in need of a glass of champagne) I contemplate the fact that try as I may there is no way I will ever match the Pol Roger consumption of this revered Prime Minister. He loved the stuff with single-minded devotion and drank few other champagnes, whereas I merely consider the house to produce some of the finest of all wines from the region.

In fact consuming many, many bottles was not sufficient. Sir Winston even named his favourite racehorse 'Pol Roger'. To this day the Churchill connection is still remembered: since his death the British labels of the non-vintage White Foil and vintage Gold Foil have had black borders. The family tradition continued. When his son-in-law, the late Lord Soames, was leading the British delegation at the Rhodesian peace talks he called a press conference at a particularly difficult point in the negotiations. When asked for an estimate of how much longer the talks would last he said, 'Thirty days.' 'How can you be so exact?' asked the surprised interviewer. 'Because I only have thirty bottles of Pol Roger left' was the reply.

The history of the house is a story of generations of a family devoted to the production of the finest champagnes and also to remaining a family-owned house. In 1849 Monsieur Pol (champenois for Paul) Roger decided to expand his smallish business of making champagne and selling to *négociants*. He established his own house, on the avenue, and the name was soon known on the British market. Fifty years later he handed over the business to his sons Maurice and Georges. They realised that their father's champagne was nearly always referred to as 'Pol' Roger, so they successfully petitioned the President of the Republic for permission to link their father's Christian name and surname together, and the company's name was established. The brothers expanded the business and the cellars. They had their share of success – and misfortune. One morning in 1900 Maurice was woken by a thunderous sound which proved to be the collapse of the new cellars and new *galeries*. Over 500 vats and 2.2 million bottles were lost!

Maurice had a son, Jacques, and a daughter, Antoinette, who married Jean de Billy. Georges had two sons, Guy and Jean. Overall control of the house passed to Guy, Jean, Jacques and Jacques' wife Odette, who met Churchill in 1944 while working as a courier for the resistance. The next generation is now in charge: Christian de Billy and his second cousin Christian Pol-Roger, and de Billy's son Hubert has recently signed on. Despite the huge increase in champagne production of the past two decades the house has proceeded cautiously, expanding its vineyard holdings to 80 hectares,* which now supply 40 per cent of its grape needs. It owned no vineyards as recently as thirty years ago.

Pol Roger maintains a close 'hands on' contact with the growers at vintage. The two Christians, together with uncle Jean Pol-Roger and Monsieur Coffinet, the *chef de caves*, are all to be found around the various vineyards from 5 a.m. until about 9 p.m., checking the quality of the crop and ensuring that the unhealthy grapes are left to rot. They don't own any press-houses; the wine is pressed locally and arrives by tanker in Epernay. First fermentation is carried out in a combination of glass-lined concrete and stainless-steel vats. Traditionally the style of the house's blend was a firm, robust wine two-thirds red grapes and one-third white, but as consumer tastes have lightened over the past thirty years so have the wines, and there is now a higher percentage of Chardonnay.

All remuage is still done by hand as the cousins have yet to be convinced of the advantages of the automatic methods. Christian de Billy quotes Monsier Coffinet who says, 'When *gyropalettes* can be as flexible and sensitive as man, then we will start using them. At the moment the design does not incorporate the artistry that is an intrinsic part of champagne-making.' Among the most obvious characteristics of Pol Roger are the incredibly fine bubbles and the superb refined aroma. The average temperature of its cellars is only 9.5°C, below most others, and this allows a slower, more prolonged fermentation.

Pol Roger has always been extremely popular on the major export markets and these have been nurtured zealously. There are no flamboyant public-relations gestures – they simply aren't needed. The cousins would rather spend their time maintaining the superb individualism of their wines and personally look after their good customers. Like Bollinger they have a degree of authority and influence which

---

*Laws theoretically preventing the exploitation of growers make it virtually impossible for a house to purchase vineyard land – but not if the growers are retained in employment after the sale to cultivate the land.

belies the relatively modest size of the operation, and also like Bollinger this has been achieved not by accident but by devotion to quality wines and by the dogged determination to remain in control of their own destiny.

'We would like to increase production, but at our own pace. The future for us is in maintaining a tightly knit family business.' With these words Christian de Billy sums up the house's philosophy. I comment on Hubert's excellent command of English, his considerable knowledge of vintages past and present and his easy rapport with the clients. A gleam of pride lights up the eyes of an essentially modest gentleman, and Christian says, 'Ah, yes. The fifth generation is learning the controls.'

THE WINES
Non-Vintage White Foil

Delicious drinking. The delicate *mousse* produces a creamy white froth and the bouquet is rich and fruity. The superb Chardonnay dominates; although only 40 per cent, it provides much fragrance and flavour, yet there is also the firm backbone of the Pinot content. One of the most consistent of all non-vintage champagnes.

Vintage Brut

Up to 50 per cent Chardonnay. Stylish, well-structured wine of intense character and a marvellous extroverted appley flavour. One of the best examples of the benefits accruing from the spending of a little extra money on the great vintage wines. Their 1971 was memorable, and the 1973, 1976 and 1979 wines were some of the very finest of their years. The house style was not overpowered by the rich, voluptuous character of the 1975 vintage; it will drink well for years to come. Not particularly typical Pol Roger but it still possesses the necessary refinements. The 1982 is quite simply magic.

Rosé Vintage

One of my favourite pink champagnes, 25 per cent Chardonnay and 75 per cent Pinot Noir including the 10 per cent added Bouzy Rouge. An almost translucent deep salmon colour with a refined, fruity bouquet reminiscent of cherries. Varies in style from year to year, but not in consistency of quality.

Blanc de Blancs de Chardonnay Vintage

Pol Roger is a house with a pronounced Epernay base and style. The grapes for this wine are from Cramant, Mesnil, Oger, Avize and Cuis. An amazing depth of flavour for a wine from these cru. The last time I enjoyed a bottle was at the house with Christian de Billy; it was the 1982 vintage and it was my forty-third birthday. A time for celebration; unfortunately the time of tasting was midday on the day after a serious fall down some cellar stairs (I promise you, before a drop had passed my lips). I arrived in agony with torn shoulder muscles and a few cracked bones. After one mouthful I felt that life was worth what would have to be very serious attempts at survival. A wonderful glass of Blanc de Blancs at its very best. There is not a lot produced, and it is relatively cheap for the superb quality. Search it out and enjoy!

The house makes two different Prestige Cuvées and I consider they suffer from the problem experienced by other great houses: the relative value for the extra money is simply not there. If pounds, dollars, yen or whatever are no object by all means purchase a few bottles of the RÉSERVE SPÉCIALE PR VINTAGE or CUVÉE SIR WINSTON CHURCHILL VINTAGE, but I confess I would keep my money and spend it on more bottles of the vintage or the Blanc de Blancs.

—— LOUIS ROEDERER ——

ESTABLISHED: 1766.
LOCATION: Reims.
YEARLY PRODUCTION: 2.5 million bottles.
VINEYARDS: 182 hectares, mainly in Avize, Ay, Cumières, Cramant, Vertus, Verzenay and Verzy.

The most important step towards appreciating the glories of this house is to buy a bottle of non-vintage Brut Premier, and taste the wine. An unforgettable balance of Pinot Noir dominance (66 per cent) and Chardonnay elegance. A powerful yeasty bouquet with a hint of oak precedes a delicious intensity of ripe fruit flavour and a soft, yet slightly austere finish. One of the greatest of all non-vintage champagnes from a family-run firm with a wealth of vineyards.

The story of the house of Louis Roederer is a fascinating saga of ups and downs. In about 1766 a company was formed by a Monsieur Dubois; he was succeeded by a Monsieur Schreider, who brought in his nephew from Alsace as a partner – Louis Roederer. In 1833 Schreider died and the company ownership was passed on to the nephew. The name was changed to Louis Roederer and this young man proved to be the first in a line of dynamic members of the family. The name rapidly became one of the best known within the district and all important new export markets were developed. Sales rocketed from around 100,000 bottles a year to 2.5 million in 1870! Roederer had also followed Moët, Clicquot and Ruinart into the lucrative Russian market where price was not of paramount importance.

Louis Roederer II succeeded his father in 1870 but died ten years later, and control passed to his sister, Madame Léonie Olry-Roederer; her son Léon assumed command later and the expansion of the house seemed assured – until 1917, the year of the Russian Revolution, an absolute disaster for this high-flying house. Not only did it lose money – the last shipments are unpaid even now, and the unpaid statements are on display in the small museum at the company's offices – but they lost a market which had grown to a massive, irreplaceable 80 per cent of Roederer's total sales.

Not surprisingly things were a little quiet for the next fifteen years but in 1933 another of the many formidable 'grand ladies' of champagne turned up on the scene, Madame Camille Olry-Roederer. The house flourished, production regained momentum, exports boomed once again and the name Roederer became synonymous with the very finest of quality wines. The remarkable Madame Camille managed to combine an innate flair for show-womanship with a more than practical attitude towards the complex tasks of guiding one of the greatest of champagne houses through some very turbulent years. The reign lasted until 1975 – some forty-three years as sole director of Maison Louis Roederer. The house has continued the family tradition. The President today is Madame Claude Rouzaud, daughter of the late Camille, and the Managing Director is her son, Jean-Claude Rouzaud. It has also continued the tradition of quality at all costs – not easily attained but all-important. It is easy to appreciate the unique class of the wines of Louis Roederer, but not so easy to appreciate just how hard the members of the house (both family and employees) work at maintaining these high standards.

Roederer owns a vineyard holding which is the envy of the rest of the champagne industry, averaging 97 per cent rating (nothing is below 95 per cent) and providing more than 80 per cent of its grape requirements. No other major house can boast a percentage anywhere near this figure. It is one of the main factors in the consistency of the Roederer style.

There is also an individualistic house method of vinification. Madame Roederer was one of the early proponents of stainless steel, and vats were introduced – but on her own terms. They were only gradually accepted as the quality of the resultant wines was assessed and reassessed. It was finally decided that all of the first fermentation would be carried out in these vats, but that they would be smaller than usual, and of varying sizes – custom-made for the produce from the various vineyards and of a size small enough to enable individual attention to the different nature of the cuvées. The company is cautious with malolactic fermentation, which is carried out 'only when necessary', as the emphasis is placed on keeping as much of the character of the wine as possible.

One of the most fascinating aspects of the champagne business is that the large houses essentially use the same methodology but vary greatly in individual details. Bollinger ferments in a combination of stainless steel and small oak and stores its reserves in magnums; Krug ferments only in small oak and stores reserves in stainless steel. Roederer ferments in stainless steel ('easier to keep hygienic, a crucial factor when avoiding malolactic fermentation') and stores its renowned reserves in large oak casks 'to add the oak background missed in first fermentation'. The casks are also a hotchpotch of different sizes, for the same reasons as the variation in the stainless-steel tanks. At least 650,000 litres of reserve wines are stored under state-of-the-art humidity and temperature controls.

All in all the house of Louis Roederer is a fascinating blend of the most up-to-date methods combined with the painstaking labour- and capital intensive traditional methods. Nothing is changed unless it improves the quality of the wine. Jean-Claude Rouzaud is an oenologist and keeps a firm control over the *cuverie* and *caves*.* A team of management and workers ensures that standards are maintained, and a devoted public in more than sixty different countries enjoys 2.5 million bottles each year.

The Wines
Non-Vintage Brut Premier

A glorious, carefully crafted and individualistic blend of four different harvests with up to a third from years of vintage standard. More Chardonnay (34 per cent) than the previous Roederer non-vintage wines. Made only from the cuvée (a little of the taille is kept for the wines with higher dosage, the rest sold).

Blanc de Blancs Brut Vintage

A Crémant wine from the villages in the Côte des Blancs, though it doesn't possess the specific characteristics of the single villages. The house considers this an attribute, but as a dedicated follower of the individual cru of the Côte des Blancs I am not quite so sure.

Brut Vintage

Usually an excellent wine, but pushed almost into oblivion by the success of Cristal. Refined, yeasty style with a fullish Pinot Noir and oak flavour, yet a gentle finish.

Brut Rosé Non-Vintage

Twenty years ago this house was one of the very few to adopt a serious attitude towards pink champagne. The vintage Rosé was one of the small number of its style worth drinking, and many a serious champagne drinker was converted to the delights of this style by a glass or three of Rosé by Roederer. The house now makes a non-vintage, as it decided that concentration on house style was all-important. The wine is made by the maceration method, a mere twenty-four hours of skin contact if the grapes are particularly ripe, and never more than forty-eight hours. The wine is delightfully Pinot Noir in flavour with a crisp, firm Roederer finish.

Rich

The same blend as the non-vintage but with addition of a 6 per cent dosage of cane sugar. I have never understood the French habit of drinking the driest of champagnes with their luscious, sweet desserts and this wine proves the point. It is a well-balanced, flavoursome dessert wine of considerable attraction and a far better accompaniment to the last course.

*The *cuverie* is where the must is unified, usually on the ground floor. The *caves* are the lower levels where storage and remuage are carried out ... although often the general term 'caves' is used to describe both.

Cristal Vintage

The unique clear bottle (well, it was unique – now there are literally hundreds of imitations within and without Champagne), the story regarding the original customer, Tsar Alexander II, and the attractive packaging have generated thousands of words of praise. Cristal rates alongside Moët's Dom Pérignon and Taittinger's Comte de Champagne Blanc de Blancs as arguably the most famous of all champagnes.

The grapes for Cristal are carefully selected from the estates and approximately 50 per cent of the blend is Chardonnay. The style is unique – a rich, luscious wine with a more floral bouquet than the other wines of the house, and a softer finish; yet there is still a considerable degree of firmness matched with the depth of honeyed fruit flavour. The wine has more vintage variation than most other Prestige Cuvées, and there have been years (particularly in the early 1970s) when I have been disappointed ... but not, I hasten to add, in the past decade.

An amazing quantity of Cristal is made in some years and overall it accounts for approximately 20 per cent of Roederer's total sales. The house is still meticulous in the selection of suitable vintages. There will be no 1987 because of lack of intensity of flavour. An interesting sign of the quality of the wine occurs when one is drawn into conversation with Rémi Krug. Usually after about sixty seconds the subject turns to the top champagnes, and later when discussing the finest made by his 'friends' (he is too polite and generous to call them the 'opposition') he invariably mentions Cristal first.

There is a small amount of CRISTAL ROSÉ made by the maceration method. If you have tasted this you are more fortunate than the author.

13

THE GREAT NAMES
OF CHAMPAGNE

—— DEUTZ & GELDERMAN ——

ESTABLISHED: 1838.
LOCATION: Ay.
YEARLY PRODUCTION: 800,000 bottles.
VINEYARDS: 40 hectares, mainly at Ay, Bisseuil, Mareuil-sur-Ay, Mesnil-sur-Oger and Pierry.

A house with great integrity, excellent wines and a low profile. I am offered regular glasses of Deutz* when in London, New Zealand, Australia, the United States, or travelling around France – but usually by fellow restaurateurs. It seems to be the caterer's champagne, which is a genuine compliment to its qualities.

The house was established by two Germans. Gelderman had the money, and his partner had the personality and the good fortune to marry a girl from Pierry who owned vineyards. The present President, André Lallier, is a descendant and the business is still family-owned. Its own vineyards provide 45 per cent of its grape requirements and Monsieur Lallier is proud of the long-established private contracts with individual growers which provide the rest. Some families have been supplying the house for more than a hundred years.

The vinification procedures are very traditional. The wines from each vineyard are made separately in small vats; there is no refrigeration equipment as the wines are left to develop as in the old days with *passage au froid naturel* – the natural fall in temperature in the *cuverie* during winter. A much slower process but the house believes the result is more flavour. Its NON-VINTAGE BRUT is a stylish Pinot-dominated blend, full of flavour and with considerable ageing potential. Its firm structure is totally opposite to the present trend for lighter, softer and less complex wines. One of the more underrated of non-vintages. The VINTAGE BRUT is a typical Ay blend of top-quality Pinot Noir with a little Pinot Meunier and about 25 per cent Chardonnay

*The name is simplified on the label these days.

from the Côte des Blancs. A sound, flavoursome wine of very consistent quality. Deutz's fragrant, creamy BLANC DE BLANCS VINTAGE is a textbook example of the subtle nuances of fine wine-making using the top-quality produce from the slopes of Avize and Mesnil-sur-Oger. The 1979 was wonderful. The ROSÉ BRUT VINTAGE is solid, rounded and easy drinking but lacking the final touch of excitement necessary if one is to choose a pink champagne. CUVÉE WILLIAM DEUTZ VINTAGE is one of the best of its genre and is sold at a more reasonable price than most. A delicately balanced, lightish wine – 50 per cent Pinot Noir, 20 per cent Pinot Meunier and 30 per cent Chardonnay.

Deutz is an interesting, slightly schizophrenic house which is a master of publicity for its other involvements – the first-rate Rhône house of Delas, Château d'Aulée in the Loire, and its worldwide sparkling-wine operations* – yet seems determined to keep its champagne known only by a minority of drinkers.

—— THE HEIDSIECKS ——

In 1780 Florenz-Ludwig (later to become Florens-Louis) Heidsieck, an immigrant draper from Westphalia, decided to dabble in the champagne business. Five years later he deserted his rather prosaic occupation for the delights of his sideline interest and the house of Heidsieck was established. It was an instant success and his reputation spread.

Florens-Louis had no children and after his death in 1828 the business continued under the direction of his two nephews, Christian Heidsieck and Henri-Louis Walbaum. Both had been in the company for some time, but their partnership lasted for only six years. In 1834 Henri-Louis left to found Walbaum Heidsieck & Co. (much later to become Heidsieck & Co. Monopole), and Christian continued the original company in association with a Henri Piper. He died a year later and his wife married Piper.

Now everything was in total confusion. The 'Walbaum' had been removed from the company name of one house, leaving 'Heidsieck & Co.', and the Piper operation was still sold under the name Heidsieck. The important American market eased the complications by referring to the very popular wines of the latter as 'Piper's Heidsieck'. The point was taken and in 1845 Piper Heidsieck was firmly established as a distinctive brand. The name Monopole first appeared in 1860, but in the meantime Charles-Camille Heidsieck, who married a Henriot, complicated matters even further by joining forces with his brother-in-law and setting up Charles Heidsieck.

The muddle intensified over the next fifty years when the most recently established of the Heidsiecks was the only firm not to change its name.

* See Chapter 16.

The images of the firms are still confusing to many champagne drinkers. They are completely different in styles of operation, with entirely different styles of wine. If you are not totally bewildered, read on.

—— PIPER HEIDSIECK ——

ESTABLISHED: 1785.
LOCATION: Reims.
YEARLY PRODUCTION: 5 million bottles.
VINEYARDS: None.

Piper is an ultra-modern house. It doesn't own any vineyards, grapes are purchased from more than sixty crus and, importantly, the wine does not undergo malolactic fermentation. The company was the innovator in computerised automatic remuage, introduced in 1978 and copied by many other houses. Its technical expertise cannot be doubted. However, I must confess to being a little puzzled by this well-known name. It produces and sells a large number of bottles (2 million are sold in the United States, Great Britain and Italy alone). Its CHAMPAGNE RARE VINTAGE is one of the great Prestige Cuvées, a delicious blend of Grand Cru grapes with 60 per cent superb Chardonnay. The BRUT SAUVAGE VINTAGE is the best of this style of wine with better balance between fruit and acid than the others. The ROSÉ VINTAGE is an attractive, fragrant wine in the more full-bodied 'pink' style – and yet I find the other wines unappealing. The VINTAGE wines simply don't match up to the high standards of most other houses. They do have the intensity but the recent vintages that I have regularly tasted (1973, 1976, 1979) have lacked the delicacy expected of wines with a 50 per cent Chardonnay content. The NON-VINTAGE is erratic in quality, sometimes full of fruit and flavour but usually rather harsh and lacking grace. Maybe these problems merely emphasise the need for considerable ageing of *non-malo* wines.

After considerable rumours about the house, the citizens of Reims opened their morning papers on 4 October 1988 to read that the firm had been taken over by Rémy Martin. Now the cognac house owns two out of three Heidsiecks.* Will they allow them their independence?

—— CHARLES HEIDSIECK ——

ESTABLISHED: 1851.
LOCATION: Reims.
YEARLY PRODUCTION: 3.5 million bottles.
VINEYARDS: None.

Charles-Camille Heidsieck was the man responsible for the music-hall song 'Champagne Charlie'. His lifestyle was envied by the likeable and wealthy characters of

*And also the only two major houses without any vineyard holdings.

Victorian and Edwardian society, and they spent their days and nights converting everyone else to the delights of 'champers'. He was a frequent traveller to the United States where his extroverted personality conquered the hearts and pockets of the champagne-drinking fraternity. Unfortunately he was also rather reckless and spent much of his business time extracting himself from a series of ill-judged ventures. He once attempted to carry a diplomatic bag across the lines during the civil war while on his way to collect a large debt in New Orleans. When captured by the Yankees he was jailed, which was not surprising as the pouch contained contracts from French garment manufacturers for clothing for the rebel army!

A certain amount of Charles-Camille's *esprit de corps* carried on through the family. All the great champagne *négociants* have been terrific ambassadors for the product, and none more so than this branch of the Heidsieck family. Their efforts have been well rewarded with 'Charlie' particularly strong on seemingly every export market in the world. As I have already mentioned, even Prohibition failed to halt the continuation of substantial sales to the United States. The British market has always been the most important and the firm's success has been helped considerably by firsthand knowledge of the United Kingdom and Eire. Jean-Charles (all members of the family who worked in the business were given a hyphenated name) was educated in Berkshire before the First World War and his son Jean-Marc spent time at Trinity College, Dublin along with the novelist J. P. Donleavy. There is a wonderful moment in *The Destinies of Darcy Dancer, Gentleman* where the hero orders a bottle of bubbly in a posh Dublin bar and muses 'Heidsieck, what a lovely name for champagne!'

Sadly, the family no longer have any connections with the company. I must admit a feeling of regret when Jean-Marc retired in 1987, and I was concerned that Rémy Martin might prove to be another short-term owner. This was a little unfair as I was ignoring the cognac firm's admirable contribution to the continued success of Krug. So far things are working very well indeed.

In Joseph Henriot's period of stewardship a beautiful (stainless steel *can* be beautiful) state-of-the-art new *cuverie* was built and the additional Rémy finance has allowed the purchase of top-class grapes. *Chef de caves* Daniel Thibault is like a child with a new toy and is making superb wines; they now have more bottle age and a higher percentage of reserves in the blend. NON-VINTAGE BRUT RÉSERVE is a glorious, yeasty, soft and flavoursome blend of equal proportions of all three varieties. It would definitely win my prize for the most improved non-vintage wine of the last decade. There is a delicious, full-flavoured BLANC DE BLANCS VINTAGE with the general characteristics of the Côte des Blancs rather than the more individualistic 'mono cru' style of many wines. The VINTAGE BRUT is so totally different from the style of the 'Charlies' of old that it takes one by surprise. Previously the wines were aristocratic – full of flavour but a little severe. At times I felt they were better appreciated in the tasting room where their intrinsic values shone, rather than when actually drunk. Not now. The wines are extroverted, warm and welcoming. The ROSÉ BRUT VINTAGE is delicate with a particularly fine *mousse* and fruity finish; 50 per cent Chardonnay, which creates the delicacy but also, according to Monsieur Thibault, allows the wine to flaunt the characteristics of the particular years. CHAMPAGNE CHARLIE VINTAGE is another Prestige Cuvée that suffers from an unfortunate package created by a designer with a mission to be different and no understanding of the traditions of champagne. If you see a bottle, don't be put off; the blend of equal proportions of Chardonnay and Pinot Noir is rich, soft and sensuous, and worth the money.

—— HEIDSIECK & CO. MONOPOLE ——

ESTABLISHED: 1834.
LOCATION: Reims.
YEARLY PRODUCTION: 1.5 million bottles.
VINEYARDS: 110 hectares, mainly in Ambonnay, Faverolles, Savigny, Verzenay and Verzy.

The house had been established for fourteen years before the brand name of Monopole was created. Despite many changes of partners and trading names of the company the wine was firmly established as Heidsieck Monopole. In 1923 the actual name of the company was officially changed to the brand name. At the same time the company was sold to the owners of a chain of grocery stores, who in 1972 sold it to G. H. Mumm, part of the Seagram champagne empire. Unlike the Perrier-Jouët connection, Mumm has exercised strenuous 'hands on' control. The adjoining cellars were connected and the wines of Monopole have been firmly treated as a subsidiary marque of the larger, more aggressive parent company. Perhaps for these reasons Heidsieck Monopole is a rather enigmatic house, capable of producing excellent wines and yet often lacking an individual presence on the major champagne markets of the world. Very underrated, which is bad for the house but great for the knowledgeable buyer!

For many years the legendary *chef de caves*, Monsieur Alfred Simon, reigned supreme, crafting rich, flavoursome, long-lasting wines with a true Montagne de Reims flavour of luscious, intense Pinot Noir. In the past two decades even the NON-VINTAGE wines have benefited enormously with keeping, and wines that initially seemed one-dimensional have dramatically changed character in bottle. Definitely *not* the champagne for drinking out of actresses' slippers. Whenever the house releases VINTAGE BRUT grab it, and keep for a few years. I always make a point of drinking most of it after the release of their next *millésime*, and keeping some back even longer. At the time of writing I am fondly surveying a couple of unopened cases of the glorious rich, honeyed 1975. Forty per cent of the blend is Chardonnay (only from 100 per cent vineyards) and the Pinot Noir is from 99 per cent and 100 per cent areas. Monsieur Simon may be retired but his spirit lives on in these glorious wines; ironically (and fortunately for us) they are often sold for little more than many non-vintage wines. The ROSÉ BRUT VINTAGE is also excellent value, refined wine made by the *addition* method with the same blend as the vintage.

The DIAMANT BLEU VINTAGE is a puzzling wine. My evaluation is perhaps not helped by tender memories of the glorious 1966 vintage which was made in a different style, and a different bottle. The new package is a squat bottle with diamond-shaped carvings in the sides. The concept may be all right in theory, but it looks hideous, like supermarket bubble-bath. However, the wine itself is usually very stylish and shows well in the lighter-style vintages when the 50 per cent Chardonnay is allowed to flaunt its elegance. The DIAMANT BLEU ROSÉ 1982 was the first release of a very limited edition (only 15,000 bottles and only for the United States). Hopefully other vintages will follow. Go to desperate lengths to secure a bottle: it is a deliciously ethereal mouthful of soft, lingering raspberry fruit with a gloriously fine *mousse*.

—— LANSON ——

ESTABLISHED: 1760.
LOCATION: Reims.
YEARLY PRODUCTION: 6.2 million bottles.
VINEYARDS: 210 hectares spread all over the main areas, including a massive 40 in Grand Cru Chouilly.

A walk around Lanson's export despatch warehouse is like a practical lesson in the geography of the modern world. Enormous stacks of cases are labelled with names that never existed when I completed my university studies, and yet my host and friend Jean Baptiste Lanson knows the 130 or so countries with the intimacy of a man who at some stage of his career has visited many of them, and always worked on the Lanson family principle of cherishing any export market, no matter where or when.

Pierre Lanson was the first Champenois I ever met. New Zealand of the 1960s was hardly paradise for either the dedicated champagne drinker or the supplier. The nation was devoted to rugby, racing, beer and little else. Pubs closed at 6 p.m. The notorious 'six o'clock swill' had to be seen to be believed. At the end of the working day, a large number of New Zealand's manhood rushed to the nearest hostelry and drank as much as possible in the available hour. They would then spill out on the streets, and the consequences were sufficiently disastrous to lend credence to the powerful Prohibition lobby. Needless to say top-class wine merchants and restaurants were few and far between, but there was dapper, debonair Pierre promoting his champagnes. I have already discussed the successful outcome of his efforts. 'If only we had more markets which drank as much Lanson per capita as New Zealand,' sighs Jean Baptiste.

Lanson Père et Fils celebrated its 225th anniversary in 1985, but the company was actually founded by a François Delamotte in 1760 and remained in his family's control for the first 100 years. The Lanson family had associations with the house for many years and in 1855 the company was taken over by Jean Baptiste, a prominent *négociant*, politician and judge who changed the name to Lanson Père et Fils. Over the early years there were a few inter-family financial skirmishes and the family firm as such really only began in 1894 when Henri Marie Lanson, a dedicated champagne man, became the sole proprietor and dedicated himself to expanding the European market. This was not too difficult for a natural businessman with a love of his product, fluent in English, German and Dutch, and holding the office of Dutch consul in Reims.

After the First World War the house expanded rapidly. In 1926 the company acquired superb cellars and land in the rue de Courlancy, and began serious purchases of vineyard land. Henri Marie's son, Victor, took control, a larger-than-life character with a prodigious capacity for his own wines, a wealth of hilarious stories and anecdotes, and the ability to transfer his enthusiasm to the most amateurish wine lover. A perfect ambassador for champagne. He was fond of claiming, 'I only make champagne for myself. What I can't drink, I sell.' Yet behind this image was a shrewd, hard-nosed businessman with an acute understanding of the industry, past, present and future.

Many doubted the future of champagne, but not Victor. The company invested heavily in land and once the Second World War was over the company was in great shape for expansion. The image of its non-vintage Black Label was promoted and soon the name Lanson was rivalling some of the more established brands. In 1976 the house of Masse, located immediately next door to Lanson's cellars, was purchased and while production is a respectable 500,000 bottles per annum it is really treated as a *sous marque*. At the same time Pierre Lanson's in-laws, the Gardinier family, bought shares in the company. They were Champenois who had made a fortune in the fertiliser business in the USA and were keen to invest 'back home'. The Lanson family had become large and unwieldy. It was fine being the largest family-owned company in Champagne in the 1970s; but unfortunately the costs of reinvestment for expansion became prohibitive. There were more than 17 private shareholders, a significant outside shareholding and a lot of squabbling. By 1979 the Gardiniers were in charge of Lanson and Pommery, only to sell them to the BSN group in early 1984. Things weren't as bad as they seemed; Jean Baptiste Lanson is quite adamant in his preference for working within the structure of 'a large group, but running a part of the operation which is reliant on the performance abilities of only a few people. It is much better than being answerable to everyone in a vast extended family.

In 1976 Lanson exported 1.5 million bottles; ten years later it was 3.6 million, and Lanson was also second to Moët on the home market. Sales are mostly of the NON-VINTAGE BLACK LABEL, an easy-drinking, fresh, fragrant blend of 40 per cent Chardonnay and 60 per cent Pinot Noir and Meunier. No malolactic fermentation is allowed – the house considers that the wine benefits 'as long as you have enough stocks to allow sufficient bottle age'. With 20 million bottles in its cellars it is without problems, but a few years ago there were times when the wines were rather green. The VINTAGE BRUT RED LABEL is often one of the best buys of all champagnes. I remember with pleasure the rich, yeasty 1976, which was selling for little more than many non-vintage wines. It was one of the few excellent wines from this year, because (like Krug) Lanson remembered the robust, high-alcohol 1959 vintage and only used grapes from the beginning of the harvest before they became overripe. The blend varies considerably as Lanson believe in accentuating the style of the year as opposed to the house style. BRUT ROSÉ NON-VINTAGE also offers excellent value, a whoosh of extrovert Pinot flavour combined with Chardonnay subtlety, and only a little more pricey than the non-vintage. There are two Prestige Cuvées: NOBLE CUVÉE VINTAGE and a 225TH ANNIVERSARY SPÉCIAL CUVÉE. Interesting wines, but the price–quality ratio doesn't match the vintage.

—— G.H. MUMM & CO. ——

ESTABLISHED: 1827.
LOCATION: Reims.
YEARLY PRODUCTION: 10 million bottles.
VINEYARDS: 220 hectares, mainly in Ambonnay, Ay, Avenay, Avize, Chambrecy, Cramant, Mailly and Vaudemanges.

The origins of this famous house are not in the midst of the Montagne de Reims, but in the heartland of the Rheingau. Three brothers – Jacobus, Gottlieb and Philipp – formed a partnership with another German, Friedrich Giesler, and a Monsieur Hauser of Reims. They established a house, P.A. Mumm & Co. The Mumm brothers were vineyard owners, wine-makers and merchants of considerable standing in the Rhine valley* and wanted to expand into the Champagne region. The firm certainly started propitiously. By the end of the first year of trading 70,000 bottles had been bought in and resold. By 1830 Hauser was off the scene and in 1837 Giesler left to found his own firm in Avize; the Mumm family were in total control and another brother Theophile was sent to Reims to run the operation – he remained until his death in 1852. The family then split into two companies; Jules Mumm & Co. lasted until 1909 and was then taken over by the other, more dynamic G.H. Mumm & Co.

Dynamic is certainly the right word. By the end of the nineteenth century the company was being run by succeeding generations of partners but totally independent of Germany. In this short time it had expanded to become the largest of all *négociant* houses, accounting for 9 per cent of the total of all champagne sales. In this first decade of the century the partners decided to invest in vineyards, a wise move as they purchased the very best, gradually building up 50 hectares, 40 of which were in the Côte des Blancs. By the start of the First World War the company was

*The 70-hectare Weingut von G.H. Mumm is superbly sited, just above Schloss Johannisberg.

——— 105 ———

remarkably successful and wealthy with solid assets and the priceless advantage of the brand Cordon Rouge being well known throughout the world – not only on the major markets. Its records of 1913 show sales to Ceylon, Indonesia, Malaysia, the Philippines, Siam, Singapore, Australia, New Zealand and even China.

Unfortunately the First World War brought even more disaster to this house than others. The partners were still German nationals and the company was sequestrated. On 28 July 1920 the state publicly auctioned the assets of the company and it was purchased on behalf of a group of investors who formed the Société Vinicole de Champagne Successeur de G.H. Mumm & Co. Georges Robinet, a previous employee and the man who had accomplished the difficult task of General Manager for the government, and René Lalou, a lawyer, friend and shareholder, were the two talented businessmen who managed to guide the company through the traumas of the recent past and the immense difficulties of the inter-war years. They doubled the vineyard holdings, restored the company's pre-war image of quality (Mumm had always been one of the more expensive of champagnes) and promoted the name Cordon Rouge rather than the Germanic 'Mumm' tag. They were remarkably successful – the right men at the right time.

But then along came the Second World War and the German occupation. For the next four years the company reverted to being German-owned and was run by the original family, who had not been slow in claiming their rights. After the war the company founded by Robinet and Lalou resumed command; the official title was now G.H. Mumm & Co., Société Vinicole de Champagne – Successeur. In 1955 the Canadian distillers Seagram bought a shareholding which eventually became 99 per cent. In 1959 they purchased 80 per cent of Perrier-Jouët and in 1972 84 per cent (later to become 99 per cent) of Heidsieck & Co. Monopole. The outside capital has allowed the group to expand dramatically, combining huge sales at home with a major export presence. The vineyard holdings are a wonderful asset and provide a solid backbone of Pinot Noir for the Mumm style. Their technical facilities are, as is to be expected, very modern with vast ranks of tanks, assemblage vats and computer-controlled *gyropalettes* which handle 250,000 dozen bottles at a time.

The flagship wine of the house, NON-VINTAGE BRUT CORDON ROUGE, is usually a very stylish, creaming soda style of champagne, surprisingly light considering the 75 per cent Pinot Noir content. (In fact, it seems to have become much lighter over the past couple of decades.) One of its many attractions is a very soft, smooth finish – an excellent aperitif champagne. The cheaper NON-VINTAGE EXTRA BRUT, which is available on some markets, is easily recognisable – no red sash – and to be avoided at all costs. In fact, I would have included the house in the previous chapter if this wine were not such a dominant force on some markets. I cannot understand the marketing policy of such an illustrious house using its well-earned name on such an inferior product. If confronted with a choice of the two non-vintage wines pay the extra; you will not be disappointed.

Mumm's VINTAGE CORDON ROUGE BRUT is usually an intriguing wine; in years that have generally disappointed they have regularly been one of the houses that have produced excellent wine. This is a tribute to the company's superb Pinot Noir sources and also to the *chef de caves* André Carré's preference for 'the wines which allow me to make wines with strong personality. By this I mean those from a Reims house.' He is a little scornful of the lighter 'new wave' wines and considers 100 per cent Chardonnay to be 'easy to make', and Pinot Meunier as 'neutral'. Only Pinot Noir from the Montagne de Reims escapes any criticism whatsoever: 'wonderful, complex wines which add atmosphere to champagne'. The 1955 fills me with nostalgia, dating back to my visit on the 1972 Champagne Academy course. In 1977 Monsieur Carré opened a magnum to celebrate my eldest daughter's first visit to the house — Jessie was only six months old and failed to appreciate the amazing toasty, rich flavour which seemed to linger on the palate forever. At a recent tasting with Carré in his blending room I was given a fascinating lesson in dosage — two bottles of their excellent luscious, rich 1982 vintage, one without and one with dosage. There was hardly any difference as 'our dosage in 1982, is very, very little. Not all vintages need the same dosage; this one certainly doesn't need our usual percentage.' Perhaps this is one of the reasons for their attractive 1976. To finish we had another bottle of the 1955, to celebrate the fact that we had enjoyed the bottle so much eleven years before. It was still rich, toasty, with a beautiful solidity of ripe fruit flavour.

NON-VINTAGE MUMM DE CRAMANT BLANC DE BLANCS is a unique 'mono cru' of 100 per cent grapes from the village of Cramant, made as a Crémant. (It was formerly called Crémant de Cramant.) Foaming, frivolous and fascinating, it started out as a private cuvée for the directors but fortunately is now a little more widely available although still in rather short supply. If you have trouble finding a few bottles you can always pop across to the superb restaurant of Freddy Giradet at St Crissier in Switzerland (telephone 021 34.15.14); he stocks it as his house champagne. The CORDON ROSÉ BRUT VINTAGE is one of my favourite pink champagnes, an attractive pale colour which belies the full, Pinot flavour. Thirty per cent Chardonnay, the rest is Pinot Noir and it is made by the *addition* method. The label was decorated with a lovely red rose designed by the well-known Japanese painter Foujita. It was missing for a number of years and rumour has it that this was a reaction to some of the more severe political measures of the early days of the Mitterand socialist regime (at one stage Reims had a communist mayor who refused to serve champagne at city banquets!). Fortunately it is back.

There are two Prestige Cuvées, made in totally different styles. The RENÉ LALOU VINTAGE is a complex, heavyweight style with a fragrant finish. A must in one's education of the amazing variety of styles within the region. The new MUMM DE MUMM VINTAGE is a lighter, more racy style. Much more lively than suggested by the funereal dark package.

—— PERRIER-JOUËT ——

ESTABLISHED: 1811.
LOCATION: Epernay.
YEARLY PRODUCTION: 3.1 million bottles.
VINEYARDS: 108 hectares, mainly in Avize, Ay, Cramant, Dizy, Mailly and Vinay.

I first stayed with this house in 1972. It was a small operation, within a large international corporate umbrella but directly controlled by a member of the original family, Michel Budin. It was internationally recognised for the quality of its wines but also well known for having a very limited production. One of my closest friends with business ties with the company at the time used to claim that they 'made less wine in total than Moët make Dom Pérignon'. Perhaps this was rather an exaggeration. Since then the size of Perrier-Jouët has changed dramatically, but its non-vintage and vintage wines still enjoy the same reputation for excellence.

In 1811, Pierre-Nicolas-Marie Perrier, a native of Epernay, founded the house Perrier-Jouët (Perrier was a common name in Champagne, so he added his wife's maiden name to create a distinction). His wines were an instant success and Pierre was fortunate to have a son who proved to be a dynamic businessman. Charles Perrier expanded the firm and developed the name, especially in Britain. PJ was a firm favourite of the court of Queen Victoria and *the* favourite of Edward VII. Charles became one of the prominent members of the Champagne community; he was elected Mayor of Epernay and lived in considerable splendour in a baroque-style house on the avenue de Champagne. Exports continued to expand; by the time of his death in 1878 the house was producing more than a million bottles a year and was a very profitable and secure business. From 1840 onwards both father and son had reinvested their profits into the purchase of substantial vineyard holdings – in one visionary transaction Pierre purchased 30 hectares in Cramant.

Charles had no son and the company was bequeathed to his nephew, Henri Gallice. Michel Budin's father Louis married into the Gallice family and in 1934 became head of the company. Michel took over stewardship in 1959 and in this very year the Canadian liquor giants Seagram took over. This was the early days of the financial manoeuvres within the industry and there was much relief when it became obvious that Perrier-Jouët was to be run independently from the G.H. Mumm holding company.

In 1974 Perrier-Jouët produced a modest 1.2 million bottles and now it is the tenth largest of all brands. Most of this increase has happened in the past five years as the United States market has taken a definite liking to the house style. More PJ is now drunk in New York than in Paris.

The wonderful spread in Cramant, plus other Grand Cru vineyards on the slopes of the Côte des Blancs, has enabled the house to expand without losing any of the individualistic qualities of the wines. The fruity, delicate NON-VINTAGE BRUT is a charmer. I never cease to be amazed that a mere 30 per cent of Chardonnay (admittedly the very finest) can be so dominant. Over the years there have been many superb years of the VINTAGE BRUT, the same zippy, fruity elegance with a little more intensity of flavour. I have fond memories of the 1964, 1966 and 1979. The flowery, beautifully balanced 1982 is absolutely stunning, possibly the best PJ vintage of my experience. BLASON DE FRANCE BLANC and ROSÉ have recently been re-released − more full-bodied wines created from a blend of vintages and aged for longer than the usual house style.

BELLE EPOQUE FLEUR DE CHAMPAGNE VINTAGE

The image of the house is very much tied to a marketing creation, the distinctive flower bottle created by the illustrious Belle Epoque glass-worker Emile Gallé. In 1902, Henri Gallice had the brilliant idea of commissioning this bottle design; others followed suit with decorated bottles (as they have done again today) but the Gallé bottle was the only real success; yet it was soon forgotten. Pierre Ernst, a director of the firm, found four Belle Epoque 1900 bottles in 1964 and the design was recreated two years later to celebrate the seventieth birthday of Duke Ellington in Paris. The cuvée was also sold commercially but only at Maxims and at the prestigious Parisian store Fauchon.

Michel Budin and Pierre Ernst decided to use the bottle for a Prestige Cuvée, and after much searching and experimentation a Parisian glass-worker Jean Bigou managed to recreate the bottle en masse with sufficient authenticity. At first in 1965 just 5000 bottles were made, and 15,000 by 1975. No one, in their wildest dreams, would have estimated that within another ten years about 600,000 bottles would be produced and sold in a good year! What about the wine? Well, the white is usually a soft, creamy, elegant wine with considerable depth of flavour provided by the 50 per cent Pinot Noir. In recent years I have tasted some disappointing bottles; hopefully these were mere aberrations. The Rosé is a delightfully smooth, sensuous wine of great finesse. The dominant Chardonnay content lightens the style but the Rosé flavour is still there.

There are few champagnes with the high profile of these two Prestige Cuvées. Hardly an episode of *Dallas* goes by without JR Ewing knocking back a bottle; no self-respecting wine retailer would consider a display of champagnes without a few bottles; a friend in Key West threw a New Year's Eve Belle Epoque Party − every guest brought a bottle and the empties had to remain for patio decorations! In a matter of a few years 'Belle Epoque Fleur de Champagne' has joined the elite trio of Dom Pérignon, Cristal and Comte de Champagne.

Michel Budin must be a very proud man and Seagram must be a very happy company; they have transformed a small *maison* into a major name with large sales of a very profitable wine. Achieved by marketing genius and superb quality.

—— POMMERY ——

ESTABLISHED: 1836.
LOCATION: Reims.
YEARLY PRODUCTION: 6 million bottles.
VINEYARDS: 307 hectares, mainly in Avize, Ay, Bouzy, Cramant, Dizy, Mailly, Mutigny, Oger, Sillery and Verzenay.

I visited Pommery regularly in the 1970s. The de Polignac family were still running the huge operation. The wines were excellent, continuing the tradition of a rich, flavoursome, long lasting style – but one did not have to be a super sleuth to realise that things were not running smoothly. Time and money were running out for the family. The huge amounts of finance needed to update the facilities and finance stocks were beyond the resources of one of France's most famous families (cousins of the Grimaldis of Monaco). An expensive process of revitalisation was needed. It was of crucial importance to both the house and the whole industry because Pommery was very much an integral part of the commercial, cultural and social history of the city of Reims.

Madame Jeanne Alexandrine Louise ('Louise') Pommery swelled the ranks of champagne widows in 1858 when her husband Louis died. She was only forty years old, inexperienced in the art of making champagne but with an astute business mind* which immediately recognised the potential of the British market. An office was opened in London as early as 1861 and Madame enjoyed the size and frequency of the orders, and also her regular visits which introduced her to the 'English Gothic' style of architecture – so much so that in 1870 when she purchased 60 hectares of land on the Butte St Nicaise, the new offices and buildings constructed were modelled on the castles of some of her best clients. These stunning buildings dominate the southern part of the city, along with the splendid Parc de Pommery donated to the inhabitants of Reims – and the splendid family home, Château de Crayères, built across the road from the commercial aspects, a superb mansion styled on the fashions of the eighteenth century and set amid beautifully landscaped gardens in the English style. It now houses a three-star restaurant, 'Boyer Les Crayères', with very superior accommodation.

Underneath are 120 Roman cellars linked by 18 kilometres of chalk *galeries* tunnelled by French and Belgian miners. The Pommery cellars have often been referred to as the 'eighth wonder of the world'. Madame was not a desk-bound manager; she paid much attention to both the work in these cellars and the preferences of her valued customers. In 1874 Louise launched the first completely

*This was fortunate because her husband's partner Monsieur Narcisse Gréno (hence the original company, Pommery & Gréno) was by all accounts a great salesman and *bon viveur*, but was not blessed with much financial acumen. Also he retired in 1860.

Brut champagne. For years she had been concerned about the high dosage, as much as 12 per cent of sugar for even the drier wines, and the gradual shift to serving champagne as mainly a dessert wine. While the totally dry, no-dosage Pommery Nature was not quite the answer, it was the forerunner of the style which has gained universal acceptance.

By 1890, when Louise died, Pommery was one of the largest and most influential of all houses, with export sales in excess of 2 million bottles to all the corners of the world. The British market was particularly important, and for the first thirty years of the twentieth century the brand reigned supreme. Madame's daughter Louise had married the Marquis de Polignac and in 1907 her grandson Melchior de Polignac was running the company. The family dynasty continued until the late 1970s.

Sadly the great house had lost its way by then. The hurly-burly of international finance seemed to be at odds with the genteel, aristocratic style of the family. In 1979 the Gardinier family, recent purchasers of Lanson, bought the house and literally poured money in. It seems that the financial requirements stretched even this wealthy family (see Lanson) and four years later both companies were sold to the French industrial conglomerate BSN whose portfolio includes yoghurt-producers, Evian and Badoit mineral waters, Kronenburg Brewery, the producers of Lea and Perrins Worcestershire sauce and the largest bottle manufacturers in Europe. The prophets of gloom and doom had a field day when this sale was announced. There had already been a noticeable drop in the quality of some of the wines on the British market where the wine press exerts considerable influence on the opinions of the rest of the English-speaking wine world (admittedly many of these problems most probably related to imperfect stock rotation as the house passed through a succession of agents − the wine seemed to possess either too much bottle age or too little). There was much sombre speculation about the influence of businessmen well versed in the art of making and marketing yoghurt, but with no experience in the unique world of champagne. In fact they have proved to be remarkably successful.

The house of Pommery is one of the most exciting places in Champagne now. Its superb vineyard holdings would average a phenomenal 100 per cent if the company didn't own a tiny vineyard within the city boundaries of Reims. Of Pommery's total staff of 300, half work in the vineyards, among the growers. They consider this a great advantage in their relationship with the people who provide half of their grape needs. The most up-to-date *cuverie* was installed a few years ago, and the gleaming array of eighty-eight computer-controlled stainless-steel vats on three floor levels nestle behind the idiosyncratic 'Scottish Baronial' façade of the original building. Like Moët and some others the house has decided it prefers the largest of vats for *assemblage* as they allow a more homogeneous flavour to be extracted, and these have just been built within another of the buildings.

Prince Alain de Polignac, a fourth-generation member of the family, is the only member still with the house, but he has the crucial position of *chef de caves* − a delightful, quiet, serious wine-maker who has never forgotten that champagne is for drinking and not just talking about. His wines show the class of the initial grapes, but also the advantages of first-rate vinification with the best equipment that money can buy. The Pommery style is very much in evidence in the NON-VINTAGE BRUT ROYALE — one-third of each of the three grapes, full flavour with evidence of plenty of age on the lees and a slightly austere, dry but fragrant finish. The VINTAGE BRUT is equal proportions of Pinot Noir and Chardonnay with only the cuvée used and only from grapes from Pommery's own vineyards. A complex wine with the fragrance of the Chardonnay prominent and yet a rich, flavoursome finish. The BRUT ROSÉ NON-VINTAGE has a fresh, delicate character with 30 per cent Chardonnay in the blend. It is made by the maceration method. Sec and demi-sec are also made for certain markets.

In 1985 the house launched its first Prestige wine — CUVÉE SPÉCIALE LOUISE POMMERY 1979, a beautiful soft, fragrant and creamy wine with 60 per cent Chardonnay content. Only three cru are used in the blend: Ay for the Pinot Noir, Avize and Cramant for the Chardonnay. The wine will only be made in years that Prince Alain considers exceptional — definitely one of the superstars worth the money. An excellent CUVÉE SPÉCIALE LOUISE POMMERY ROSÉ VINTAGE has been created after years of consideration of the blend and method of vinification. It is a blend of 50 per cent Chardonnay from Avize and Cramant and 50 per cent Pinot Noir from Ay, with a light touch of maceration for colour and fruit extraction. Excellent, beautifully made refined pink champagne.

If I were writing this book a few years later I have no doubt that Pommery would be added to the chapter of my absolute favourite houses. By then, the four quality hiccups of recent years will have been forgotten. The new regime has the organisation and the heritage to restore one of the greatest of names to all its former glory. As Prince Alain says, 'We are not volume-hungry [a rather modest statement from a wine-maker supervising the production of these vast numbers of bottles] but we are image-hungry. Champagne is a rare commodity, we have only a limited supply of top-class grapes and therefore we must be conscious of quality and image.'

—— RUINART PÈRE ET FILS ——

ESTABLISHED: 1729.
LOCATION: Reims.
YEARLY PRODUCTION: 1.3 million bottles.
VINEYARDS: 18 hectares in Brimont and Sillery.

It seems very strange that one of the Moët–Hennessy group of companies can be best described as relatively unknown and definitely underrated. It just doesn't go with the corporate image. It could be that this smallish, individualistic establishment is overshadowed within the group.

Dom Thierry Ruinart was taught the art of sparkling champagne-making by his friend Dom Pierre Pérignon. He confided the secrets to his nephew Nicholas Ruinart, who founded the first champagne house in 1729 (Gosset has documents to prove it was the first *négociant*, but Ruinart claims to be the first company commercially involved in only 'sparkling wine'). Soon afterwards Nicholas's son Claude joined the company and they moved to enormous Roman cellars. Claude was the first to use *crayères* for champagne production and storage.

The first house was also extremely popular both at home and abroad. It was one of the most enterprising of all the early exporters. When other houses first visited distant markets they would usually find that a member of the Ruinart family had already called, and the Ruinart wines were firmly established as the finest of champagnes. The family continued their control over the business but while the quality remained of high standard the previous dynamism was lacking and the firm missed out on benefiting from the increasing sales of champagne.

In 1963 Moët & Chandon purchased the house but it has retained a degree of independence. Expansion has been gradual, the house has yet to capture the image to match its quality. As pricing of champagne depends on both factors there have been some bargains. Wine-lovers have been counting their blessings while enjoying the Dom Ruinart range of wines, and hoping that the wines would remain a secret known only to the astute few. A wine-tasting group which meets regularly at Methuselah's has been happily quaffing the Blanc de Blancs for years, 'the same high quality as its stablemate Dom Pérignon ... at a much more affordable price,' they say. It can't last forever.

The NON-VINTAGE R.DE RUINART BRUT is a fullish-flavoured blend of roughly equal quantities of all three grapes. Pleasant drinking but it lacks a real definition of character; I wouldn't like to attempt to pick it in a blind tasting, whereas the individualistic house style of many others makes the task a little easier. The VINTAGE R.DE RUINART BRUT is a totally different story – a 'big', rich toasty wine with a robust Pinot character. An excellent mouthful of real flavour. The ROSÉ R.DE RUINART has a pronounced raspberry bouquet and an attractive balance of full Pinot Noir flavour softened with 20 per cent Pinot Meunier.

There are others in a somewhat confusing portfolio of wines, but the focal point of the house is the superb quality of the two Prestige Cuvées. The DOM RUINART BLANC DE BLANCS VINTAGE has a complex Chardonnay style, luscious, smooth and lemony with a subtle depth of flavour provided by a percentage of rare white grapes from the Montagne de Reims. Many aficionados agree with those already mentioned and consider that the 1975 was the finest champagne of all produced in that remarkable year. The DOM RUINART ROSÉ VINTAGE is also one of the very best of its style – a light salmon-pink colour with an elegantly balanced blend of Chardonnay from both the sources used in the Blanc de Blancs and Pinot Noir from Bouzy. I usually prefer my Rosé champagnes youthful and extroverted but this refined, mature wine with at least seven years' bottle age is a delightful exception.

—— TAITTINGER ——

ESTABLISHED: The house of Fourneaux in 1734, Taittinger in 1931.
LOCATION: Reims.
YEARLY PRODUCTION: 4.2 million bottles.
VINEYARDS: 250 hectares scattered throughout the main regions, plus a considerable amount of land in the Aube.

Pierre Taittinger was a young man from Alsace who spent the First World War on the staff of General Joffre. He had the good fortune to be stationed at the luxurious Château de la Marquetterie at Pierry where, centuries before, Brother Jean Oudart had experimented with the creation of the sparkling wine of Champagne at about the same time as that other well-known Benedictine, Dom Pérignon. He was impressed with both the mansion and the region. Alsace no longer appealed, so he returned to Champagne and bought the Château and its vineyards and in 1931 the old-established house of Forest-Fourneaux (the widow Clicquot had turned to a Fourneaux when she needed blends in the early days of her reign). The house of Taittinger–Mailly was formed in the midst of very difficult times, yet has never looked back.

Pierre Taittinger was not a man to be satisfied with gentle progress. In 1933 he moved to Reims and purchased two cellars, one under the Benedictine Abbey of St Nicaise. The building had been destroyed during the Revolution but the monks had extended the Roman *crayères* and created superb cellars. Later there was an added bonus; when workers were removing rubble they discovered a few dozen empty bottles with a pot-bellied shape. These were later reproduced and used for Comte de Champagne.

The benefits of one of the largest of all vineyard holdings are enormous. A few competitors are inclined snobbishly to denigrate the holding in the Aube, but they admit that the non-vintage has an attractive Chardonnay flavour which is partly provided by grapes from the south.

A few years ago the NON-VINTAGE was a little bland – a safe selection which would not disappoint but neither would it stimulate the taste buds. The wine seems much more stylish now, elegant and soft with a delightful lemony finish. The VINTAGE is an excellent example of the glories of intense, ripe Chardonnay flavour, a consistent high-flyer in blind tastings. Taittinger was one of the few houses to make an excellent wine in 1980, and the 1982 was a wonderfully vivacious wine of ripe fruit flavour and yet finishing very softly in the mouth. A wine to convert the most sceptical sipper. The

TAITTINGER VINTAGE COLLECTION is a series of 'limited editions' of cuvées considered unique. The wines really play second fiddle to the lacquered bottles designed by famous artists – the first three releases were the work of Victor Vasarely, Arman and André Masson. You either love them or hate them ... the designs that is!

COMTE DE CHAMPAGNE has already been mentioned frequently, one of the few truly great Cuvées de Prestige. Nothing is left to modern technology for these blends. The company is more than happy to avail itself of the benefits of state-of-the-art equipment and the most modern methods for other wines but the Prestige Cuvées are still sealed by *liège et agrafe* and remuaged by hand. In fact the cellars under the Abbey are devoted to only these wines.* The stocks, in bottles, magnums, jeroboams and methuselahs, are a magnificent sight, especially when *en pupitre*. The BLANC DE BLANCS VINTAGE is simply one of the most perfect of all champagnes, a rich mouthful of flavour and elegance. The only trouble is that after one bottle I start wondering when I will be fortunate enough to drink another. The ROSÉ is, like the Dom Ruinart, one of the rare pink champagnes which benefits from keeping. It is made by the maceration method from grapes from Ambonnay and Bouzy; as is to be expected these cru provide a wine of considerable depth balanced with fragrance. A wine to be savoured and worth every penny.

---

*The house is reluctant to disclose the actual volume of sales of these unique wines. A figure of 900,000 'in a good year' was mentioned to me but when I quoted this around Reims there was a good deal of scepticism ... or was it jealousy?

14

OTHER NAMES OF
IMPORTANCE

—— AYALA ——
(Ay)

The history of the house always seems more interesting than the rather unexciting wines. The beginnings of the firm were romantic. In the 1860s Edmond de Ayala, the son of a Colombian diplomat, was sent to stay with a friend of his father's, the Vicomte de Mareuil. Not only did young Edmond enjoy the region, he also fell in love with and married one of his host's nieces, who had the good fortune to inherit a reasonable chunk of vineyards. This was the beginning of Ayala, and the firm flourished, particularly on the British market. The house was definitely one of major importance; books on wine written in the 1930s attest to the qualities of Ayala. Nowadays the house makes nearly a million bottles a year of straightforward, usually correct wines but the image of Ayala seems to have lost its lustre.

—— BARANCOURT ——
(Bouzy)

I have watched the development of this house with fascination. In 1966 three twenty-year-old members of well-known *récoltant manipulant* families in Bouzy pooled resources and bought some land still unplanted after phylloxera. A few years later they were able to amalgamate the new plantings with the family holdings, and Jean-Paul Brice, Pierre Martin and Raynald Tritant had converted three small family operations into an international house with considerable potential. Expansion was 'softly, softly', with the original family cellars used and the family traditions continued. The scale of the operation was still small; Jean-Paul's father was the *remueur* for the wines at the Brice cellars. I well remember a leisurely Sunday lunch in the middle of the halcyon summer of 1976 sitting in the Brice courtyard, right in the heart of Bouzy, drinking many a bottle of champagne and then following with

—— 116 ——

some of the rare top-class Bouzy Rouge from a number of vintages, including one from the First World War. After about eighteen bottles (there were only three of us, but a few more of them) Jean-Paul confided that while expansion was planned, it would not be rushed and quality was more important than increased sales.

This sounded just fine at the time, but didn't work out. Over the next decade expansion definitely kept to schedule, new cellars were built just outside Bouzy and the partnership became *négociants*, the French food and wine magazines extolled the virtues of the wines, yet I felt the quality had dropped. There was an earthy character and an erratic quality. Fortunately these growing pains seem to have been sorted out and the full-bodied ROSÉ BRUT, THE CRAMANT GRAND CRU 100% and the newest wine, CUVÉE DES FONDATEURS 1983 (50 per cent Pinot Noir from Bouzy and 50 per cent Chardonnay from Cramant) are worth searching out. The aforementioned Bouzy Rouge is one of the very few Coteaux champenois worth the money.

—— BESSERAT DE BELLEFON ——
(Reims)

Edmond Besserat created his own house in Ay as early as 1843. The establishment was small and was content to stay that way, but later when Edmond's two sons took over stewardship (one married a Mademoiselle Bellefon, hence the new name) expansion occurred. But there was insufficient capital to achieve the required growth and in 1959 the family company was sold to Cinzano. Then expansion really began with a move into ultra-modern facilities on the outskirts of Reims. Financial control was taken over by the giant French drinks conglomerate Pernod–Ricard in 1976 and production rocketed. The house now makes in excess of 2 million bottles a year. Nearly all the grapes are bought in as the vineyard holdings are a mere 10 hectares of Pinot Noir in the Vallée de la Marne.

Pernod-Ricard, with its vast interests in other drinks from vermouths to cognac, has a massive well-organised distribution network within France and Europe and not surprisingly Besserat de Bellefon features accordingly on wine lists of prominent hotels and restaurants. The two Crémant wines are the interesting ones. CRÉMANT BRUT and CRÉMANT DES MOINES ROSÉ are light, stylish wines with a soft finish – easy, uncomplicated drinking at a reasonable price. These two wines account for just over 40 per cent of total production and there will definitely be nomenclature problems when the decree comes into power banning the name Crémant within the Champagne appellation. The non-vintage and vintage are unexciting, the GRANDE CUVÉE B. DE B. is a reasonably attractive Chardonnay-dominated blend of vintages.

—— BILLECART-SALMON ——
(Mareuil-sur-Ay)

People have been telling me about this house for years and years, yet I just never seemed to get around to tasting the wines. Finally, in the interests of research, I have done so. They are splendid!

The Billecart family have been in the village since the sixteenth century, and the marque Billecart-Salmon was first registered in 1818. The fifth generation is currently at the helm, but production is modest – approaching 500,000 bottles a year. You won't find any bottles in the discount bin of the local wine retailer. The wines offer a very good example of the individuality of a small family concern where the tastes of the modern market-place are hardly likely to be discussed at board meetings (that is, if they have such things).

The family used to own vineyards but they were sold this century in the interest of financial survival; they now buy grapes from all three main regions. I particularly enjoy the NON-VINTAGE BRUT, a full, rich, Pinot-dominated wine with a surprisingly light, soft finish. The superb intense flavour is a characteristic of all their wines and the family claim it is the result of bucking the trend – instead of the rapid first fermentation at about 18°C favoured by most houses they prefer it more leisurely at a much colder 8°C. The delicate, fragrant, salmon-pink ROSÉ NON-VINTAGE BRUT is becoming the fashionable drink among those champagne-lovers who appreciate superb value for money.

The profile of the house is low. It will never experience the trendy wine and food journalists beating a well-trodden path to its front door. Neither will it expand production to such a dramatic extent that it becomes a well-known international brand. It will carry on making excellent wines with real style and finesse.

—— BOIZEL ——
(Epernay)

I have enjoyed many decent bottles of Boizel in many different countries, sometimes under their own label but often under one of their many others. This low-profile family firm makes 1.2 million bottles per annum, exporting half to the major markets. The fifth generation, Evelyne and Christopher Roques-Boizel, run the operation and things are changing. They have a new, young oenologist and new equipment, with premises on the prestigious avenue de Champagne. It is not demeaning to note that a large percentage of Boizel wines are sold as good value for money, cheap without being by any means the cheapest – they simply sell well-made wines at the right prices.

—— F. BONNET PÈRE ET FILS ——
(Oger)

Over the past fifteen years I have participated in most of *Decanter* magazine's blind tastings of champagnes. Usually the points awarded to the top wines are reasonably uniform with a number of wines scoring relatively similar marks; perhaps one or two will nudge out the others for pride of place. This wasn't the case in the 1983 tasting of vintage wines when the glorious BONNET 1976 BLANC DE BLANCS was an overwhelming winner, a gorgeous, luscious, superbly balanced glass of creamy, appley fizz – the finest from the Côte des Blancs. Exciting wine.

The house is one of the smaller *négociants*, and was founded as recently as 1922 by Monsieur Ferdinand Bonnet, a *récoltant manipulant*. The business is still totally controlled by the family and is now run by the third generation under the direction of Mademoiselle Nicole Bonnet; they own 9 hectares in the Côte des Blancs, with an average rating of a glorious 99 per cent (accounting for approximately two-thirds of the production of just over 160,000 bottles per annum). The average age of the wine is four to five years for non-vintage, and five to seven years for the vintage. A small house such as Bonnet has a much more fluctuating annual production; much depends on the characteristics and the quality of the harvest. For instance in the 1976 vintage, which favoured the Côte des Blancs, 50 per cent of Bonnet's production was vintage, and even 1979 was 30 per cent. One of the unique *négociant* houses.

—— BRICOUT ——
(Avize)

The first time I tasted a bottle or three of the wines from this house was in the cellars of the Kupferberg sparkling-wine operation in Mainz, Germany. Not really surprising because they own Bricout. The house was founded in Epernay in 1878 by Arthur Bricout, who was married to Constance Kupferberg. The German connections were furthered when Bricout moved to Avize and merged with Charles Koch, a native of Heidelberg who had established his own firm as early as 1820. The house of Bricout & Koch was established and based in the splendid Château d'Avize. The Koch side of the firm disappeared at the beginning of this century but the name remained until recently. Kupferberg bought the establishment in 1966 and proceeded to revolutionise a smallish house with the great assets of 40 hectares of prime territory in Avize, Mesnil and Vertus. Production is concentrated on five wines, three of which are non-vintage. CARTE NOIRE is a blend of 40 per cent Chardonnay, 40 per cent Pinot Noir and 20 per cent Pinot Meunier, and CARTE OR is 60 per cent Pinot Noir and 40 per cent Chardonnay. The differences in the wines are subtle, but significant – I always seem to prefer whichever I am drinking at the time. The ROSÉ is perfectly adequate, light and delicate as is to be expected from a pink wine made from 85 per cent Chardonnay plus the addition of 15 per cent Bouzy or Cumières. The VINTAGE is the same blend as the CARTE OR, but the scene-stealer is the Cuvée Spéciale ELÉGANCE DE BRICOUT, a racy, fragrant yet full-flavoured wine, 50 per cent Chardonnay from Avize and Cramant and 50 per cent Pinot Noir from Ay and Verzenay. This was launched with the superb 1982 vintage. It will be interesting to see future wines when the fruit is not quite as outstanding.

—— CANARD-DUCHÊNE ——
(Ludes)

Owned by the Veuve Clicquot group since 1978, this house makes a carefully calculated style of wine for a certain style of market. Well crafted, with definite character and good bottle age and yet not expensive – a much better glass of champagne than many of its competitors in the same price range. The rather industrial cellar building, more reminiscent of the most commercial of New World wineries than the *caves* of sleepy, staid Champagne, dominates the tiny village of Ludes, close to its better-known neighbour Mailly in the northern part of the Montagne de Reims. The house does not have traditional cellars close by; they were established in the village as long ago as 1868, but little of consequence happened until the last thirty years, during which sales have skyrocketed. Canard-Duchêne now produces nearly 3 million bottles a year, mostly non-vintage sold as value-for-money champagne through the supermarkets and more price-conscious outlets on the home market. Only 15 per cent is exported.

The NON-VINTAGE BRUT is a perfectly agreeable glass of casual drinking champagne with a generous proportion of grapes from the Aube region. There are many producers who pompously denigrate all wine from this region yet make wines inferior to Canard-Duchêne's.

One can happily consume many bottles and still stay friends with the bank manager. The 1982 is particularly attractive. The Prestige CUVÉE SPÉCIALE CHARLES VII, with Chardonnay and Pinot Noir from the Marne, has no great plusses, nor any great faults. Personally, I would prefer to spend the money on a bottle of the parent company's vintage.

—— CHÂTEAU DE BOURSAULT ——
(Boursault)

Champagne is not exactly the most picturesque countryside. Dull, undulating plains and modest slopes offer no great scenic beauty, except for the vast spreads of beautifully nurtured vineyards. Similarly, the succession of wars have left little in the way of ornate architecture to compensate – but there are a few gems: Moët's Château de Saran at Choilly is one and Château de Boursault, nestling among the highest vineyards of the southern slopes of the Marne at Château-Thierry, is another.

The present neo-Renaissance Château stands on the site once occupied by a fortified castle, the stronghold of the Barons of Boursault. It was destroyed by invaders, rebuilt and, as is the fashion of the region, destroyed again. Madame Clicquot purchased the ruins in 1819 and in 1843 she was persuaded by her son-in-law Louis de Chevigne to build this magnificent, hugely expensive monument. A rather uncharacteristic gesture of grandeur from a hardnosed businesswoman who watched every sou. However, it was not all fancy; it became her home for the rest of her life, and afterwards her granddaughter and family lived at Boursault until its sale just after the First World War. The Château was bought by an Armenian gentleman, Nourhan Fringhian, in 1927; he was murdered in 1955 and the property passed on to his three sons. One, also named Nourhan, bought out the others and is now the sole proprietor and maintains a sizeable spread of 18 hectares of grapes.

The wine is in very short supply as production of the two wines, non-vintage and Rosé, is limited totally to grapes from the Château's own vineyards. It is the only estate in Vallée de la Marne allowed to use the name 'Château'.* Sometimes I wonder whether my attraction to this champagne is practical – it is a well-balanced, mature blend of approximately 50 per cent Pinot Noir, 35 per cent Pinot Meunier and 15 per cent Chardonnay – or because it is the house bubbly at my favourite London restaurant, Tante Claire. It is well worth searching out – elegant, refined champagne at a most reasonable price.

—— DE CASTELLANE ——
(Epernay)

Epernay doesn't have the spectacular splendour of the Cathedral or Basilica of St Rémi, which dominate the Reims skyline, but the city does have the weird de Castellane Tower which owes more in origin to North Africa than to northern France.

The house was established in 1880 by the Vicomte de Castellane, who didn't last long. The business was soon in the hands of Fernand Mérand, who created a major house of reputation which flourished at home and abroad during the twentieth century. Times became rather tough in the 1970s; Laurent Perrier bought a 20 per cent share in the company in 1984, and nowadays through shareholdings of the Nonancourt family holds a controlling interest.

The house owns no vineyards but has contracts with growers in about eighty different crus, mainly in the Montagne de Reims and Côte des Blancs. Production is about 1.5 million bottles per annum, half of the must is still fermented in oak casks and all remuage is done by hand. The NON-VINTAGE CROIX ROUGE is of sound quality,

---

*Because the wines are all produced on the estate. There is a considerable surplus of grapes, which is sold under contract to Moët.

with a pronounced Chardonnay flavour despite containing 40 per cent Pinot Noir and 30 per cent Pinot Meunier. Of the other wines the VINTAGE BLANC DE BLANCS is excellent value; a stylish, creamy and delicate wine with at least six years' bottle age.

—— DUVAL LEROY ——
(Vertus)

This house, established in 1859, owns nearly 10 hectares of vineyards, many in the best parts of the Côte des Blancs, and produces about 4 million bottles per annum. One of the top six champagne exporters to the United Kingdom, it is still family-controlled – and still unknown. The reason is quite simple – over 70 per cent of its wine is sold as Buyer's Own Brand to Sainsbury's and other 'new wave' UK champagne retailers. The wines are well made, full of fruit, and rarely suffer from the gut-wrenching excess acidity of the supermarket champagnes of the old days. They are wines that can be trusted and much of our thanks is due to the Duval family's meticulous approach to large-scale production of inexpensive champagne.

—— GOSSET ——
(Ay)

The labels proudly proclaim, 'La plus ancienne Maison de Vins de la Champagne'. Pierre Gosset traded as both a *récoltant* and a *négociant* in 1584 and the family have been firmly based in Ay ever since. The firm has never been large. In fact in the early 1980s a modest production of about 250,000 bottles per annum was achieved; nowadays it is around 400,000. It has also maintained traditions: up to 60 per cent of the total production is fermented in oak casks and malolactic fermentation is discouraged.

The present two generations running Gosset are involved in businesses outside Champagne including the excellent Château de Grille Chinon and a boat-building company at La Rochelle. While they have been reluctant to part with traditional methods of production they have never been afraid to part with assets when offered a good profit. In the early 1970s they sold much of their vineyard land at a huge price to Krug and now own a mere 10 hectares. In 1980 they bought the house of Philipponnat but sold it to the liqueur firm Marie Brizard in 1987.

The image of the house is complicated by the number of different wines produced. There is an 'ordinary' range of BRUT EXCELLENCE NON-VINTAGE, BRUT ROSÉ and VINTAGE which offer good-value wines with considerable depth and character. The Rosé, incidentally, was the first to be bottled in clear glass – as recently as 1947. The 'Antique Range' are bottled in a reproduction of the traditional eighteenth-century bottle – a BRUT GRANDE RÉSERVE NON-VINTAGE, the GRAND MILLÉSIMÉ and GRANDE MILLÉSIMÉ ROSÉ are even more complex, yeasty wines.

Unmistakable, but to me it is rather dubious whether these wines are worth the extra money. Except one very special wine. The late and dearly missed Etienne Gosset and *chef de caves* Jean Pierre Mareigner created a sublime blend, CUVÉE QUATRIÈME CENTENAIRE, to celebrate the 400th anniversary of the house, twenty-three different wines from prime sites in the Montagne de Reims and Côte des Blancs. Four vintages were included, 1971, 1973, 1978 and 1979, and after some settling time the wine blossomed out and became one of the finest champagnes I have tasted, a fitting tribute to the creativity and vision of Etienne. Only 2500 cases were made – I am still eking out the last few from my collection. Perhaps brother Antoine will repeat the exercise.

—— GEORGES GOULET ——
(Reims)

A curious house with a chequered career, some great ups and some downs. Victorian and Edwardian Britain loved it and it was one of the big sellers of the time. The house maintained a presence on both the domestic and export markets with, by all accounts, solid workmanlike wines. In 1960 the firm was purchased by the house of ABEL LEPITRE, which soon became a holding group, Les Grands Vins de Champagne, and also included another well-known brand, ST MARCEAUX. The wines in the late 1960s and early 1970s were excellent, the 1973 CRÉMANT and VINTAGE and the Prestige CUVÉE DE CENTENAIRE all possessed a delightful creaming soda style. The tricky 1976 vintage was not handled well, the wine was overblown and sweetish, lacking the bite and steeliness of finest champagne. Since then there have been many changes in management and company structure. I drink the wine reasonably regularly and sometimes it is very good indeed, other times not so.

—— ALFRED GRATIEN ——
(Epernay)

One of the houses with a considerable international reputation. The NON-VINTAGE qualities are revered by the wine trade, hardened wine writers on blind-tasting panels go misty-eyed when the old vintages appear, and the public seems to appreciate all the wines. Obviously there is a demand for mature (dare I say slightly oxidised?) champagnes made in the traditional manner. Wherever I travel in the world and talk about older vintages, the subject invariably turns to Alfred Gratien. And yet the house is one of the smaller *négociants* producing only about 250,000 bottles a year.

Alfred Gratien established his champagne house in Epernay in 1864. At the same time this dynamic entrepreneur also formed a sparkling-wine company in Saumur. He was later joined by a refugee from the strife in Alsace, Jean Meyer. The firms still exist as separate entities and are managed by the Seydoux family, descendants of the founders (and relatives of the Krugs). The extremely successful Loire operation dwarfs the Epernay establishment in size, but not in prestige.

The whole emphasis of Champagne Gratien is based on tradition. The sales boom of the past twenty years has passed them by; their sales have only slightly increased. As Alain Seydoux says,

> We are traditionalists ... 'old school' champagne makers. All our wine is still fermented in oak, we do not allow malolactic fermentation, the vintage wines are still stoppered with a cork as they receive much more ageing on the lees than most other houses. Yes, we are small, but if we are not known by everyone that is an advantage. There is no pressure to increase production dramatically and turn out youthful, neutral wines. We believe that the most important part of the *méthode* is the ageing on lees and that requires patience, and capital. But it also produces wine with complexity and style. Then champagne is the greatest wine of all, it is both exciting and serious – it has no equal.

The firm doesn't own any vineyards: 'We are small, with a good name, and consequently have no trouble obtaining the maximum co-operation from the growers. who like to see their grapes made into high-quality wine.' The house style is not only monitored by the Seydoux family, their *chef de caves* Jean-Pierre Jaeger is the third generation of his family to hold the all-important position. The NON-VINTAGE is definitely not for casual slurping. It is full, toasty and has a slightly austere, but still fruity finish. The ROSÉ is considerably softer and yet still firm, an interesting example of this style.

The house doesn't believe in Cuvées de Prestige. Instead it places great emphasis on its VINTAGE wines – often aged for more than six years and made to continue ageing gracefully. At the time of writing the London agents still stocked bottles from the 1964, 1966, 1969, 1970, 1973, 1976 and 1979 vintages. I have recently tasted the last two and they were wonderful, still full of fruit and flavour.

—— JACQUESSON ——
(Dizy)

Jacquesson is one of the oldest houses still in existence, and is still making excellent champagnes, admittedly less than half as much as in the last century. Claude Jacquesson and his son Maurice founded the house in 1798, in Châlons-sur-Marne. The house thrived and within a matter of years was in the same league as the original big names of the industry – Moët, Ruinart and Clicquot. In 1810 its spectacular new cellars were visited by Napoleon, who was impressed. Not only did he take a generous quantity away reputedly to drink on the eve of battle, but he awarded the firm a gold medal 'pour la beauté et la richesse de ses caves'. This wonderful promotional asset has never been ignored and it features prominently on the labels.

Maurice's son Adolphe took over control in 1836, and offered partnership to his friend and employee, a certain Joseph Krug, and the firm continued to grow with considerable export sales throughout Europe as well as success on the home market. Adolphe married an English girl, Louise Jaunay, in 1839, and two years later Joseph married her sister Emma. Everything was going along very smoothly, but suddenly Joseph left the firm and went to Reims to set up Krug & Cie. Jacquesson continued to expand, especially the exports. One of its proudest achievements is the sale of 1 million bottles at the 1867 Universal exhibition, a vast amount of wine considering that total champagne production was only around 13 million bottles per annum at this time!

Adolphe died in 1875 and so did the male lineage. The various family descendants showed little interest and the house gently faded, almost away. Fortunately in 1920 Léon de Tassigny, a broker, purchased the firm and moved it to Reims. The dramatic sales figures had disappeared by now but de Tassigny was able to restore the quality. On his death in 1952 control passed to his wife, who was quite *formidable*, in the grand tradition of the champagne widows. Her great love of frequent glasses of champagne no doubt contributed to her long life, and she died in her eighties. The company was purchased by Jean Chiquet, who moved it to Dizy where he and his son Jean-Hervé continue the tradition of excellence.

Jacquesson owns 22 hectares of vineyards, 11 in Avize and the rest in Ay, Dizy and Hautvillers, which provide approximately 60 per cent of its annual production of 360,000 bottles. The range of wines offers a fascinating breadth of styles. I adore the meaty, robust PERFECTION BRUT NON-VINTAGE which has a large Pinot Meunier content. The BLANC DE BLANCS BRUT NON-VINTAGE from its Grand Cru vineyards has a strong varietal flavour and yet the bottles I have tasted have lacked the delicacy associated with this style. The ROSÉ BRUT NON-VINTAGE, made with Pinot Noir, Pinot Meunier and a dash of Chardonnay, is perfectly respectable if rather unexciting. The VINTAGE PERFECTION BRUT is a real mouthful of intense Pinot Noir and Pinot Meunier flavour lightened with 30 per cent Chardonnay. It wouldn't quite qualify as one of my all-time favourites, but the excellent-value SIGNATURE BRUT VINTAGE certainly might, made of equal quantities of Pinot Noir and Chardonnay from only the cuvée. I have tasted both the 1976 and the 1979 and they were delicious, well-balanced, beautifully made champagnes.

—— MARNE & CHAMPAGNE ——
(Epernay)

'The Bankers of Champagne'. An unknown name in its own right and yet the third-largest producer of all. This privately owned firm makes ten or more million bottles a year, under hundreds of different labels. A percentage of the production is sold *sur lattes*. A vast amount of wine is sold as BOBs — companies actually claim to exist when all they are doing is buying *marques auxiliaire* wines from Marne, even labelled, packaged and despatched by them!* Much is also sold slightly upmarket as *sous marques* owned by the company. These include Eugène Clicquot, Gauthier, Pol Gessner and A. Rothschild. While connoisseurs of the finest of champagnes may not approve of either the quality of Marne & Champagne wines or the methods of business, no doubt the company's bank managers are delighted – low overheads, fast turnover in enormous quantities and the realisation that there will always be a huge domestic demand for wines of these standards and prices.

—— MERCIER ——
(Epernay)

Eugène Mercier was a man of extraordinary energy and ideas. In 1858 he founded his own house, Maison Mercier, Union de Propriétaires, a Paris-based amalgamation of five champagne houses destined to concentrate on supplying large quantities of champagne of reasonable quality. His natural markets were not part of high society, but were more everyday folk, and to this end he set about self-promotion with a series of spectacular events. A giant 200-ton, 200,000-bottle-capacity cask which took 250 Hungarian oak trees and twenty years of work was built in Epernay and transported to Paris for the 1899 World Exhibition. Twenty-four oxen were needed to transport it and in certain places en route houses had to be pulled down to allow passage, but the publicity achieved made all the hard work worthwhile and afterwards it was returned to Epernay where it was used for blending until 1947. Eugène was not interested in traditional cellars; he saw the need for space and over thirty years custom-built 18 kilometres of wide, easily worked *galeries*. In the early days horse-drawn carriages passed through; more recently there was a car rally. Now more than 150,000 fascinated visitors receive a guided tour of the cellars and an explanation of the champagne-making process while being transported by train.

Mercier became a giant amongst giants by bucking the accepted trend and concentrating on the domestic and nearby markets. Even to this day approximately 90 per cent is consumed in France. The company is now owned by Moët and is part of the giant LVMH group. Two hundred and twenty hectares of vineyard land with a preponderance of Pinot Meunier plantings provide only a small percentage of the grapes needed for the annual production of about 5 million bottles.*

The wines are perfectly sound and agreeable drinking. The Pinot Meunier dominance doesn't contribute a great deal of grace but it helps create a zippy, youthful, soft, easy style. The non-vintage rosé is a particular delight, good enough to rate in the top wines at a recent *Sunday Express* magazine tasting. Eminently drinkable champagnes at the right price. I drink regular bottles – for elevenses, at

*The degree of compromise in the new regulations means that consumers will still not know when the source is this company.

noon, early-evening revivers, late evening for no reason at all, on picnics, in the members' enclosure at Lords cricket ground, on the patio at home. In fact, that is the joy of Mercier and the other cheaper champagnes that I mention. If one avoids snobbishness, regular champagne drinking does become much more affordable!

—— OUDINOT ——
(Epernay)

You almost need to be an investigative financial journalist to chart the recent history of this producer of unpretentious, sound, good-value wines. The house was established in Avize at the turn of the century by a family of *récoltant manipulants*. Business was built on the sound base of top quality vineyards in Avize, Cramant, Chouilly, Bouzy and Tauxières and in 1979 the company JEANMAIRE was purchased. In 1982 the Trouillard family, who had sold their TROUILLARD–DE VENOGE house, but not vineyards, to the HENRIOT–CHARLES HEIDSIECK group, bought Oudinot and added another cluster of highly rated vineyards.

Present-day Oudinot–Jeanmaire, which also includes a subsidiary BEAUMET, now owns 65 hectares of vineyards and produces about 700,000 bottles per annum under the various names. Jeanmaire offers drinkable champagne at the cheaper end of the market, whereas the Oudinot wines are more fragrant and stylish. The VINTAGE ROSÉ is particularly attractive – delicate flavour, soft and very smooth.

—— PHILIPPONNAT ——
(Mareuil-sur-Ay)

Another house much enjoyed by members of the wine trade of the world. When prominent trade personalities are asked to name their favourite champagne houses the names Krug, Bollinger and Roederer are always mentioned along with some of the other big names, then usually one or two from the less well-known establishments such as Billecart-Salmon, Alfred Gratien, Gosset – and Philipponnat.

The family were initially wine-growers around Mareuil-sur-Ay, and in 1910 Pierre Philipponnat created a *négociant* house, acquiring excellent cellars beneath the chalk along the banks of the Marne. In 1935 he purchased the renowned Clos des Goisses vineyard, 5.5 hectares of vines in one single hillside vineyard with a short, steep south-facing slope. The exceptional vineyard has developed a reputation matched only by Krug's Clos de Mesnil and Salon's vineyard at Le Mesnil. Obviously the intense, rich, single-vintage wine from this single estate is the company's flagship. It is very rare, and very expensive. A must, at least once in the life of any serious

*See Chapter 11 for Mercier's supply contract with the CVC.

champagne drinker!* But one mustn't ignore the other fine wines of the house – in particular a well-structured, full-flavoured NON-VINTAGE ROYALE RÉSERVE BRUT, which has approximately 60 per cent Pinot Noir and 30 per cent Chardonnay, and the full-flavoured ROSÉ ROYALE RÉSERVE BRUT. I have never considered the vintage wines to be worth the extra cost when compared with the excellent non-vintage.

The house is quite small, with an average production of just under 500,000 bottles per annum. Twenty-five per cent of its grape supplies come from its own vineyards. The family sold to Gosset in 1980. In April 1987 it was sold to the liqueur company Marie Brizard, which considers that a quality house of this style will strengthen its already considerable hotel and restaurant business throughout Europe. One can assume that the name Philipponnat will become an even more regular feature on the wine lists of the most prestigious of dining rooms. There is no need to compete with the larger houses on the mass retail market.

—— JOSEPH PERRIER ——
(Châlons-sur-Marne)

In the 1800s the thriving town of Châlons-sur-Marne was right in the heart of the champagne industry; thirteen houses of significance existed. Nowadays the hub has moved closer to the major focal points of the finest vineyards around Epernay and Reims, and Joseph Perrier is left virtually alone in Châlons: not that this seems to worry it. The house was established in 1825 but the family ownership was shortlived and Paul Pithois purchased the business in 1888; the same family still owns the firm, with nephew Jean-Claude Fourmon, one of the true gentlemen of Champagne, in charge.

I must confess to a long-lasting love affair with the wines of Joseph Perrier. The house owns 20 hectares of vineyards on the northern slopes of the Vallée de la Marne, in the villages of Verneuil, Damery, Hautvillers and Cumières (the source of Pinot Noir of sufficient quality almost to match Bouzy as a producer of still red).

Obviously with these top-quality vineyards providing 30 per cent of annual grape requirements there is a significant black-grape content, but it is one of the houses which happily acknowledges the importance of Meunier. Year in, year out, the NON-VINTAGE CUVÉE ROYALE BRUT is one of the best-value champagnes – oozing rich, luscious Pinot flavour (35 per cent Noir and 30 per cent Meunier) and yet still possessing the light touch of Chardonnay; with at least three years' bottle age. I have never tasted a disappointing bottle.

The vintage wines are full of character and never short of age. Their CUVÉE CENT CINQUANTENAIRE first created in 1975 to celebrate the 150th anniversary of the house is an attractive blend of top vintage Chardonnay and Pinot Noir in roughly equal

*No one can quite match the French for pretentious wine writing. I quote a review of the Clos des Goisses 1980 in the December 1987 issue of *GaultMillau* magazine. I think it is better left in the original: 'Un champagne qui fait beaucoup fantasmer, mais que l'on associe, essentiellement, à des lieux sportifs: le bord d'une piscine, par exemple, ou un chalet savoyard, le soir, devant un feu de bois.' Funny, I thought it was for drinking!

quantities, but I would rather keep my money for more bottles of the stunning CUVÉE ROYALE BRUT ROSÉ, a unique wine with a deep colour and rich raspberry flavour.

—— SALON ——
(Le Mesnil-sur-Oger, Avize)

An idiosyncratic house of tiny proportions, making 'mono cru' wines from one grape, Chardonnay, in only the finest of vintages (in fact only twenty-two vintages in the last sixty years). Sales are strictly limited to 60,000 bottles a year.

The house was established in unusual circumstances. Eugène-Amie Salon was a Champenois who went to Paris as a young man and made his fortune as a furrier. His sister married the *chef de caves* of a firm in Le Mesnil-sur-Oger. Whenever Eugène-Amie drank his brother-in-law's wines he noticed the super fragrance and intensity of the Mesnil grapes. He was intrigued, so be bought grapes from several growers in Mesnil and in 1911 began making his own wines as a hobby, happily drinking them with his friends and business associates. Later he purchased his own vineyard and started to treat the whole business more seriously. He even started putting labels on his bottles. During the 1920s heyday of Maxims, Salon was the house Champagne.

Monsieur Salon established sources of supply from the finest growers, only in Mesnil, and established a unique set of principles which have not changed over the years, even though the company was owned by Besserat de Bellefon, and now Laurent Perrier. Not only are the majority of vintages regarded as unsatisfactory (the parent company is then the happy recipient of the grapes), but in the few suitable years only the cuvée is used. Fermentation is carried out in vats but maturation is in oak barrels. There is no malolactic fermentation and the management considers that the wine needs anything from eight to ten years to mature. Dégorgement in the modern manner was tried and rejected. The wine is obviously not easy to find – try Harrods, Fortnum & Mason's (if the staff haven't drunk it all), or Neiman-Marcus in San Francisco – and it is not cheap.

—— THE CO-OPERATIVE BRANDS ——

The influence of the co-operatives is growing. There are now nearly 150. Only a few specialise in marketing a specific range of wines. Establishments of interest include:

NICOLAS FEUILLATTE
(Centre Vinicole de la Champagne)
(Chouilly)

Yes, there is a man called Nicolas Feuillatte. Rumour has it that he was a grower before turning socialite. He is very elegant in a manner that only the French can acquire – relaxed, charming, with the slightly aloof manner of a world-weary sophisticate. Everything is superb, until he starts talking about 'my wines' while we are sitting in an office underneath the giant co-operative sign. I am treated like a numbskull as he launches into a dissertation on how he was a hard-working grower who wanted to expand and needed the technical expertise of 'the finest house in Champagne'. I point out that we are not in a *négociant*'s establishment and he changes the subject by introducing himself to the lady sitting next to me and enquires how she enjoyed her visit. She happens to be the Centre's European sales manager! I realise that Monsieur Feuillatte impresses many people. I wasn't one of them.

The brand was created as recently as 1986 when the organisation decided to 'create a wine with good quality, reasonable price and brand recognition'. Sales are already exceeding a million bottles a year, the home market and New York State accounting for a significant proportion. The wines are of a more than satisfactory standard – a well-balanced, yeasty NON-VINTAGE, a gentle, fragrant ROSÉ and excellent BLANC DE BLANCS. The wines are not downmarket. Director Jean Pierre Darrault considers that 'We must strive for quality, but it must be at the right price. We are not in competition with the major houses, but are filling the needs of a new market created by the media through an incredible amount of attention to champagne.'

JACQUART
(Coopérative Régionale des Vins de Champagne)
(Reims)

This co-operative sells in excess of 8 million bottles per annum, and 2 million of these are sold under the Jacquart brand. The distinctive label with a partially unclothed woman astride a flying horse has certainly been successful on the domestic market, where the price–quality balance has appealed. There are many cheaper wines than Jacquart in French supermarkets and stores but they are most inferior. The NON-VINTAGE BRUT TRADITION is usually a sound, crisp, fresh and reasonably delicate glass of everyday champagne. The VINTAGE is perfectly acceptable although I am yet to be attracted to the ROSÉ. Now that the brand is firmly established at home the management is turning its attention to the export markets and I have drunk many a bottle in the United States, New Zealand and Australia as well as Great Britain.

MAILLY-CHAMPAGNE
(Société de Producteurs Mailly-Champagne)

Seventy members with access to 70 hectares of Grand Cru vineyards. About 500,000 bottles are produced each year, and, uniquely, it is all sold under the co-operative label – none goes back to the growers. A number of Pinot Noir-dominated blends are made; I have found them lacking in subtlety but other tasters enjoy the full flavour.

OTHER NAMES OF IMPORTANCE

PALMER
(Société Coopérative de Producteurs Grands Terroirs de Champagne)
(Reims)

This co-operative was founded in Avize in 1947 and the brand Palmer was created in 1948. Expansion was rapid and the society moved to larger premises in Reims in 1959. There are now 220 hectares in vineyards from fifty different crus and the annual production is now just over 1 million bottles per annum. Only a small percentage is sold under the Palmer label, but this is growing as exports to Great Britain and other European markets increase. Once again I repeat my eternal thanks to the better co-operatives who are able to produce easy-drinking, everyday champagne at an affordable price. Palmer is one of these establishments.

PANNIER
(Château-Thierry)

Champagne Pannier was established in Dizy at the turn of the century by Louis Eugène Pannier and his son Gaston. Their business soon outgrew its modest facilities and the firm moved to a new site in Château-Thierry — two levels of ancient stone quarries. Pannier added another two levels and now benefits from excellent premises with a natural temperature control of a constant 10°C all year.

Alongside these traditional working spaces are large areas containing the most up-to-date equipment, because this is no longer a small house. Ten years ago the operation was family-owned and produced 250,000 bottles per annum. Then it was sold to a group of its grape suppliers and a co-operative was formed. Now there are 190 grower members, mainly in the Marne, but a few from the Montagne de Reims and Côte des Blancs, and production is now 2.5 million bottles a year. Now that is expansion!

Only about 40 per cent is taken back by the members. The Pannier label is being promoted assiduously with sales mainly in France, but they are growing in Great Britain and Germany. POL DE BREUIL and DE BRIENNE are old-established names still in use, but gradually being phased out. The wines offer good value for money and a good example of the drinkability of Pinot-Meunier-dominated blends.

—— OTHER HOUSES AND GROWERS ——

The structure of the champagne industry encourages thousands of labels. Some apply to houses that are almost dormant, 'shell companies' owned by other houses and used when a secondary name is required. Many are making (or buying in) dull uninteresting products, and the majority of names mean little to the serious lover of champagne. Yet there are many worthy houses making attractive wines.

Houses that I have not tasted often, but have enjoyed over the years are CHAUDRON

(Vaudemange), CHAUVET (Tours-sur-Marne), in particular their delicious Cachet Vert Blanc de Blancs, ROLAND FLINIAUX (Ay), HÉRARD ET FLUTEAU (Gye-sur-Seine-Aube), HOSTOMME (Chouilly), LAURENTI (Les Riceys-Aube) LARMANDIER PÈRE ET FILS (Vertus), LECLERC BRIANT (Epernay), R. & L. LEGRAS (Epernay), RAPENEAU (Epernay) and DE TELMONT (Epernay).

As I have explained, growers are much more difficult to assess. I have tasted literally hundreds of their wines and enjoyed many. Yes, consistency is often lacking, sometimes also balance. But the best offer interesting wines of considerable individuality. Recently I have particularly enjoyed wines from MICHEL ARNOUL (Verzenay), PAUL BARAPB (Bouzy), ALEXANDRE BONNET (Les Riceys-Aube), especially the unique still wine of that area, Rosé des Riceys, ANDRÉ CLOUET (Bouzy), JACQUES COPINET (Côte de Sézanne), LAUNOIS PÉRE ET FILS (Le Mesnil-sur-Oger), PIERRE PETERS (Le Mesnil-sur-Oger), especially his Vintage Blanc de Blancs, JACQUES SELOSSE (Avize) and JEAN VESSELLE (Bouzy).

15

NAMES TO SEARCH OUT

The years of expansion since the huge harvest of 1970 have caused problems as well as pleasure. Many of the large houses have been able to finance sufficient stocks to take advantage of the increased availability of supplies of top-quality grapes, albeit often only by means of allowing financial takeover. Some, such as Moët, Clicquot, Lanson, Mumm and Pommery, have flourished, building upon the centuries of self-promotion and top-class products. Others, such as Charles Heidsieck, ran short of capital and quality, suffered many changes of ownership and yet are now thriving. Fortunately for 'Charlie' the status of one of the best-known names of the Grande Marque houses was eagerly desired, something which has not always been accorded lesser names which have been consigned into oblivion and destined at best to appear occasionally as a *sous marque*.

Happily there are also many positive stories among lesser-known names belonging to both large, old-established houses and much smaller, younger operations. I have spent much time in Champagne during these years of change – always tasting the wines of the Grande Marque houses, and always searching for splendid, individualistic wines from names not easily found even in the most adventurous of wine merchants.

—— HENRI ABELÉ ——

ESTABLISHED: 1757.
LOCATION: Reims.
YEARLY PRODUCTION: 600,000 bottles.
VINEYARDS: None.

Fancy talking about the third-oldest house still trading today in this chapter. The firm was initially founded by Théodore Vander Venken, a fabric and linen dealer from Lille. No one seems to know how he got involved with champagne but he was certainly a success story and a soundly based operation was passed on to his family. In 1876 Henri Abelé inherited the business and came to live in Reims. Within eight years the firm had pioneered the freezing brine system of dégorgement, rapidly taken up by other houses.

Just as the champagne market really began to expand, Abelé lost its way and meandered along. In 1942 the company was taken over by a large organisation controlled by the father of Monsieur Lafay, who is now Directeur-Général. When the present generation arrived ten years ago the organisation was in a mess: 'Martini & Rossi, through their Saint Raphaël subsidiary, had financial control but didn't understand the champagne industry.' Sales were a respectable 1.2 million bottles, mainly sold by mail order, but the quality left much to be desired and the necessary capital expenditure needed to upgrade the facilities was a formidable sum: 'The house needed rejuvenation and I had no option but to search for a different majority shareholder.' Not an easy task for a house in decline; in fact it seemed to many observers within the trade that Abelé was soon to become another of the many houses of former glories, absorbed by one of the major league more for the benefits of extra cellar space than extra market penetration, and destined to join the vast numbers of forgotten names to be spied only on posters on the walls of the restaurant Le Vigneron.

But things were to change dramatically. In 1985 Freixenet, Spain's largest wine group, bought the house, and many Champenois were aghast. Not only was the owner foreign, but it was a sparkling-wine maker of massive size: the whole champagne industry makes little more than three times as much wine as Freixenet's Penedes operations alone. Its Cordon Negro cava is one of the largest-selling wines in the world — around 12 million bottles in the United States every year, which is nearly as much as the total for the whole of Champagne. It owns its own distributors in America, the United Kingdom, Germany and Australia. It owns a winery in Mexico and has recently established the prestigious California winery Freixenet Sonoma, which makes quality sparkling wines from Chardonnay and Pinot Noir.

No wonder the locals were a little worried; after all, the worldwide Freixenet reputation has been created by reasonable, undemanding wines at cheap prices. Would they downmarket the image of champagne? Would they understand the philosophy and economics of making the ultimate of sparkling wines? In fact, no one needed to worry. As Monsieur Lafay says, 'Freixenet are definitely more sympathetic to the ways of the champagne business than were the Saint Raphaël group.' At present the production level has been halved as a complete reorganisation takes place. The extensive cellars are being renovated and extended and the 2 kilometres of *caves* are being readied for full occupancy. The house has the luxury of 1.3 hectares of central Reims ground space, and construction of a spectacular series of buildings is under way.

All this expenditure would be fruitless without decent wines. Happily Freixenet and Monsieur Lafay are fully aware of this. The house style has softened considerably; the NON-VINTAGE LE SOURIRE DE REIMS is an attractive, delicate, flowery wine with pronounced Chardonnay character. The GRANDE MARQUE IMPÉRIALE VINTAGE is not perhaps the finest of its type available but the post-takeover wines are yet to be released. The ROSÉ NON-VINTAGE is a serious, full-bodied wine with plenty of zip and rich Pinot flavour.

Lafay is justifiably pleased with the new direction:

> Freixenet now controls the worldwide distribution for Abelé . . . already we are second to Moët in the growing Spanish market. In 1986 exports accounted for 40 per cent of our output, now it is 70 per cent. At present we have retracted to a medium-size house in order to ensure that quality comes first. We will soon have the most modern of facilities for expansion, and then our plans for the future will be gradually realised . . . but never at the expense of quality.

—— A. CHARBAUT & FILS ——

ESTABLISHED: 1948.
LOCATION: Epernay.
YEARLY PRODUCTION: 1.8 million bottles.
VINEYARDS: 53 hectares, mainly in Avenay, Ay, Bisseuil and Mareuil-sur-Ay.

At the pinnacle of his success it was claimed that David Frost had 'risen without trace'. One could use the same term to describe the incongruity of the rapid development of the house of Charbaut, achieved without any of the seemingly obligatory high profile. The firm was only started after the war and yet is now firmly established on the avenue de Champagne. The main reason for its relative anonymity is that much of the business was previously devoted to own labels and *sous marques*. A large part of this is being phased out. Now, finally, the more specialist wines under their own name are drawing more than favourable critical praise both at home and abroad.

André Charbaut was born locally, at Fère-Champenoise. He started work there, not in the champagne business but for a brewery. After military service he changed occupations and in 1930 went to work as Commercial Director for Champagne Ducoin, a position he held for twenty-eight years. He then founded the house A. Charbaut & Fils. Some vineyards were purchased but the limited expansion offered as a *récoltant* didn't appeal, so the firm became *négociants*. During the 1960s André purchased his former employees, Ducoin in Mareuil-sur-Ay, and things really started to move.

René Charbaut, André's son, joined the firm at the tender age of eighteen, and was followed by brother Guy. The operational base had been moved to Epernay and business boomed with numerous styles of wine of varying degrees of quality being sold to the various market sectors under a proliferation of labels. Many of you readers have drunk many a bottle of Charbaut, but under many names – De Courcy is a well-respected label with prolific sales in the United Kingdom, and major wine retailers such as Sainsbury have availed themselves of Charbaut BOB supplies for many years.

In 1983 a significant development occurred – the firm moved into the illustrious avenue de Champagne, proudly taking its place alongside such well-established names as Moët & Chandon, Perrier-Jouët and Pol Roger. Quite a feat for a company in only its thirty-sixth year. The old cellars inherited with the purchase are very historic – nineteenth-century workers have carved their names along the chalk walls of the 4 kilometres of *galeries.* But, although perfect for a film set, they are narrow and unsuitable for modern equipment, and incapable of storing the projected quantities of bottles. New cellars, totally functional and devoid of romance, have been built and more are on the way. At the moment pressing, vinification and bottling are all done in the original buildings at Mareuil-sur-Ay and the expansion at headquarters is just to keep up with the increased production. Remuage is done mainly by hand and there are a few antique machines, forerunners of the *gyropalettes.* They look the same, hold the same pallet, yet are turned by hand. Interestingly they remuage half-bottles, magnums and even jeroboams. As the production of these is reasonably limited they are all dégorged by hand. They specialise in the larger bottle sizes – when they fill a twenty-bottle nebuchadnezzar they use one bottle just to give the new bottle a final rinse out!

I cannot pretend always to have been a fan of the large, sometimes confusing, range of wines, but things have improved dramatically over the past few years. The excitement in the non-vintage wines lies with the delightful BLANC DE BLANCS – a flowery nose, delicate Chardonnay flavour, yet still quite a sturdy finish. The reason for this unique style is the Marne vineyard owned by the house. It has planted Chardonnay in a predominantly Pinot region as a safeguard in poor years. The result is consistent yields of top-notch standards with a fuller, richer varietal flavour.

The house motto may well be 'We believe in Rosé'. I have never visited cellars with such a large percentage of Rosé; admittedly it is rather obvious as it is all in clear bottles (René thinks Charbaut is the only customer for clear-glass jeroboams). The ROSÉ NON-VINTAGE is made by the maceration method. It is an excellent wine, a real blast of raspberries on the nose and a wonderful length of flavour. A wine that is far superior to many other wines of this style which cost much, much more. Charbaut make two Prestige wines, the CERTIFICATE ROSÉ and CERTIFICATE BLANC DE BLANCS. Both thoroughly justify the *de luxe* tag: superbly made, individualistic wines of great character. Both are a little more expensive than vintage wines, but are much cheaper than many others in this range. The Rosé has an alluring nose, more delicate than the non-vintage and yet still full of the charm of a summer's day on the terrace. The flavour is incredibly soft and luscious yet finishes with plenty of zip. A wine for seduction! In a recent *Decanter* magazine blind tasting I gave my highest mark to the 1979 Blanc de Blancs, arguably the best-value Cuvée de Prestige on the market. The beautiful pale-yellow colour is highlighted in the clear bottle, and has an attractive lemony nose with superb, rich Chardonnay fruit. Champagne to be savoured.

I tasted these wines with René, at the end of what had been a tiring working day for both of us. After the 'business' was finished and a glass or two poured, René relaxed. A gentle, reflective smile came to his face as he said, 'It's good to unwind with a nice glass of champagne.' A great understatement as he was drinking a glass of Certificate Blanc de Blancs! The house prides itself on being a traditional *affaire familiale* which has undertaken rapid expansion but paradoxically achieved this with considerable caution; 'We could have built the new cellars under construction along with the others four years ago . . . but we don't like owing the bank too much.'

Future plans are for more emphasis on Charbaut and less on the other labels (De Courcy will obviously continue its successful career). A New York State winery operation is in the experimental stage, and there is a consultancy agreement with a co-operative in the Maharashta district near Bombay. In the midst of all this René remains proud but realistic: 'We are only a success as long as we continue satisfying our customers.'

—— GARDET ——

ESTABLISHED: 1895.
LOCATION: Chigny-les-Roses.
YEARLY PRODUCTION: 600,000 bottles.
VINEYARDS: None.

Discovering this small, modest house has been one of the great delights of my champagne-drinking of the past few years. The family-owned establishment is one of the region's better-kept secrets, tucked away in a tiny village in buildings that are not exactly historic – they had the misfortune to be close to a German V2 rocket base in the Second World War and the Allied bombers proved rather effective.

Grapes are bought in from all three major vineyard regions and a large portion are Pinot Noir. The NON-VINTAGE BRUT SPÉCIAL is a rich, creamy mouthful of flavour with at least four years' bottle age. Approximately 30 per cent of the total production is VINTAGE and the full, luscious wines are released a year or two later than most – the family consider that their house style needs more bottle age than others. They were one of the few houses to make a top-notch wine in the awkward 1976 vintage – a wonderful honeyed wine of considerable intensity. At no stage did the wine become blowsy as beautifully balanced acidity counterbalanced the lightly excessive ripeness. The 1979 was the most powerful, structured wine I have tasted from an essentially lightweight vintage. The ROSÉ is certainly not delicate, a full-bodied 100 per cent Pinot Noir made by the maceration method.

Over the years I have shown Gardet wines to numerous champagne enthusiasts and the responses are fascinating. Most adore the 'classic' style more similar to wines of the 1950s than the 1980s ... and yet the few that don't appreciate this are very positive in their dislike. The wines are extremely good value (the vintage is little more expensive than many well-known non-vintages), so it is well worth seeking out a bottle or three and making up your own minds!

——— PAUL GOERG ———

ESTABLISHED: 1950.
LOCATION: Vertus.
YEARLY PRODUCTION: 600,000 bottles in total, only a percentage sold with the Paul Goerg label.
VINEYARDS: The eighty-five-member co-operative controls 115 hectares around Vertus and Mesnil.

The profile of La Goutte d'Or is more that of an old-established medium-sized *négociant manipulant* than of a co-operative. The cellars and offices are right in the heart of the Côte des Blancs, traditional buildings of a modest size. Initial production was a mere 20,000 bottles; things have changed considerably since but it is still a relatively small operation – a fascinating contrast to the giant Centre Viticole de la Champagne just along the road at Chouilly.

The co-operative has traditionally supplied the most prestigious houses with top-quality Chardonnay Vin Clair. Both management and members became aware of the pronounced consumer interest and in 1982 they decided to make and sell their own range of 'specialist' wines. While the name Paul Goerg may seem rather unappealing (though a journalist friend of mine is convinced that 'Gurgle with Goerg' is a great advertising slogan) it does have a significant historical context. Monsieur Goerg was an important nineteenth-century *négociant en vins de Champagne* who led the village's resistance to the German invasion of 1870 and was imprisoned for his trouble. Later he became Mayor of Vertus, a member of the regional council of the Marne and Chevalier de La Légion d'Honneur.

A majority of the vineyards are 100 per cent but Vertus itself has an *échelle* of 95 per cent, so the Paul Goerg wines are Premier Cru. Director Daniel Aubertin is conscious of the responsibility in handling the produce of some of the finest cru of the Côte des Blancs. His firm is interested not in the light, rather anonymous Blanc de Blancs designed for a market which requires 'easily made, nondescript, cheapish champagne' but in producing the best possible. The grapes are pressed in Vaslin presses and *only* the cuvées are used in the wines selected for the Paul Goerg label, certainly never the deuxième taille. Aubertin is rather condemnatory of the present system: 'I don't consider that the deuxième taille should be allowed to be part of the prestigious *appellation* of champagne. I am sure there are many others who would echo these sentiments but restrictions of business operations prevent many doing so publicly.'

Fifty per cent of the wine is remuaged in the traditional manner, the rest courtesy of the sixteen *gyropalettes*. It is interesting that for a co-operative the stockholding is extremely large – 2.5 million bottles, over four years in average. They keep the non-vintage for at least three years, preferably four, and the vintage for at least five years. The cellars are mostly traditional with the original section blessed with perfect natural temperature control and used for the storage of reserve wines, vintage wines and the collection of older vintages.

The BRUT TRADITION NON-VINTAGE is a perfectly acceptable wine with 40 per cent Pinot Noir content, well balanced and with a concentration of flavour. It seems rather unfair to comment that despite the qualities of the wine it doesn't quite match up to the rest of the Paul Goerg range. I have tasted the BLANC DE BLANCS NON-VINTAGE several times in the past few years and the quality is very even. A flowery nose with a delicate, yet vivacious appley flavour. An excellent example of varietal character. The BRUT ROSÉ NON-VINTAGE is delightful. La Goutte d'Or is one of the few houses to make pink champagne with no Pinot Noir in the initial blend. Ten per cent Vertus Rouge is added to the Chardonnay; the result is a delicate almost translucent colour with a subtle but definite Pinot nose and a lovely strawberry creaming soda finish. A perfect aperitif on the patio when Great Britain produces one of its rare summer days! I defy the finest of champagne palates ever to pick the VINTAGE as a co-operative wine; it is stunning – reeking of Chardonnay fruit and flavour with a soft finish only achieved by the correct combination of top-notch fruit and the requisite ageing on yeast. A no-compromise wine which shows the glories of the Côte des Blancs. The CUVÉE SPÉCIALE CENTENAIRE has a 5 per cent touch of Pinot Noir in a blend of selected vintage years, the first release uses 1979, 1980 and 1981.

Daniel Aubertin co-ordinates a remarkably successful operation; he is a youthful man with impressive technical qualifications who is an unashamed lover of the Chardonnay grape and its achievements in Champagne. He likes to point out that he is not on his own – there are many other people within the industry who share his views: 'After the frosts of 1985 quite a number of growers have replaced their Pinot Noir plantings with Chardonnay. That's when you know the choice is unbiased ... when the decision has no complications. It is a simple choice of one or the other.'

He is justifiably proud of La Goutte d'Or's achievements: 'We are still very small – not surprising when you consider that the Côte des Blancs consists of only 3000 hectolitres and the Centre at Chouilly controls 800 hectares of this! We have raised standards by offering our members easy access to the technical resources to make better wine. We are confident that at least a third of our production will be sold as Paul Goerg wines.' The members have recently purchased a tiny walled vineyard in Vertus, near their cellars. CLOS DU VERTUS will receive separate vinification, and only be released in years of special quality. I have tasted the Vin Clair of the 1988 harvest – superb!

An interesting aside is introduced to the lunchtime conversation as he serves with the cheese a bottle of Vertus Rouge La Goutte d'Or 1976, a decidedly interesting wine with no oak whatsoever and by common consent a decade too old – yet the Pinot flavour still lingered. At the turn of the century Vertus was planted solely with Pinot Noir, but thanks to the neighbouring Mesnil the growers became aware of the delights of Chardonnay and its suitability for the area.

At present it is not easy to find bottles of Paul Goerg on sale, but they are worth seeking. Times are relatively recent – 400 years later on to the market-place than Gosset for instance – but the German and United Kingdom markets are growing. Hopefully others will follow and we champagne lovers will long continue to benefit from a well-crafted range of wines with an individualistic, well-balanced style of Chardonnay at its best, and at a reasonable price.

—— LANDRAGIN ——

ESTABLISHED: Still growing and in a state of flux.
LOCATION: Verzenay.
YEARLY PRODUCTION: Also changing rapidly.
VINEYARDS: 25 hectares in Verzenay, Beaumont-sur-Vesle, Sillery, Tauxières and Villers-Allerand, and growing.

The Landragin family have been growers in Verzenay since 1772, and another branch of the family originates from Hautvillers. No one could ever accuse them of being newcomers to the region, yet you will find no reference to them in any articles or books about Champagne because for generations the family were quite happy selling most of the crop to the major *négociant* houses and making and selling a small percentage of their wine locally. This anonymity will not last for much longer. Things have changed dramatically within the family structure and a whole new set of wine-making and business principles are being established by a young 'man of both hemispheres', Dominique Landragin.

Dominique's father Pierre took over the family vineyards between the wars, and continued the family tradition until the 1960s, when he gradually increased their commitment to building the family's brand. Young Dominique trained at Montpellier and gained practical experience in various cellars, but as the youngest of four children (albeit the only son) he was frustrated with his lack of prospects, so in the mid-1970s he took a job in Australia, making sparkling wines for the giant Seppelt company. It was a totally new environment for him and his wife Anna and he could have either slipped into a routine of mediocrity or become disgruntled and scuttled back home with his tail between his legs. He did neither. The original job didn't

A new wine-world for the houses – Napa Valley, California.

If you are awarded a gold medal in 1810 – keep flaunting it!

Mumm's marketing masterstroke – instantly recognisable.

Created in 1864, this label has been recently resurrected to dignify an excellent wine.

Understated classicism for a unique wine.

The essence of simplicity which has spawned countless garish imitations.

Designer-marketing makes Belle Epoque the success story of the last decade.

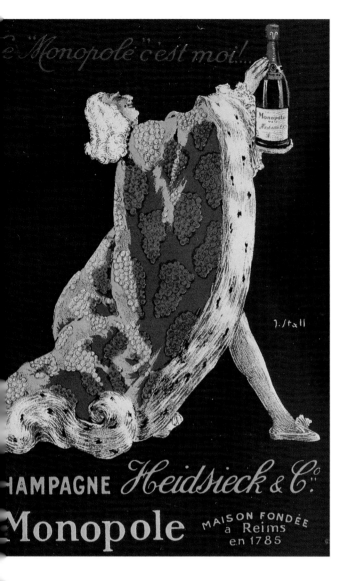

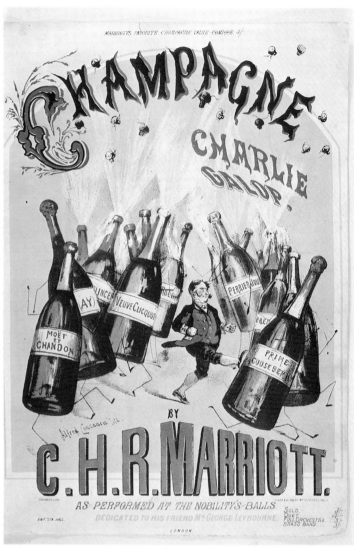

kling marketing from the 1890s to the 1920s.

Source of top quality grapes for the joint Deutz–Montana venture.

OPPOSITE ABOVE *Even in the most intimate moment, the first duty is 'product placement'.*

OPPOSITE BELOW *Years of spraying the stuff around rewarded Jackie Stewart with a directorship of Moët London Ltd!*

RIGHT *This long-running campaign fosters notions of high-living and exclusivity.*

ABOVE *Champagne marketing is infinitely adaptable – this ad of the late 1980s is stylish and non-élitist.*

Dom Pérignon.

appeal so he formed a partnership with Ian Home to make Yellowglen *méthode champenoise* wines in Victoria. I can't say the wines ever appealed to me, but the Australian public loved them, and they drink a lot of wine. The company was an instant success. Within a few years the partners sold out to a large national wine company. Dominique stayed on for a while but has recently begun his own operation in the same state. Down-under, top winemakers are accorded a superstar status normally reserved for chefs in his native country, and this likeable extrovert has thrived on the challenge of the relaxed but fiercely competitive Australian wine scene, but also enjoys supervising his family interests.

Now there is a deal with a number of other growers in Verzenay and the group sell a range of superbly crafted, individualistic styles under the 'Landragin' label.

The BRUT NON-VINTAGE is an attractive blend of 80 per cent Pinot Noir and 20 per cent Pinot Meunier with beautiful, rich varietal character balanced with a zippy fresh fruit. Excellent drinking. CRÉMANT is the same blend as the non-vintage, with not only less atmospheres pressure but a little more dosage which produces a softer wine with a yeasty, luscious character. ROSÉ BRUT. A real Montagne de Reims Rosé. The Pinot Noir shrieks on the nose and on the palate, a real mouthful of strawberries, plenty of fizz and a dry, clean finish. BLANC DE BLANCS CHARDONNAY. There are considerable parcels of Chardonnay in the Montagne de Reims. In fact Bouzy, which can be considered the real heartland of Pinot Noir territory, has 12 per cent of its vineyards planted with this outsider. Dominique has produced a delicate, fragrant wine ... perhaps lacking a little of the finesse of the Côte des Blancs Chardonnay but gaining a little more flavour. BLANC DE NOIRS PREMIER CRU. Not always a style of wine that I enjoy often but I have appreciated many a bottle of this full, yeasty wine. One of the few champagnes I would happily drink with a red-meat course. Twenty per cent of the blend is fermented in cask. VINTAGE BRUT 1982 is the first year released, 100 per cent Grand Cru Pinot Noir from Verzenay. Once again 20 per cent fermented in cask. Full flavour with the creamy soft finish typical of the vintage. CHAMPAGNE ANNA LANDRAGIN 1979. Once again 100 per cent Grand Cru Pinot Noir from Verzenay and 20 per cent fermented in oak. An intense 'traditional' Pinot champagne flavour with a surprisingly fresh finish. It is not planned to release a consistent style of wine with this label; instead it will be used only for vintages of special character.

Of course it is rather easy to extol the virtues of the first of the 'new' Landragin wines – after all, the non-vintage wines are from the remarkable 1982 and 1983 vintages. Nevertheless they have achieved a fascinating range of styles from a very small regional spread of vineyard holdings. He has managed this by different technical approaches to different blends and by concentration on the different varietal flavours. Further expansion plans are under way and an Australian wine-maker is to be installed as *chef de caves*. This may seem rather like taking coals to Newcastle ... but Dominique is convinced that the combination of a high-tech 'no faults' wine-making training (necessary in a country where excessive rather than insufficient heat is a common problem) plus the perfect natural soil and climatic conditions will be a stunning success. Who knows?

Definitely a label to watch.

——— BRUNO PAILLARD ———

ESTABLISHED: 1981.
LOCATION: Reims.
YEARLY PRODUCTION: 300,000 bottles.
VINEYARDS: None.

Bruno Paillard – the new kid in town. Handsome, engaging, with a winsome smile, and articulate. The youngest of all *négociants* (and definitely the most recent)*, he is also one of the smallest, but it would be a mistake to under-estimate him. In fact the image of his premises sums up the style of the man – small building and big sign! I am not denigrating Bruno, its just a fact that his flair for publicity, marketing and selling has enabled quite an amazing new development to thrive despite the harsh rigours of the present commercial world.

Bruno was born as recently as 1953, of good Champenois stock. The family have been growers for generations (they still own a vineyard in Bouzy) and father was a successful broker. Bruno joined the family business in 1975, and also acted as export consultant to Marne & Champagne, the largest suppliers of BOB wines in the region. The early years of his trading career were very successful but, in Bruno's own words, he was 'occasionally frustrated when I went to some of the really top producers who had small quantities of really fine wines available, but they were far too good for BOB purposes'.

Not the person to resist a sound commercial opportunity, he began buying these parcels and selling them under his own name with *marque d'acheteur* status. By 1981 this side of the business was of sufficient size to enable Bruno to become a *négociant manipulant*. Sales are now up to 300,000 bottles a year and growing rapidly. 'I may be small compared to the giants but production is already half of Krug's total' is one of his favourite phrases. Only 5 per cent is sold on the home market, 'just a few select *cavistes*** and about forty restaurants'. The largest markets are Switzerland followed by Belgium and the United States, with the United Kingdom improving.

The fermentation and storage cellars are more similar to the CVC than to the traditional houses – no romance whatsoever. Computerised *gyropalettes* but also huge towers of stacking pallets right up to the high ceilings – remarkably

*The other house is Vranken.
**'Boutique' wine shops.

space-effective. There is a huge 'very expensive' air conditioning plant which ensures that the temperature never varies by more than 0.4°C.

It is still rather early on to make firm value-judgements on the whole range of wines. I have usually found the NON-VINTAGE (approximately 50 per cent Pinot Meunier, with Pinot Noir and a little Chardonnay) pleasant – clean, fresh and full of fruit. Easy, undemanding drinking. The BRUT ROSÉ is made by the maceration method with 10–15 per cent Chardonnay added at the end, plenty of zest and delicate flavour. I consider the best of all the range is the CRÉMANT BLANC DE BLANCS, very refined with subtlety – an ideal aperitif champagne.

VINTAGE wines are treated in a different manner at Paillard. The blend is never remotely the same. Bruno chooses the balance which he considers emphasises the varietal character which has been most successful. For instance the 1976, 'the super summer' which produced very rich wines, is 60 per cent Chardonnay and 40 per cent Pinot Noir whereas the 1979 is 80 per cent Chardonnay and the 1981 is 90 per cent Pinot Noir. The individual characteristics of all three are appealing, particularly the fragrance and vivacity of the 1979. Also *all* vintage wines have the dégorgement date on the label. Bruno considers that 'Champagne should be fully mature at the time of dégorgement. In my opinion the wine is never as good two or three years later. The buyer should always know this important date.'

Not only does Bruno have a boundless enthusiasm for making champagne, he also has a keen sense of marketing. The range of non-vintage wines have stylish packaging but the vintage are something totally new for champagne – a different original oil painting adorns the label of each vintage à la Mouton Rothschild. Bruno instructs the artists by describing the vintage. His description of 1979 as 'youth, colour and movement' was translated into a village fair enlivened by a merry-go-round of children. The rich 1981 was described in one word, 'exuberance', and was translated by a metamorphosis of the Smiling Angel of Reims Cathedral into the image of Bacchus. This works well on the labels, and allows Bruno and his wife to decorate the walls of their house with superb paintings!

Obviously future expansion is at the forefront of this dynamic young man's mind – there is plenty of land available on the industrial estate for more buildings – but source of quality produce is paramount. 'At our size we have a future only in the rarity of the high-quality grapes in the products.'

─── DE VENOGE ───

ESTABLISHED: 1837.
LOCATION: Epernay.
YEARLY PRODUCTION: 1.5 million bottles.
VINEYARDS: None.

It may seem a little strange placing an establishment of this size and age in this chapter, but affairs have not always run smoothly at this major house, and it is a pleasure to report that things are definitely improving.

When Henri-Marc de Venoge established his own house in Mareuil-sur-Ay he had been in the champagne business for fifteen years, knew the trade well and had no trouble establishing his own marque – within two years he moved the operation to Epernay. In 1845 he was joined by his son Joseph and the gradual growth of the early years was replaced with much more dynamic expansion, both at home and abroad. De Venoge soon became one of the better known names on the British market. By 1864 things were really booming and Joseph registered the two trademarks, Cordon Bleu and Champagne des Princes, which have been the focal sales-points of the firm. In the same year he was the first in Champagne to create a Crémant Rosé. His son Gaetan joined the family firm in 1869 and business continued to expand to such an extent that at the time of Joseph's death in 1898 de Venoge was one of the largest houses, producing in excess of 1 million bottles a year (similar to Moët & Chandon at the time). The family continued the business traditions and in the process the house moved to the prestigious avenue de Champagne.

This was the pinnacle of achievement in the history of the house. From this point on there was a gradual decline. The house became a public company in 1926 and branches of the family continued to exert considerable financial and management influences. In 1958 the company was taken over by the Trouillard family but the house began a rather chequered career, changing ownership frequently, and in 1986 the two houses, Trouillard–de Venoge, were sold on to a large industrial company with interests as diverse as banking, insurance, canned foods and sugar milling. Trouillard was sold in 1987 and the House of de Venoge is back on its own.

Over the years de Venoge had suffered from a lack of image. The wines were perfectly acceptable but lacked class. Production was large (over 3 million bottles a year in the 1970s), yet the name was not exactly well known. The frequent changes of owners, wine-making and marketing strategies had taken their toll – the house had lost its way just when the competition was really hotting up. Something had to change, and it certainly has. The new President Directeur-Général Thierry Mantoux has initiated a 'process of revitalisation' which aims to present the wines at the upper end of the market and to reassert the reputation for quality.

Mantoux is an interesting character to be sitting in the avenue presiding over one of the major houses. For a start he is only in his early forties, and he is not Champenois by birth or training. The past few decades have seen the gradual erosion of importance of the champagne families' social connections in favour of the more pragmatic commercial qualifications. Mantoux is one of the most highly visible of the recent 'business school graduate' appointments. He has some champagne experience with Joseph Henriot in his Charles Heidsieck days, but the rest of his postgraduate time has been spent in other industries. He is also the author of the best-selling book *BCBG. Le guide du bon chic bon genre*, a Gallic version of the tongue-in-cheek *Sloane Ranger Handbook* which claims to be the style arbiter for the over-achieving French yuppie.

The changes have been swift and far-reaching. The senior management are closer to the age group of record industry executives. The *chef de cave* and Export Manager are in their thirties and the French Sales Manager is the same age as the boss. Concentration is now on the production of a much smaller quantity of individualistic wines. Two of Mantoux's first decisions were to sell off all deuxième taille and *all* of the poor 1984 vintage. Stocks have been trimmed to only the wines the team want in their cellars. In three years production has been halved, and what a difference in the wines! As Mantoux says:

> We believe in investment in the product. We don't own any vineyards, but are very happy with the contracts with our growers ... one has been with the house for over sixty years. We are buying the finest of grapes, selling off the surplus and making economic sense with a realistic production of wines that command a realistic price. I don't have to go begging to Head Office for permission for most policy decisions, but if the Chairman of the group has a bottle of Cordon Bleu and doesn't like it ... then I am really in trouble and all hell would break loose.

The new NON-VINTAGE CORDON BLEU is a revelation. It is 75 per cent Pinot Noir, yet the character of really top-notch Chardonnay shows through. The result is a beautifully balanced, mature wine with much of the complexity of vintage champagne.

Only time will tell with the 'new wave' vintage wines. The 1982 is superb, but I will withhold judgement until I can sample the product of a less spectacular year. In the past I have not been enamoured with the BLANC DE BLANCS DE CHARDONNAY, but recent tastings confirm a lighter, more flowery varietal style. CUVÉE DES PRINCES is an elegant, subtle Blanc de Blancs from Cramant, Mesnil and Avize. One of the Prestige wines with real style and flavour, and — dare I say it – worth the money. The only pity is the bottle, which is in the shape of a decanter and even comes with a glass stopper. Marvellous for the olive oil in the kitchen, but it rather denigrates such a classy champagne. The most interesting of the special de Venoge wines is the CRÉMANT ROSÉ, a recreation of the wine first developed in 1864 by Joseph. An outstanding zippy, flavoursome yet soft wine; Chardonnay with a small amount of Pinot Noir added (the blend obviously varies according to the characteristics of the wine at the time – but the 'recipe' is guarded as zealously as the Coca-Cola formula). The transparent glass bottle highlights the pale pink colour *gorge de pigeon* and is complemented by a replica of the original label.

Obviously a house in the midst of dynamic change, with some superb wines. The only cloud on the horizon is the lack of ownership of vineyards, but that hasn't worried a number of other large houses. Mantoux and his team are confident that the 'new' image will create success as the champagne-lovers of the world rediscover an old friend.

—— GEORGES VESSELLE ——

ESTABLISHED: 'For generations,' says M. Vesselle, with a gallic wave of his hand.
LOCATION: Bouzy.
YEARLY PRODUCTION: 150,000 bottles (much of this is Coteaux champenois).
VINEYARDS: 17 hectares in Bouzy – 2 Chardonnay, the rest Pinot Noir.

Georges Vesselle is a larger-than-life character in an industry with a history of such people. He is Vineyard Director of the G.H. Mumm–Perrier-Jouët–Dry Monopole group, controlling over 420 hectares; renowned for his management skills, he has been the guiding force behind many of the group's technical innovations. He is also the latest of a long line of members of his family who have held the position of Mayor of Bouzy. These tasks would be more than sufficient for any ordinary person, but not Georges. He also runs his own *récoltant manipulant* operation, which possesses a substantial reputation among the local cognoscenti.

The Vesselles have been around Bouzy for centuries. The village is not large but there seem to be many gateways with the same surname on the brass plates proudly announcing the title *'Viticulteur'*. They all make mouth-filling, solid, sturdy Pinot-Noir-dominated champagne – excellent drinking. But the wines from Georges are special.

There is nothing particularly imposing about the establishment either above or underground. Georges inherited his house and cellars (but not vines); Madame Vesselle inherited the vineyards and cellars dug by her great-grandfather. The latter were conveniently just across the road and now they have been joined by a narrow, snaking gallery. The cellars are quite basic, but very typical of the villages of the Montagne de Reims. I dread to think of the consequences of a severe earthquake as the buildings are virtually perched on top of a series of man-made rabbit warrens.

Despite being the man in charge of the glorious Mumm and Perrier-Jouët Chardonnay vineyards, he is a staunch believer in the superior qualities of the Pinot Noir grapes, and those based in his home village: 'Bouzy has a unique microclimate, south-facing slopes which miss both the northerly and westerly winds. The grapes receive just that little extra warmth – not too much, mind you. The quality is unique.'

When I comment that this sounds just like Dominique Landragin's claim for the superiority of Verzenay he readily agrees that this is the other great cru of the Montagne de Reims and then adds, 'Perhaps Ambonnay also.' But then again Mumm and Dry Monopole own large holdings in all three.

The 'Establishment Georges Vesselle' employs only seven people. It is not exactly space-age like the large houses; the cellars are rather disorganised with both stainless-steel tanks and oak casks scattered through a series of unprepossessing rooms. The casks are made from Hungarian oak and originate from Alsace. They are of varying sizes and each is named: the largest is 'Monsieur', the next 'Madame' and the smaller ones after the children. These contain some of the very finest Bouzy Rouge. Methods of vinification of this still wine are very traditional. The fermentation tanks have a *chapeau couvert* on top – a Bordelais piece of equipment which is a wooden tray with holes. As fermentation begins the skins rise to the top. To prevent this and maximise the flavours the *chapeau* is repeatedly pushed down the tank, taking the skins with it. The wines destined for champagne remain in stainless steel and undergo malolactic fermentation.

The dégorgement, bottling, labelling and packaging are all done by hand. 'Really this business is an amusement ... it is *très artisanal* and I have great fun playing with the wines. I can create any blend I wish and I don't need to fill in a series of memos and wait for a decision from high up!'

Nevertheless, the wines are *très serieux*. The NON-VINTAGE is a surprisingly light colour considering it is 90 per cent Pinot Noir. It has a very fine bead with a delicious full-flavoured nose and an intensity of flavour which in most years can easily be confused with a vintage wine. It always improves with laying down for another year or two. The VINTAGE BRUT GRAND CRU is invariably powerful, rich and luscious – possibly the best 1973 I have tasted, a glorious classic 1975, one of the most full bodied yet beautifully balanced of the 1979s. The 1982 recently tasted was a wonderful experience, reeking of ripe fruit and plenty of Pinot flavour with considerable backbone and years of life ahead. The ROSÉ BRUT GRAND CRU is nectar, glorious strawberry flavour with a good deal of character counterbalancing the soft, creamy finish. Georges has definite views on the production of Rosé:

> People don't realise just how much the quality of the finished product depends on the still red wine. Also the best Rosés are made from 100 per cent Pinot Noir [well, coming from Bouzy he would say that!]. Interestingly in the terrible years of 1972 and 1984 I blended poor still red with poor champagne and for some reason on both occasions produced very good wines.

The new CUVÉE PRESTIGE BLANC DE NOIRS LA JULINE is a blend of vintages; the first release is 1979, 1980 and 1982. An alluring golden colour with a very fine bead. I tasted it in Georges' office, which had two large vases full of sweet-smelling roses, but when the bottle was opened the bouquet completely overpowered the scent of the flowers and a glorious champagne aroma filled the room. A soft, mature wine with a warm, lingering finish.

This is not a book on the Coteaux champenois but mention must be made of the fine BOUZY ROUGE, in particular the CUVÉE VÉRONIQUE-SYLVIE, which is a blend of the best years. A 'burgundian' nose with a fruity violet flavour. The present wine is a blend of 1979, 1981 and 1985. I ask Georges if he has a favourite vintage or two – he sits back and says, 'Ah yes: 1943, '47, '59, '64, '66 . . . and of course '76.'

I have been vigorous in my arguments against 'mono cru' champagnes, but there are always exceptions to the rules. Georges and Madame Vesselle certainly prove this.

16

THE FUTURE OF CHAMPAGNE HOUSES OUTSIDE THE REGION

The last decade has not only been marked by an explosion of champagne exports. Many of the major markets have also enjoyed a comparable boom in consumption of other sparkling wines, and not necessarily those products at the cheapest end of the price spectrum. The public's taste for bubbly has been particularly pronounced in the United States, where champagne and sparklings were the only types of wine with a growth in consumption in 1985. In the early 1960s farsighted strategists recognised the problems of the limitation of expansion options within Champagne and began to diversify into operations where the years of experience, costly experimentation with new technology and careful honing of market skills could be used to increase turnover – hence the ever-increasing number of houses which have established sparkling-wine facilities (and of course other business enterprises) outside the region.

There have been ventures within France and nearby European countries. In the Loire alone Deutz owns Château d'Aulée, Bollinger owns Langlois Château, Gosset is justifiably proud of Château Grille, Taittinger owns Bouvet Ladubay and the Seydoux family of Alfred Gratien established the renowned sparkling Saumur house Gratien & Meyer at the same time as the champagne firm. Moët & Chandon, G.H. Mumm and Deutz have factories in Germany (the latter's involvement dates back to 1904) and Moët is also involved in making sparkling wine in Austria. There are many other interests within and outside the wine world. Many houses are involved in other *de luxe* fields such as perfume and haute couture. The Taittinger family's business interests include hotel chains.

However, the really interesting developments have taken place much further away.

In 1960 Moët established itself in Argentina. One thousand acres now produce in excess of 3 million bottles of equal quantities of sparkling and still wine. In 1974 a 200-acre vineyard was created in Brazil, with Cinzano as minority shareholders, which produces bottles of wine. These two sizeable operations are of no particular significance in terms of quality but are of tremendous interest all the same as they were the first long-range diversifications by a champagne house, and are presumably profitable.

—— THE UNITED STATES ——

The most significant development was the creation of Domaine Chandon, which started in 1973. It is indicative of the comparative recentness of the export of skills and capital that this 'mission to establish and grow an integrated sparkling-wine business in the USA' (Moët's words) was treated with a great deal of circumspection by most of the other houses, which sat back and waited for the results before taking any action themselves. Dare I suggest that a number of houses would not have been disappointed if the venture had failed? As it happened, the first wines were released in 1977 and the critics were happy and the wine-drinking public voted with their pockets. A new era was born!

DOMAINE CHANDON
(Yountville, Napa Valley)

Moët is quite frank about its decision – it was to enable the company to obtain a much larger market share than it could ever achieve with only champagne. Robert-Jean de Vogüé realised that there were limits to growth, even for the giants, through the exporting of more bottles. At the time there were many mutterings around the dining tables of Reims and Epernay. I remember well a rather tense evening when a volatile discussion raged after a youngish member of the champagne trade dared suggest that Moët's action need not necessarily denigrate the name champagne. He was correct. Whereas the South American connections were planted with a hotchpotch of undistinguished varietals .(Chasselas, Ugni-Blanc and Riesling Italico to name but a few), the Napa winery was to use only traditional high-quality varietals – Chardonnay, Pinot Noir and some Pinot Blanc. In those times (and regrettably it is often still the case) American wineries were most extravagant with the term 'Champagne' and liberally splashed the word all over labels of anything with a sparkle. Domaine Chandon was the first California producer of *méthode champenoise* not to abuse the hallowed name. Interestingly, many top-quality California producers have since followed.

The first wines were made totally from grapes bought in from a number of growers, including Trefethen, where the wines were initially made. The huge, modern and stunningly beautiful winery was completed in 1977 and two storage extensions have been added since. Domaine Chandon owns 1600 acres of land, including a 900-acre range in Carneros, just on the Sonoma County border, 150 acres on Mount Veeder, 220 acres surrounding the winery in the heart of the Napa – and they are still buying.

Under the guidance of Moët's Chief Oenologist, Edmond Maudière, many of the traditional methods are used. Particular attention is paid to maturation of the grapes, which are picked slightly under-ripe to achieve levels of acidity normally frowned upon in the Napa. The champenois selective pressing with most of the deuxième tailles discarded and separate vinification is rigidly controlled. The *assemblage* is carried out by Maudière and interestingly reserve wines supply up to 30 per cent of the final blend. Yet there are also major innovatory features. Picking is done by giant machines at night when the coolest temperatures encourage less colour extraction from the Pinot Noir grapes. The remuage is carried out by massive *gyropalettes* – parts of the winery are more reminiscent of a horror movie set than of the parent establishment in the avenue de Champagne.

Three wines are produced. CHANDON BRUT, a blend of Chardonnay, Pinot Noir and Pinot Blanc with a minimum eighteen months' age in bottle 'on the yeast'. Over the years I have been pleased with the consistency of quality and style, a tribute to the skill of the blender. BLANC DE NOIRS is a blend of Pinot Noir grapes from various microclimates of the Napa. The gentle pressing still allows a very delicate tinge of pink – not a Rosé by any means. The wine has two advantages: a gorgeous pastel colour and a soft, slightly fuller finish. CHANDON RÉSERVE is a limited-quantity release of a Pinot-Noir-dominated blend with considerably more bottle age, much more intensity, and a much higher price tag. It is interesting that despite the fact that Stateside wine drinkers are more vintage-conscious than most (Laurent Perrier insists that the finest possible cuvée it can make for its premium wine Grand Siècle must be made from a blend of vintages, yet is sufficiently pragmatic to provide a single-vintage wine for this market), Domaine Chandon refuses to compromise and continues only to make wines with these large proportions of reserve wines, even though it deprives them of the chance of a year on the label. Good for them.

At no time would I suggest these wines are of comparable style and quality to Moët & Chandon. They are what they claim on their labels, Napa Valley Sparkling Wine Method Champenoise, and perfectly acceptable. The sheer volume of sales, which have rocketed to 5 million bottles a year, suggests that the planning, capital investment and dedication are being amply rewarded.

PIPER-SONOMA
(Healdsburg, Sonoma)

This company was established in 1980 as a joint venture between Piper Heidsieck and its US importers Renfield, who also owned Sonoma (now called Rodney Strong) vineyards. The winery opened its doors in 1982 and now produces over 1.5 million bottles a year, the majority being the uncomplicated BRUT. Small quantities of BLANC DE NOIRS and TÊTE DE CUVÉE are also made. Unlike Domaine Chandon, these wines are made from single years and are therefore vintage-dated. In 1987 Piper bought out its partners, and it will be interesting to watch the future developments now that Michel Lacroix, its *chef de caves*, is in total control.

MAISON DEUTZ
(Arroyo Grande, Santa Barbara)

There are few things in life less pleasant than attending a social gathering and having a glass of wine thrust in your hand followed by the words 'You're the expert – tell us what this is.' The poor expert is on a hiding to nothing – if he or she manages to answer correctly it is 'only to be expected' and there are no plus points to be gained. But heaven forbid if, as is most likely, the beleaguered individual surrounded by inquisitive people gets it wrong. The reaction then is, 'I told you so. These people don't know what they are talking (or writing) about.'

It happened to me at a recent Sunday gathering in the heart of Surrey. A glass of bubbly was proffered and instant judgement required. The *mousse* was fine and constant, the bouquet quite floral with none of the 'old socks' smell of Chenin Blanc (in the Loire). Neither did it smell hot country (i.e. Spain). In fact there was a delicate hint of the classic yeasty nose prevalent in many good champagnes. Next, the taste – soft and fragrant with a subtle creamy finish. The wine was a pleasure to drink and yet did not possess the intensity of flavour nor the steeliness to be the real thing. I was nonplussed as I was running out of choices, especially on reflection that there was nothing of this elegance being produced in Australia or South Africa ... yet. That left California. When I offered this as the answer there was a hush (the guests actually stopped talking about the problems of their children's schooling, their marriages and other such small talk). I presumed I had really messed things up, but the quiet was due to annoyance rather than glee – I think I actually gained credibility.

The wine was MAISON DEUTZ BRUT CUVÉE. In 1983, 800 acres were purchased and 150 planted (40 per cent Pinot Blanc, 30 per cent Pinot Noir, 25 per cent Chardonnay and 5 per cent Chenin Blanc) in an area closer to Los Angeles than to San Francisco and many, many miles away from the Napa and Sonoma. André Lallier, the great-great-grandson of the founder of Deutz, had searched the length and breadth of the California wine regions and considered the ideal geographical assets for making fine sparkling wine were here, just north of Santa Barbara. The soils are chalky with limestone outcroppings offering excellent drainage and the climate is relatively cool, thanks to ocean breezes and cool morning and evening fogs. The operation is not exactly in the Domaine Chandon class. Although the giant Swiss food conglomerate Nestlé has a third equity, there is nothing gigantic or space-age about Maison Deutz. Picking is by hand and the grapes are pressed in small quantities in a *coquard* press imported from 'home' – the only one in the United States. Selective pressing is carried out and the wine goes through a malolactic fermentation (very rare in California) and *all* remuage is done by hand. The wine I tasted was from the first release, a modest production of 55,000 bottles from bought-in grapes. By the time the firm's own vineyards are 'on stream' an estimated 400,000 bottles will be produced per annum and a vintage Blanc de Noirs will be added.

DOMAINE MUMM
(Rutherford, Napa Valley)

I have discussed the positive financial and directional contributions of the Seagram ownership of G.H. Mumm, Perrier-Jouët and Heidsieck Dry Monopole. Yet it is interesting to note that outside Champagne the company's wine interests have been extremely uncompromising; the House of Ricasoli (including Brolio Chianti), New Zealand's innovative Montana Wines, New York State's Taylor, Gold Seal and Great Western, plus huge wineries such as the Taylor California Cellars and Paul Masson have all bitten the company bullet in recent years. Yet operations that are presumably more profitable and offering a more positive future are given the care, attention and financial backing which denote serious attitudes towards the wine industry. Domaine Mumm is its latest.

Originally the intentions were simply to utilise facilities at its classy Napa winery, Sterling Vineyards, buying in superior grapes. The success of certain other premium California sparkling wines persuaded the corporate powers-that-be to expand their horizons. In 1981 Epernay-born and trained Guy Devaux was appointed General Manager, Michel Budin of Perrier-Jouët was brought in as consultant, and the development was under way. Devaux spent three years creating a blend of 60 per cent Pinot Noir and 40 per cent Chardonnay selected from twenty vineyards. Secrecy was all-important to the company and the 1986 debut of MUMM CUVÉE NAPA was worth the wait – a fragrant, soft and yet full-flavoured wine.

In the words of Bernard Ganter, G.H. Mumm's North American Director at the time, 'We were overwhelmed with positive comments from coast to coast, although limited in our sales efforts by the initial limited availability.' Since then Seagram has purchased 80 acres of the prime of the Napa in Rutherford at a reputed US$42,000 per acre and is building a winery of sufficient size to cope with revised production levels. I am sure this will not be the last of the Domaine's vineyard purchases, despite the incredibly high market prices for good land.

ROEDERER ESTATE
(Anderson Valley, Mendocino)

Roederer purchased 570 acres in 1982 and immediately planted 370 and built a winery. Fabrice Rosset of Roederer is very enthusiastic and talks of an eventual production of 12 million bottles, a blend of Chardonnay and Pinot Noir. He is the first to admit a few mistakes with the firm's experiences of making wine in a hot climate, but is very confident of the success of the operation and initial reactions to the first release have been more favourable.

BOLLINGER has a small interest in what initially seems a rather unholy alliance with United Kingdom brewers Whitbread and Italian superstars Antinori. Rumours abound regarding just about every other major champagne house – yet I can't help but feel that the pace may be a little slower. The houses will need either the financial backing of Domaine Mumm or the ability to select cheap(ish) vineyard land like Deutz. One thing is for sure: no one will be able to emulate Moët. I doubt whether even the financial might of the Moët–Hennessy group would be prepared to outlay the necessary money for such major expansion at today's costs.

RENÉ CHARBAUT has purchased some land in the Seneca Lake winery region of New York State and planted Chardonnay and Pinot Noir. He has been most impressed with some of the wines from the newer, more innovative, wineries in the region and is quick to point out that, unlikely as it seems, the climate is not much different to that of Epernay – a little colder in mid-winter and a little hotter in mid-summer. With the typically cautious family approach, René is renting wine-making facilities until the family has enough experience of a few harvests before making the big decision and building a winery.

—— AUSTRALIA ——

Now here is the country with many of the answers to the problems of expansion costs. In recent years Australia has proved more than capable of producing superb wines at reasonable prices. A recent Australia v. USA wine tasting in Sydney with eminent judges from both countries (plus Hugh Johnson and Oz Clarke from England to ensure fair play) voted 213–83 in favour of the Australian wines ... and the cost difference per bottle was almost as much in favour of the Australians.*

With a few exceptions, until now the only distinguishing feature of Australian sparkling wines has been their mediocrity. In the past the word 'Champagne' was abused even more than in the United States, but things are getting better. Now Australian wine-makers are allowed to use the term only when the contents of the bottle are made by *méthode champenoise*. Some houses are beginning to take sparkling wine more seriously. Dominique Landragin's efforts at Yellowglen when it was his own winery are highly rated by Australians. I have spoken to many wine-makers about the poor quality of their sparkling wines and most agree that they are many years away from developing their own industry with the right grapes in the right areas and the right equipment.

Well, they had better move a little faster because the Champenois are about to repeat the California success story.

*The Californians claimed that their wines were suffering from travel sickness and demanded a rematch on their own territory – same result.

THE FUTURE OF CHAMPAGNE HOUSES OUTSIDE THE REGION

DOMAINE CHANDON AUSTRALIA
(Victoria)

Once again Moët is the dominant, driving force. Land has been purchased in the Yarra Valley, close to Melbourne and a 'Domaine' is being constructed. They have already been experimenting with cuvées made from grapes bought in from a number of coolish-climate regions of Victoria and South Australia. John Wright, President of Domaine Chandon and the originator of the idea for the California operation, first suggested Australia in 1981. The ubiquitous Monsieur Maudière has managed to supervise the various *assemblages*, and Domaine Chandon's wine-maker, Dawnine Dyer, has been out Down-under every year since 1984. Yves Bénard has recently visited Australia (funny that it coincided with the Melbourne Cup Horse Race!)

There have been no rushed decisions because the California experience has been put to good use. First make sure of the qualities of the blend using other people's facilities, then purchase the vineyards and build the winery. This time around Moët is not even wasting the chance of a sales return on the initial blends – they are being marketed back in the USA as still varietals.

Domaine Chandon plan on producing only a small proportion of its own grapes and will buy in the rest from Mansfield, Mount Macedon, Coonawarra and Tasmania, but it is a little worried about the problems of supply of suitable Pinot Noir. Whizzkid wine-maker Tony Jordan, for many years a fellow director of a technical consultancy business with the soon to be mentioned Brian Croser, is the Managing Director.

Things seem to be going smoothly, and the scale of investment is rather different from that in present-day California. Rumours place a total establishment cost of winery and vineyard land at below the figure Seagram paid for the 80 acres in the Napa.

BOLLINGER–PETALUMA
(Adelaide Hills, South Australia)

Bollinger owns 40 per cent of this exciting vineyard and winery. Petaluma is the brainchild of the country's most talented wine-maker, Brian Croser,* who has established a cult reputation in the past fifteen years. Many of the current technical innovations of the Australian wine world were pioneered by him. He and his partners purchased 100 acres in the Piccadilly Valley and planted Chardonnay and Pinot Noir. They bought and restored an old flour mill with considerable cellarage. Bollinger invested, but the decisions are Croser's and his name appears on the label. The first wines showed considerable promise and have improved with each new release. A great factor is that Australians are patriotic and in 1988 it was more difficult to track down a bottle of Croser than a dozen bottles of the French interest's RD.**

*Croser has independently formed a partnership in Oregon to establish a sparkling-wine operation.

**The incredible speed with which Down-under wineries have achieved such status can be illustrated by a recent conversation with Arnould d'Hautefeuille of Bollinger who reminded me that I introduced him to Australian wine in 1977 on his first business visit to London. He remarked 'Who would have thought that we would have been investing in the Australian industry a mere ten years later.'

THE GLORY OF CHAMPAGNE

LOUIS ROEDERER–HEEMSKERK
(Tasmania, Australia)

This beautiful island just south of Australia has a cool climate, and a few wineries are making elegant wines in a style much lighter than those on the mainland. The comparative isolation of the region is an obvious drawback, but initially Roederer claimed to have done its homework, tasted initial blends of Chardonnay and Pinot Noir and decided that the quality was sufficiently superior to override all the problems. But the house forgot about the wind and was seemingly unaware of just how bad the climate really is (any mainland Australian would happily have offered this information quite freely within the first thirty seconds of any conversation about 'offshore territory'). Roederer has now come to the conclusion that its original vineyard will only be blessed with a good vintage one year in every four, and has purchased another 40 hectares in a less exposed situation. The powers that be in Reims still assure me they have faith in the area: 'It will take a few more years than expected. At present we are not too worried about the problems: our immediate concern is the success of the California operation.'

——— WHERE NEXT? ———

Moët has just announced a joint venture with its agents in Spain (it holds a significant number of shares in the local company). Despite much consternation and at times downright hostility from many cava producers, accompanied by dark mutterings from the native workers between the cathedrals of stainless-steel vats of the Penetes, Domaine Chandon Spain is to be launched. At present they own only a small amount of land, but they are looking at new areas for more Chardonnay and perhaps Pinot Noir. The wine will be nearly twice the price of the Spanish-made sparklings and Moët is hoping to capitalise on its well-known name and quality image – it supplies nearly 50 per cent of the total champagne sales in this burgeoning market.

Bombay millionaire Sham Ghougule employed Champagne Technologie, a subsidiary of Piper Heidsieck, as consultants to his *méthode champenoise* winery in the Indian state of Maharashta. Believe it or not, the wine fooled many a discerning palate. The future quality is a little uncertain as both the Reims company and its wine-maker have extricated themselves from the deal. The wine-making countries of South America offer scope for expansion, and even China is receiving close attention. Deutz, in partnership with the mammoth local distillery, have released Grandjoie, Korea's first drinkable sparkling wine.

I am much more excited about another Deutz joint venture, with Montana winery in New Zealand. My homeland has made remarkable progress in the past two decades and its best vineyards are producing superb fruit. Montana is at the forefront of the revolutionary technical developments in this small country, which appears rather sleepy but possesses some of the finest wine-makers in the world. The wine, made from Chardonnay and Pinot Noir, will be made in relatively small quantities – 120,000 bottles a year, and sold only on the home market. Both Deutz and Montana are very confident that the initial results will be highly satisfactory and are already planning to increase production and sell the wines through the New Zealand winery's very successful export division. The country may be comparatively isolated but a weak dollar means relatively cheap investment costs for the Champenois, and the surging 'Pacific Rim' wine-drinking market is very close. Who will be next?

17

CONCLUSION

Before the Second World War champagne represented more than 30 per cent of the world's total production of sparkling wine. Despite the dramatic increase in production it now accounts for only 10 per cent. Pessimists are eager to point out that major growth markets for sparkling wine, such as the United States, now purchase much more cava than champagne. This may have been a cause for concern a few decades ago when the vast majority of cheap bubbly produced was unpleasant and the marketing was usually a deliberate attempt at confusing the consumer about the true nature of the product. Now the making of quality sparkling wine is a much more serious business with less emphasis on passing off a cheaper product as the genuine article.

The rising popularity of sparkling wines should be treated as a bonus. I doubt whether the regular consumer of the mass-market $5-a-bottle 'champagne' in the United States will ever graduate, but the more sophisticated wine-drinkers accustomed to tasting the 'premium sparklings' are aware of the ultimate product and will willingly pay the extra for champagne on special occasions.

The future is rosy for the Champenois – as long as the unique quality of their wines remains. Perhaps this seems rather didactic, but there are factors which threaten the industry's wellbeing. In the twenty years I have been closely involved with the world of champagne there have been three major worries: the relationships between growers and the *négociant* houses; the financial structures of the houses; and the need to ensure that *all* the industry concentrates on the quality of the wines.

The perennial problem of balance between stock and sales is not different from that in other regions but, because the stocks must be mature before sale and are from a number of vintages, things are more complicated. Ideally the region holds stock in excess of three years' sales: much more and the growers are at the mercy of the houses, much less and the reverse is the case.* In the 1960s and 1970s, when the local

---

*Age of stocks is not all-important. The best wines benefit enormously from considerable age but growers holding stock of wines from lesser areas and/or unattractive vintages cannot expect to hold the wine indefinitely and command high prices.

market was growing at an astonishing rate, 'grower power' was a threat to the houses as the growers were more than prepared to keep their grapes and sell the finished product themselves. At the moment things are better balanced – the sales growth at home seems to have peaked while exports, controlled by the houses, have boomed. The high prices for grapes certainly act as an incentive for the growers to sell to the houses even if, as the sceptics suggest, it merely makes them sufficiently affluent to afford the necessary stockholding to become *récoltants manipulants*.

The financial affairs of the houses have been ever-changing. When I first visited Champagne the commercial aspects were very different. The Champagne Academy was still run by the families. Christian Bizot of Bollinger takes a degree of pride in not being a product of the business-school system:

> I always tell my sons, 'I hope you are better in school than I was.' I didn't even receive my initial training in Champagne – instead my father sent me to work in the cellars of London wine merchants Corney & Barrow, and later to Liverpool, where I spent time as a salesman.* Then I was ready to return to Champagne, but to another series of hard physical tasks in the cellars. Eventually I was considered ready for travel to the United States for experience in marketing the family product. The theory was that I would learn the various tasks within the wine trade 'on the shop floor' and only then would I be capable of always reacting to the business from the family viewpoint.

Is there any wonder that the spirit of Madame Jacques is still very much in evidence? However, within a comparatively short time Bollinger has become a rarity, a family-owned business in control of its own destiny.

This manner of education is virtually impossible now. The corporate system has taken over and the business-school graduates are exercising control. There was little reaction to the first modern takeovers, when Moët purchased Ruinart in 1963 and Mercier in 1970 – after all the purchasers were Champenois. Things were very different in 1972 when Seagram became majority shareholder of G.H. Mumm and purchased Heidseick Monopole; to many within the industry it was a major threat to their independence. Little were they to know that it was merely a beginning. Despite the large number of individual houses, and the pleasing variety of house styles, the inescapable fact is that Bollinger, Laurent Perrier, Pol Roger and Taittinger are the only family-controlled houses mentioned in Chapters 12 and 13 of this book.*

The largest and most recent example of the fluctuating financial groupings in Champagne has occupied vast column inches in the financial pages of the world's newspapers – the initial establishment and consequent boardroom battles of the Louis Vuitton–Moët Hennessy–Veuve Clicquot group, LVMH. The 1987 merger of two industry giants with six major houses (Moët, Mercier, Ruinart, Veuve Clicquot,

*Not even the staunchest of Liverpudlians would claim that their bomb-ravaged city in 1950 was the greatest time or place to be learning wine salesmanship!

Canard-Duchêne, Henriot) and many other interests caused much surprise. Despite the benefits of combining strengths* to avoid the rumoured takeover attempts, many knowledgeable observers were sceptical about the claims from both sides that they were a natural merging of like-minded interests. Well, it was not long before the Moët–Hennessy and Vuitton–Clicquot camps were at each other's throats. After many public rows and a final battle that culminated with an insider dealing inquiry on the Paris Bourse, 'Jacques Rober', a company jointly owned by whizz kid Bernard Arnault's 'Financière Agache'** and Guinness, now own at the time of writing nearly 45 per cent of LVMH. Chevalier had resigned and Arnault is Chairman, with Guinness represented on the board. LVMH shares have nearly doubled in the past two years, they are now the largest public company on the Bourse.

Fortunately the actual running of the LVMH champagne companies has not been affected by these affairs, and so far each sector has been run with the necesary independence.

Fortunately the new owners have proved to be either totally sympathetic to the industry, or good listeners. Claude Taittinger has firm ideas: 'We have to be pedagogues and teach the newcomers how to behave in our society. So far our attitudes and theirs have worked well together.' No one drinking a bottle of the present Charles Heidsieck, Lanson or Pommery could help but be thankful for outside interference. Neither have the other major houses suffered. Many wine-trade analysts are still amazed by the uncharacteristic style of management exerted by Seagram when in Champagne. The relatively relaxed, patient approach has paid off and the recent achievements of Perrier-Jouët are universally admired and envied.

There is no doubt that the style of champagne has changed. New methods which allow a subtle concentration of fruit flavours and aromas (not too much of either – it would spoil the blends) has allowed the more flowery, lighter Chardonnay styles to flaunt their pedigree. Even stalwarts of the Pinot Noir such as Krug and Louis Roederer have increased the Chardonnay content in their non-vintage wines. There is no doubt that this is the style the public prefers – did they change the blends or did the new styles change their tastes?

The considerable rise in grape yields and the increase in vineyards have enabled production to keep pace with, or even surpass, sales. In 1982 CIVC introduced a new regulation, a system of compulsory stocking called the 'blocking mechanism'. In certain bumper years when the yield was in excess of *appellation* laws an extra 10 per cent could be kept, but it would have to be stored separately and without *appellation* ('blocked'), which could be used in short years in the near future. This has added a little stability to the quantity of wine available, but obviously will by no means regularise the production in a cool region where the size of the crop fluctuates wildly.

*They account for 33 per cent of the total exports of champagne and 12 per cent of the total domestic market.
**The man who in 1984 at the tender age of thirty-four bought the Marcel Boussac empire – the largest bankruptcy since World War II, and made it profitable within three years.

CONCLUSION

Alain De Corseulles, of Moët, says that being a champagne salesman is not a simple task. 'After the relatively modest harvest of 1988 we made a decision not to increase Moët's sales in 1989. I am the man who has to explain to the agents that we are part of the agricultural world and *not* an industrial product. Obviously we are profit-motivated, but not at the expense of quality.'

There are many people who would like to see the CIVC extend the delimited area. They argue that there is a considerable amount of land available for planting which is as suitable for grape-growing as the existing lesser vineyards. Needless to say most of these people own the land in question! There may be valid justification for some of the claims but at this moment the CIVC's attention is firmly focused on maintaining, or if possible, improving, the quality of champagne.

In 1988 the CIVC's *Charte de qualité* was produced. Representatives of all aspects of the trade had worked for two years to provide more up-to-date regulations for grape-growing and wine-making. The *Charte* specifies methods of soil-replenishment, selection of varieties in respect of the soil and rigid control of replanting. There are around 2000 press-houses, and these are to receive detailed attention, with the substandard ones being closed down. Most importantly, the CIVC is to allow a much more flexible start to the vintage with the communes being allowed to commence when conditions are correct for them, as opposed to the whole area.

The CIVC points out that this may not appear particularly revolutionary, but the whole industry has joined together to ensure that the unique qualities of these magical wines are retained. The hard work of the previous centuries is not about to be negated. I think that's worth celebrating with a bottle of champagne!

GLOSSARY

HOW TO MAKE THE MOST OF YOUR CHAMPAGNE

A large section of this book has been a description of the different styles of Champagne and the incredible amount of tradition, skill, care and financial attention that has contributed to the final product. Now the responsibility is yours, the consumer. Champagne is a relatively easy wine to buy, store and serve – much less trouble (and cheaper) than sorting through the classed growths of Bordeaux or the minefields of the Côte d'Or. Follow a few simple principles and you will ensure that you receive the maximum value for your money.

PURCHASE

I buy approximately 2000 dozen bottles of champagne each year . . . but that is business! When I am staying in the South of France, or holidaying in the United States, Australia, New Zealand, or wherever, I follow a few guidelines. I always buy my bottles from shops which obviously have a healthy turnover of stock. No wine takes kindly to sitting upright under bright display lights, and unfortunately champagne is the one most likely to be placed in the most prominent position by the retailer who doesn't understand the fragile nature of his fine wine stock.

The degree of bottle age after degorgement is a personal matter of taste, but it is undeniable that the wines do benefit from extra scope for development, creating more intensity of flavour. Many of the large houses keep their wines in their own cellars for this purpose, but with the cheaper wines it is up to the consumer. I have a friend who buys his Christmas champagne every year from the local Waitrose supermarket – but to maximise his value for money he purchases it in February. Storage is obviously a problem, but even a modest cupboard under the stairs away from hot water pipes and radiators will suffice.*

*The late Freddie Hilliard, a contributor to *Decanter* magazine and fellow taster at many a great tasting of the 1970s, preferred his champagne with a great deal of bottle age. He claimed to have once bought 100 dozen bottles for his personal consumption – in order to best appreciate the wines!

GLOSSARY

SIZE OF BOTTLES

A tricky subject as the abnormal sizes are usually not subject to secondary fermentation in the bottle, but filled under pressure from a larger source (*transvasage*). Quarter bottles may seem like a good idea at the time but although improvement in specialised bottling equipment has vastly improved quality they are better left for their major customers, airlines.* Many half-bottles are treated in the same manner and are not recommended for keeping (anyway they are a little too small – oh, for the pre-EEC days before the bureaucrats abolished the British Imperial Pint, sufficiently larger than a half to satisfy a thirsty solitary diner, or a marvellous aperitif size for two). Bottles are obviously an excellent size and are easy to store but Magnums offer even better quality as the amount of air contained compared to wine is the lowest. Mind you Victor Lanson had a less scientific reasoning, 'The Magnum is the perfect size for two people – the wine waiter and me!'

A number of houses such as Charbaut and Pommery take particular pride in hand *remuage* of even the largest bottles and are only too happy to specially degorge and label for the individual customer. Marvellous for a special occasion but the wise purchaser will order well ahead.

The Larger Sizes:

Magnum	2 Bottles
Jeroboam	4 Bottles
Rehoboam	6 Bottles
Methuselah (Methusalem)	8 Bottles
Salmanazar	12 Bottles
Balthazar	16 Bottles
Nebuchadnezzar	20 Bottles

TEMPERATURE

In an ideal world we (or our man-servant) would have plenty of time to gently chill the bottle for about 25 minutes in an ice bucket filled with both ice and water. A temperature of about 8°C is perfect ... just a shade too cold for my liking but this is quite important because the wine invariably warms in the glass. However, I must admit that more than 60 per cent of the bottles served in my house, in particular at dinner parties where the conversation and kitchen duties are also vying for attention, are from the convenience of the fridge, (whilst I always have a bottle of everyday drinking fizz ready chilled, I don't make the mistake of leaving the better wines in there for long periods). I have even been known to put the odd bottle or three of non-vintage in the ice box for about fifteen minutes.

One of the most important aspects is not to overchill the wine and lose the aroma and flavour. Restaurateurs invariably do so as they take the wine out of the fridge and then

*As an independent member of the travelling public I became infuriated with airlines that served economy class wines in their much more expensive business class. One of the most satisfying achievements of my life was persuading *Business Traveller* magazine to allow me to organise the first of their comparative tastings and ratings of wines served in business class. The criticism levelled at those who offered quarter bottles of champagne was sufficiently trenchant to change the policies of many carriers who now proudly advertise that they pour from full bottles.

place it in an ice bucket. This practice is even carried out in Champagne. No doubt some gentle chilling is necessary if a couple is sharing a bottle over a meal but temperature should be carefully monitored. The relatively new plastic insulated wine coolers offend the eye but they are reasonably effective in maintaining the fridge temperature.

OPENING THE BOTTLE

A relatively straightforward operation, but take care. The Londoners' Diary page of *The Evening Standard* reported*

> Barmen throughout Britain will commiserate with Lady Vesty who nearly lost an eye the other day when a champagne bottle was uncorked six inches from her face.
>
> A doctor friend at Moorfield Eye Hospital tells me there's a disturbing increase in champagne-induced casualties . . . 'We get at least two victims of champagne corks a week and often have to operate,' he says.

Never point the bottle at anyone, and never open without a napkin over the cork. Hold the bottle at a 45° angle to minimise the chances of the wine foaming everywhere, and then hold on to the cork and wire, gently turning the *bottle.*

I don't know whether the mishap to Lady Vesty was the fault of a waiter or perhaps a careless friend (then again, I wonder if she has friends that open their own bottles), but I do know that I am frequently horrified in restaurants, including some exclusive establishments in France, where the staff remove the wire cage and wander off to attend to some other detail whilst the equivalent pressure of a London bus tyre waits to unleash itself.

TASTING

I realise that the most dedicated champagne drinker has no desire to turn every glass into an intellectual exercise, but a little thought after the first sip certainly heightens awareness. What is the first impression? It may be a rich, biscuity flavour emphasising a dominant Pinot content, or it may be light and ethereal with a hint of apples which suggests a fair percentage of Chardonnay from close to Epernay. Hopefully it will not be my pet hate – fat, blowsy wine with considerable sweetness added to mask poor fruit or Deuxième Taille.

Taste is very subjective. I am not alone in disliking the non-dosage wines but many others enjoy this style. I recently poured a trade friend a glass of a first rate 1982 wine from the Côte des Blancs. Initially he thought the wine too sweet, but I managed to convince him that this was incorrect. Yes, there was a degree of richness not always apparent in other years or leaner styles of champagne, but the wine was no sweeter than others.

Nothing can replace experience through tasting as wide a range of wines as possible – unless it is a surreptitious look at the label!

GLASSES

There are many styles of glasses suitable for the enjoyment of champagne. One is perfect, it is not particularly expensive, nor more fragile than many others, but it is the most

*6 October 1988

difficult to purchase. The tall, long-stemmed tulip glass with a narrowing base at the bowl is used by the houses themselves. The unique features of a well-balanced wine and the excitement of the fizz are highlighted (and so are the blemishes of poor stuff). Mark Kernick of Veuve Clicquot shares my misgivings regarding the much more readily available style of smallish flute often used by the houses as promotional gifts – 'We know they are not ideal, but they are more suitable than most and are inexpensive to manufacture.'

I prefer the other two shapes of flutes illustrated because, as they are taller, the wine receives much more direct contact with the glass and keeps sparkling until the very last drop. The 'Pomponne', designed to ensure that the fun-loving aristocracy could never put down their glasses whilst a drop remained, are fun to use.

I needn't dwell on the harm done to champagne by the notorious saucer glass which found considerable fame despite the fact that it rapidly demolished the sparkle, but there is one other great enemy to bubbles once in the glass – any trace of detergent will immediately kill the vivacity of the wine. Always rinse out glasses in clean, hot water before serving (also ridding them of storage smells) using a clean, detergent-free cloth, and please *never* chill the glass – it must be completely dry otherwise the dampness helps dissipate the sparkle.

WHAT FOOD WITH CHAMPAGNE

Remi Krug dashes around the world promoting his wonderful wines. No one does the job better. He also promotes the matching of food with champagne by example – a few years ago he hosted a sumptuous banquet at the Mandarin Hotel in Hong Kong to prove the ideal combination of 'Nouvelle' Chinese cuisine with champagne. Last time we shared a bottle he was dashing up to Paris to confer with Joel Robuchon about a 'Seafood and Krug Spectacle'.

There is no doubt that champagne gracefully accompanies many more dishes than is often recognised. Visitors to the restaurants of the region are delighted when offered superb ranges of fish, poultry and lamb with subtle sauces, but even the most dedicated champagne lovers prefer red wine with the main course (especially if it is beef). It eases the digestion and allows a necessary respite from the bubbles. If you don't believe me ask Remi – he provided the first bottle of claret I ever drank in Champagne.

—— TOURING CHAMPAGNE ——

One of the region's many attractions is accessibility. It is the closest wine-growing region to Great Britain, a mere few hours leisurely drive along splendid roads from the port of Calais. Lunch in Reims, transport by motor car and hovercraft, concluded with dinner in London, is not a particularly arduous travel task.

The Paris–Metz autoroute whisks the traveller from the centre of the capital into Reims in one and a half hours, and the drive from Roissy (Charles de Gaulle, Paris) Airport, which misses the congestion of the metropolis, takes a similarly short time.* There is a regular train service from the Gare de l'Est to both Epernay and Reims. If you wish to visit in style, Reims military airfield is open to private planes by arrangement and diners at Boyers Les Crayères may use the restaurant's heliport!

Having arrived, by whatever means of transport, a car is desirable as it is difficult to understand the region by merely visiting the cellars. The spirit of Champagne is to be found amongst the spread of tiny, picturesque villages which nestle amongst the vineyards; non-drivers must hire a car and driver for at least a few hours.

HOTELS

My ideal visit includes a stay in at least two of four excellent hostelries in different locations.

LA BRIQUETTERIE (telephone 26.54.11.22) in Vinay, 5 miles south of Epernay. A beautifully appointed establishment set amongst lush gardens. One of the best restaurants in the region.

ROYAL CHAMPAGNE (telephone 26.51.11.51) at Champillon, 3 miles north of Epernay is an eighteenth-century inn with modern additions. Comfortable rooms and excellent food in the restaurant which flaunts one of the finest panoramic views of the wine world – the huge picture windows overlook a magnificent spread of acres of meticulously nurtured

---

*Hopefully one has time for the more leisurely and picturesque route along the banks of the Marne through Meaux, lunching at the splendid Auberge de Condé at la Ferté-sous-Jouarre, then through Château-Thierry and on to Epernay and Reims.

vineyards, a moving picture show which even manages to fascinate in the depths of winter. Reasonably expensive but worth every penny.

CHEVAL BLANC (telephone 26.03.90.27) at Sept-Saux, 16 miles east of Reims. A friendly, good value country inn run by the fifth generation of the Robert family. Comfortable, unpretentious rooms and a relaxed, but sophisticated, atmosphere in the restaurant; L'Écrevisse from their own stream, vegetables and herbs from their own gardens. An excellent choice for those staying *en famille*.

AUX ARMES DE CHAMPAGNE (telephone 26.68.10.43) at L'Épine, 6 miles outside Châlons-sur-Marne. Another charming, relaxed *auberge* – comfortable rooms in attractive surroundings, good food and modestly priced.

Reims possesses a number of agreeable hotels, the most comfortable are the LA PAIX (telephone 26.40.04.08) and the ALTEA (telephone 26.88.53.54) which are within walking distance of the major tourist attractions. There are the rather anonymous but agreeable comforts of mid-price chain hotels on the outskirts of the city. I often stay at the modern and remarkable value CAMPANILE (telephone 26.36.66.94); the beds are comfortable and the money saved pays for dinner!

In Epernay, LES BERCEAUX (telephone 26.55.28.84) is an inexpensive, central hotel-restaurant-wine bar run by an amiable couple, Luc Maillard and his English wife Jill. In Ambonnay, on the Montagne de Reims, there is the delightfully rustic AUBERGE DE ST VINCENT (telephone 26.57.01.98). The rooms are fine but the bonus is that Jean Claude Petellier presides over a kitchen dedicated to the traditional 'bourgeoise' cuisine of the region. Amazing value.

Be warned. For a popular tourist region there is a shortage of hotel rooms, therefore book well in advance, especially in mid-season.

RESTAURANTS

The cuisine of Champagne is essentially 'International French'. The region was not previously renowned for its restaurants. When I first began visiting most of the Champenois entertained 'in house' and whilst they were justifiably proud of a few good restaurants they were always a trifle apologetic about the lack of excitement in the fare offered to the public.

Things have changed dramatically, beginning in the 1960s when a wonderful, genial Parisian restaurateur Gaston Boyer moved to Reims and created the first of the 'new wave' restaurants, La Chaumière, later renamed simply Boyer (the first – and only *Guide Michelin* 3-star restaurant in Champagne). His son Gerard has since moved it to a much more grandiose operation, BOYER LES CRAYERES (telephone 26.82.80.80), a splendid refurbishment of the Pommery château on the slightly higher ground atop the Butte St Nicaise. It is the most spectacular restaurant I have ever visited, superbly decorated rooms overlooking seventeen acres of immaculate gardens, landscaped by the artist Redon, and Reims Cathedral in the background. It would be very easy for the surroundings to overpower the food and the wines, but not so. Gerard's beautifully crafted, delicate dishes are the perfect accompaniment to the fine champagnes in the cellar. There are sixteen bedrooms, many with even more spectacular views; the ultimate luxury is enjoyment of a wonderful dinner, a digestif in the bar before retiring upstairs. Needless to say all the *Michelin* stars have been transferred!

There are many other excellent establishments in Reims. My other favourite is LE GRAND CERF (telephone 26.97.60.07), on the road to Epernay. Inventive food in a delightful garden atmosphere with the added bonus of the genial, extroverted Alain Guichaoua supervising the kitchen and darting out to greet guests. Very popular with the more affluent growers. LE FLORENCE (telephone 26.47.12.70) and LE CHARDONNAY (telephone 26.06.08.60) offer food and wine of a similar standard. LE VIGNERON (telephone 26.47.00.71) is invariably packed with locals enjoying robust, flavoursome food and selecting their bubbly from the most amazing of lists – more than 100 producers are represented. Some of the decor is a little 'fake rustic' but it is saved by Herve Liegent's remarkable collection of original advertising posters. LA GARENNE (telephone 26.08.26.62) is a relaxed, informal restaurant owned by a young chef Laurent Laplaige. Older readers with an interest in motor racing may remember the building as the 'Auberge de Circuit' from the days when Reims hosted an annual Grand Prix.

The dining out scene is not as exciting in Epernay, although visitors to JEAN BERIN (telephone 26.51.66.69) will not be disappointed. LA GRILLADE, commonly known as the 'Moët Sales Staff Canteen', is one of those marvellous, unpretentious but atmospheric restaurants that are a delightful feature of rural France – simple starters and excellent meat cooked on an open wood fire.* I cannot understand why the health inspectors of Great Britain consider open hearth cooking a health hazard. Deliciously informal fare complemented by a wine list strong on the good value red wines from the rest of France ... a welcome respite from the surfeit of sybaritic delights of the region. LE MESNIL in Vertus (telephone 26.57.95.57) is a delightful, welcoming, sunny room right in the heart of the Côte des Blancs. Definitely worth a detour. If you spy the young chef proprietor in animated conversation with an enthusiastic gentleman diner say hello ... he is most probably Daniel Aubertin of Champagne Paul Goerg!

VISITING THE CELLARS

At many stages of this book I have praised the balance of superb public relations, marketing ability and canny business acumen of the Champenois. So often the first with new ideas, and the abilities to make them work. They were the first in the world of wine to open their cellars *en masse* to the wine-drinking public. Each year vast numbers of visitors pass through their doors.**The welcome may differ, the degree of education may vary, and the hospitality may finish at the end of the tour or it may include a glass of the product or a series of different wines. Whatever, the guest leaves the region with a firm impression of the *méthode champenoise* and a perspective of the uniqueness of the product.

Many of the major houses are geared to receiving vast numbers of visitors and have well-organised regular multi-lingual tours most days (check beforehand if planning a weekend visit). I have been visiting the houses for nearly two decades and recently toured all of them anonymously in order to rate their efforts at instruction.

In Reims, Pommery and Mumm both offer excellent audio visual presentations followed by tours with guides who take great care in clarity of description. Pommery have the advantage of the spectacular background of their wonderful Roman cellars. Veuve Clicquot are equally hospitable and Piper Heidsieck use electric trains to transport

*Not to be confused with the mediocre imitations which belong to national catering companies and are dotted around the country close to major roads.
**Moët and Mercier alone account for more than 250,000 visitors per annum.

people around their long galleries. In World War II these cellars were also used for hiding arms for the Resistance (the workers and members of the d'Aulan family were betrayed with the inevitable consequences). The Taittinger cellars at the Place St Nicaise are well worth visiting for their historical significance, dating back to the fourth century.

In Epernay, Mercier are supreme. Electric trains whisk fascinated enthusiasts around a reasonable amount of the cellars and the latest laser technology is now used as part of the educational experience. Moët are, needless to say, very active with a detailed explanation of the region and the *méthode* followed by a tour of a small part of their cellars.

Others are a little more reticent but only too happy to provide a more personalised insight into their operation provided you telephone in advance and make an appointment. I would suggest you visit a couple of the aforementioned tours and then visit another few from the following: Bollinger at Ay (telephone 26.55.15.11 for an appointment) is fascinating and a marvellous contrast to the large houses. Charles Heidsieck (26.07.39.34), Lanson (26.40.36.26), Laurent Perrier at Tours-sur-Marne (26.59.91.22), Joseph Perrier at Châlons-sur-Marne (26.68.29.51), Louis Roederer (26.40.42.11), Pol Roger (26.51.41.95) and Ruinart (26.85.40.29) are all highly recommended ... and, of course, Krug (26.47.28.15).

There are three main *Routes des Vins* following the principal regions. They are clearly signposted and many of the smaller producers in the villages are delighted to show arriving visitors around, thereby offering another important insight into the world of champagne.

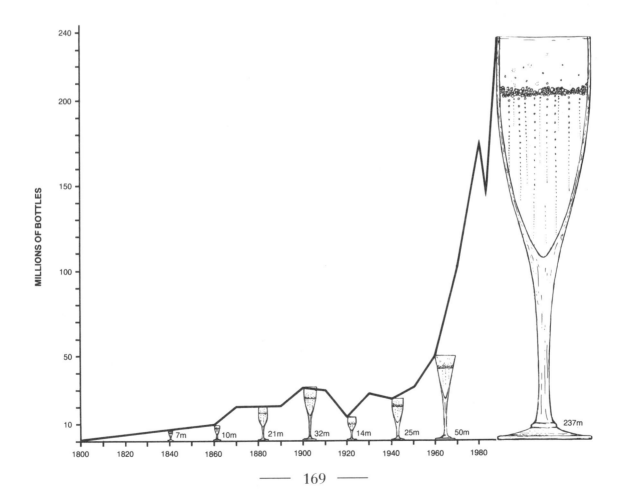

Other Tourist Interests

Wine-related places such as the Champagne Museum in Epernay and the Abbey at Hautvillers are of obvious interest, but there are many other interesting sites. The region has a vast number of churches of considerable interest.* Of course in Reims the CATHEDRAL and the adjoining archbishop's residence the PALAIS DU TAU with its museum are a must, but the eleventh-century BASILICA SAINT REMI and adjoining museum is inspiring. The SURRENDER ROOM, where General Eisenhower accepted the German capitulation, is preserved in the old Headquarter Building of the Allied Forces, just behind the railway station. Vintage car enthusiasts can visit the CENTRE DE AUTOMOBILE FRANÇAISE, a splendid collection of historic vehicles, and in summer adventurous sightseers are able to view Champagne from the air in a flight by hot air balloon – the spirit of Eugène Mercier lives on! (CHAMPAGNE AIR SHOW, 26.82.59.60.)

—— ORGANISATIONS ——

L'Ordre des Côteaux de Champenois

A commercial organisation with its roots back in the halcyon days of the court of Louis XIV when a group of noble Champenois landowners vowed to vigorously promote their own wines. The records of the L'Ordre are full of praise for the efforts of these enterprising salesmen. I would like to thank them even if only from the biased viewpoint of a present-day member who enjoys the superb banquets.

The Champagne Academy

There are thousands of members of the L'Ordre des Côteaux spread across the world. The Academy is a much more exclusive group established in 1957 and consists of less than four hundred wine trade graduates of a course of lectures, tastings and practical cellar visits which take place at the vintage (the members are possibly the only outsiders actually welcomed amongst the bustle and tension of harvest-time). A final exam ensures that the participants have done their homework. The houses which form the Academy are Bollinger, Charles Heidsieck, Veuve Clicquot, Krug, Lanson, Laurent Perrier, Moët & Chandon, Heidsieck Dry Monopole, G.H. Mumm, Perrier-Jouët, Piper Heidsieck, Pol Roger, Pommery, Louis Roederer, Ruinart and Taittinger.

The Comité Interprofessionel du Vin de Champagne

The statute of 1941 grants a wide range of powers to the semi-public organisation 'to administer the common interests of Champagne wine-growers and merchant-producers. Regulating the relationship between the two complimentary activities involved in transforming raw materials into the finished product, namely the agricultural stage and the industrial (or semi-industrial) stage.' It all sounds rather pompous, but in actual fact guarantees peaceful coexistence.

*A copy of the Green Michelin Guide will provide all the details.

GLOSSARY

A 'consultative commission', comprising six growers and six merchants, advises a 'permanent commission' made up of the Government Commissioner and presidents of both growers and merchants.

The CIVC runs a technical department with research laboratories and experimental vineyards. They undertake professional training and advise vineyard owners and oenologists. They protect the appellation by supervising tasting committees with the power to block substandard wines and keep a careful eye on new developments which may or may not be in the interest of better quality.

The crucial task is to maintain both quality control and economic balance for an industry where the yield of the harvests varies dramatically and the ultimate aim for quality is dependant upon maintaining stocks which represent several years' shipments. No mean feat!

One of the most important factors in the dynamic growth of Champagne sales in recent years has been the absence of wildly fluctuating prices. Granted, the cost of a bottle has steadily risen but not in the erratic nature of wines from other classic regions. This has been achieved by the effectiveness of the rational but complicated system of agreement of a binding price for the grapes. The committee also helps achieve a degree of stability of supply and demand regarding grapes; growers and merchants are persuaded to sign long-term undertakings and are rewarded for doing so. In years of surplus the growers who have signed contracts are granted priority and in years of shortfall the participating merchants receive similar status. There are many grumbles from both sides, after all any form of discipline is never universally popular, but they are minor and the desired coexistence is relatively peaceful.

The CIVC is predominantly funded by levies on the harvests of the growers and on the bottle sales of the merchants.

INDEX